Country Roads of
NEW MEXICO

*Drives, Day Trips, and
Weekend Excursions*

Sally Moore

COUNTRY ROADS PRESS
NTC/Contemporary Publishing Group

Library of Congress Cataloging-in-Publication Data

Moore, Sally, 1936 –
    Country roads of New Mexico : drives, day trips, and weekend excursions / Sally Moore.
        p.   cm. — (Country Roads)
    Includes index.
    ISBN 1-56626-203-8
    1. New Mexico Tours.   2. Automobile travel—New Mexico Guidebooks.   3. Rural roads—New Mexico Guidebooks.   I. Title.   II. Series: Country Roads (Series)
    F794.3.M66   1999
    917.8904'53—dc21   99-25112
                                                                           CIP

Cover and interior design by Nick Panos
Cover illustration copyright © Todd L. W. Doney
Interior site illustrations and map copyright © Leslie Faust
Illustrations based on original photographs by Sally Moore
Interior spot illustrations copyright © Barbara Kelley
Picture research by Elizabeth Broadrup Lieberman
Typesetting by VARDA Graphics, Inc.

Published by Country Roads Press
A division of NTC/Contemporary Publishing Group, Inc.
4255 West Touhy Avenue, Lincolnwood (Chicago), Illinois 60712-1975 U.S.A.
Copyright © 1999 by Sally Moore
All rights reserved. No part of this book may be reproduced, stored in a retrieval system, or transmitted in any form or by any means, electronic, mechanical, photocopying, recording, or otherwise, without the prior written permission of NTC/Contemporary Publishing Group, Inc.
Printed in the United States of America
International Standard Book Number: 1-56626-203-8
    99 00 01 02 03 04 ML 18 17 16 15 14 13 12 11 10 9 8 7 6 5 4 3 2 1

To Ian
Wam-sivin-mēcava
"Let your heart take the lead"
—Havasupai saying

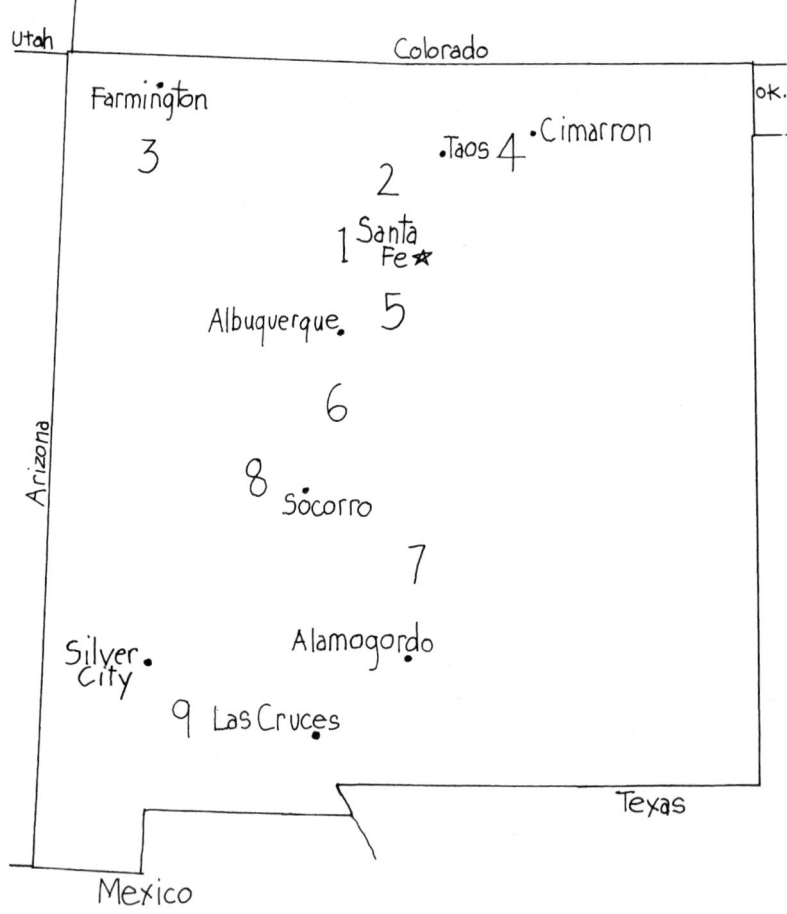

New Mexico Country Roads
(Figures correspond with chapter numbers.)

Contents

Introduction   vii

1 A Jemez Journey   1

2 Georgia O'Keeffe Country   23

3 Trading Posts and Ancient Cities   47

4 From the Mountains to the Plains   69

5 The Turquoise Trail   89

6 Savoring the Salt Missions Trail   105

7 Billy the Kid Territory   121

8 Mining Towns and Mountains   145

9 The Silvered South   169

Other Sources of Information   205

Index   211

Introduction

"The minute I saw the brilliant, proud morning shine high up over the deserts of Santa Fe, something stood still in my soul, and I started to attend. There was a certain magnificence in the high-up day, a certain eagle-like royalty . . . Ah, yes, in New Mexico the heart is sacrificed to the sun and the human being is left stark, heartless, but undauntedly religious."
—D. H. Lawrence

New Mexico is a seducer of the most potent sort, a wily beguiler whose siren lure would captivate even a born and bred Easterner like myself whose roots go back to 17th-century Massachusetts. Many years ago when I first came to New Mexico, I knew at once that it was home. Time passed, as it will, taken up with the necessity of managing a family and job. Eventually the circumstances were right, and with hardly a glance back, I returned to the land that had beckoned me for so long and in which I had traveled extensively.

This guide is the result of a love affair with New Mexico. Not every place is represented, and you may wonder at the exclusion of Santa Fe, Taos, and Albuquerque. So much has been written about these cities that another guide centered on their considerable attractions seems redundant.

The choices are selective. Routes frequently cover many miles and require more than a single day's journey. Basically, I've aimed at giving you, the reader, a sample of the many elements of geography, history, and wide cultural diversity that make up "The Land of Enchantment."

A word about the land itself. It is not all desert, or mountains, or forests. It is all of the above. With 122,666 square miles, it is the fifth-largest state. New Mexico has a diverse landscape which includes sections of the Rocky Mountains, the Great Plains, the Colorado Plateau, and six of the seven climatic life zones, from the Lower Sonoran (2,876 to 5,000 feet) to the Arctic/Alpine (higher than 12,000 feet). Each zone has its own cast of plants and animals, and often it is possible to detect your elevation by checking the landscape from your car window.

The Rio Grande, which runs from its headwaters in southern Colorado to Brownsville on the Gulf of Mexico, cleaves the state in two from east to west. In its more northern reaches, or Rio Arriba, it can be a raging torrent, but once it reaches the plains, or Rio Abajo, it slows to a broad, silty stream. The lifeblood of many civilizations from Archaic to modern times, the river has been indispensable to the state's development.

The history of man in New Mexico begins around 12,000 B.C. or earlier. Crude tools and animal bones of prehistoric big game hunters were found at Sandia Cave, near Albuquerque, and finely chipped projectile points were discovered at the Folsom Site in the northeast and the Clovis Site near Anderson Basin.

Toward the latter part of the Archaic period, the concept of agriculture filtered up from Mexico, and dependence on game lessened. Groups became more sedentary and built semi-permanent dwellings such as pit houses. Over time these evolved into the cliff dwellings and freestanding apartment complexes of the Mogollon and Anasazi.

By the 1500s rumors of great Indian civilizations and gold brought the Spanish to New Mexico. Their first encounter with Native Americans occurred in 1539, when a Franciscan friar, Marcos de Niza, led a party from northern Mexico into today's Arizona and New Mexico. At Háwikuh, near Zuni, his advance party was repulsed and the good friar fled back to Mexico.

In response to the priest's exaggerated tales of riches, in 1540 Francisco Vásques de Coronado, governor of Nueva Galicia, Mexico, led 300 soldiers and 800 Indians from Compostela to Háwikuh. He found no cities of gold, only the pueblos whose straw-enriched adobe glistened in the sun.

Following the Entrada (Spanish entry), Don Juan de Oñate marched north accompanied by troops, priests, colonists, and cattle to secure New Mexico by the cross and the sword, and in 1609 Don Pedro de Peralta established Santa Fe as the capital of the region.

The Spanish maintained dominance until 1680, when under the leadership of Popé, a San Juan Indian living at Taos, the pueblos revolted, expelled their oppressors, and killed many of the priests. The Spanish reestablished control in 1692, when Captain General Diego de Vargas Zapata Lujan Ponce de León y Contreras led a small army from El Paso, subdued the pueblos along the way, and easily wrested control of Santa Fe from the Indians.

With the signing of the Treaty of Córdova on August 23, 1821, Mexico received its independence from Spain, and New Mexico became a part of the new nation. The Mexican regime lasted until 1846, when U.S. Army Brigadier General Stephen Kearny led the Army of the West down the Santa Fe Trail and declared New Mexico a U.S. territory. This was ratified at the end of the Mexican War by the Treaty of Guadalupe Hidalgo.

During the long territorial period, the people of New Mexico tried many times to gain admittance into the Union, but it wasn't until January 6, 1912, that President William Howard Taft signed the bill admitting New Mexico as the 47th state.

With its history, it is easy to see why New Mexico is so culturally diverse, its Hispanic, Anglo, and Indian population supplemented by a 20th-century infusion of African Americans, Middle Easterners, and Asians. This rich cultural tapestry makes for an intricate and complex society.

The state's Indian population can be divided into three major groups: Pueblos, Navajos, and Apaches. Of the three, the Puebloan people have been here the longest, tracing their ancestry, as they do, to the Anasazi who built the old cities of Chaco, Aztec, and Bandelier. The Navajos and Apaches came much later, probably not a great deal before the Spanish Entrada.

The Pueblo Indians live in 19 villages, most located in the northern part of the state bordering the Rio Grande. They speak five distinct languages: Zuni (Zuni), Towa (Jemez), Tewa (Nambe, Pojoaque, San Ildefonso, San Juan, Santa Clara, and Tesuque), Tiwa (Isleta, Picuris, Sandia, and Taos), and Keresan (Acoma, Cochiti, Laguna, San Felipe, Santa Ana, Santo Domingo, and Zia).

They are a deeply religious and private people, always gracious, but preferring to keep their beliefs secret. Many practice the arts, whether the medium is clay, silver, or stone, and their contributions to Southwestern creative vision is legend.

If you wish to visit a pueblo and be a welcome guest, keep the following cautions in mind:

- Native American territory is part of a sovereign nation. Observe all posted requests or regulations, especially speed limits and prohibitions against photography, sketching, or recording. Photography is an especially sensitive issue. If permitted, images are only for private use, not to be reproduced or sold without written permission from the tribe, a difficult and time-consuming process.
- Many pueblos charge an admission fee. Some charge a photo fee, while some allow no photography, sketching, or recording at all.

- Try to check in at the tribal office or call the pueblo governor's office or the tourist center prior to visiting. Some pueblos welcome visitors, others do not except on feast days.
- Certain areas of the pueblo may be off limits, and they may or may not be posted. Generally these include cemeteries, kivas, and private homes.
- Tribes hold traditions, customs, and religion in high regard. Some actions and/or questions may be offensive. Dances are religious ceremonies, not performances. When attending, remain silent and do not applaud. And do not walk across the dance area, look into kivas (ceremonial chambers), or talk to the dancers or onlookers during the ceremonies. Photography of dances is generally not allowed due to their religious nature.
- The best time to visit a pueblo is on feast days, which are held annually, regardless of the day of the week.
- Do not bring alcohol or drugs onto the pueblo.
- Finally, remember these communities are not theme parks. They are people's homes and should be treated with respect.

Unlike the Pueblo people, most Navajos do not live in towns but prefer to space their hogans over the 25,000-square-mile reservation in the Four Corners area. They are consummate metalworkers, crafting in silver and turquoise ornate bracelets, necklaces, rings, concha (shell) belts, and other jewelry. Navajo women are world famous for their beautiful rugs, which they painstakingly weave on traditional upright looms.

The Apaches are from the same linguistic stock as the Navajos. Fiercely protective of their people, land, and customs, they suffered intense persecution during the settlement of the West. Today fewer than 4,000 live on two reservations in New

Mexico: the Jicarillas, with 800,000 acres between Chama and Farmington, and the Mescaleros, with 450,000 acres in the White Mountains south of Ruidoso.

No guide to New Mexico would be complete without a discussion of the cuisine. Do not confuse New Mexican food with Tex-Mex or Mexican. It has a flavor all its own, which owes its distinctive nature to its Hispanic–Native American blend. From the Indians we have the trinity—corn, beans, and squash. This translates into tortillas, refried beans, and *calabacitas*. No meal is complete without chile, and New Mexicans are most serious about their capsicums, both red and green. Utilized in many strengths from the mild, meaty poblanos to the mouth-blistering habeneros, they are found in salsa, gracing a plate of enchiladas, or in the marinade for carne adovada. Many consider green chile stew the signature New Mexican dish, and when natives return from far away, that's likely to be the first meal they crave.

Before setting out on your New Mexico adventure, you should be aware of several idiosyncrasies endemic to Southwestern travel. Life proceeds at a slower pace, attuned to its own internal rhythms. In small towns business hours frequently are flexible, change with the seasons and sometimes with the whim of the owners. If something is a "must see," a call ahead forestalls disappointment.

Every part of the state receives abundant sunshine, but the climate varies from place to place, often depending on the elevation. Snowfall ranges from less than two inches in the Rio Grande Valley to almost 300 inches in the north-central mountains. During the monsoon season in July and August, thunderstorms are common.

During any day, the temperatures may vary by 30 degrees, so it is always wise to be prepared and dressed in easily adjusted layers.

In an arid climate, dehydration is a concern, and the wise traveler always carries a supply of water. If you're going to be driving long stretches on little-traveled roads, an emergency stash is good insurance, and if you plan moderate day hikes, a quart per person is recommended. In addition, it's a good idea to tote a reserve of nonperishable food in the very real eventuality that you are miles from the nearest café when hunger strikes.

In spite of every effort in making the routing clear, there's always the possibility of a wrong turn. Wise road warriors carry a simple compass, mounted on the dash, and avail themselves of detailed maps, especially if they plan to try any of the state's many back-country byways. *New Mexico Road & Recreation Atlas*, published by Benchmark Maps of Berkeley, California, is the best of the bunch and may be purchased in almost any New Mexico bookstore.

Finally, dust off your curiosity, put aside preconceived notions, and open your heart. You are about to have an adventure in an extraordinary and mysterious land, as Marian Sloan put it in her book *Land of Enchantment* (University of New Mexico Press, 1981), "a land of vast spaces and long silences . . . a land of enchantment, where Gods walked in the cool of the evening.[1]

---

[1] Land of Enchantment: Memoirs of Marian Russell along the Santa Fe Trail, Marian Sloan Russell, University of New Mexico Press, ISBN 0-8263-0571-7.

1

A Jemez Journey

Getting there: From Albuquerque's Big I, take I-25 north 20 miles to exit 240, Bernalillo. Take NM 313, East Avenue, .6 miles to NM 473, and turn right on Camino del Pueblo, which intersects with NM 44 north of town. Follow NM 44 northwest 24 miles to San Ysidro. Bear north on NM 4 through Jemez Springs to the edge of the caldera, where the road completes a horseshoe turn southeast to Bandelier National Monument. Leaving Bandelier, follow NM 4, and turn west on East Jemez Road to Los Alamos. From the city, NM 502 skirts San Ildefonso Pueblo and ends at U.S. 285, Pojoaque, 24 miles north of Santa Fe.

Highlights: A journey of a day or longer takes you off the interstates into some of New Mexico's most spectacular mountain country—from canyons once sheltering ancient cliff dwellers to the city the atom built, Los Alamos. Along the way you'll visit historic Bernalillo and Valles Caldera, the 15-mile-wide basin formed by surface collapse in an area of once-primal volcanic activity. Native American pueblos, hot springs, two wineries, and the tiny All-American city of Jemez Springs round out your Jemez Mountain encounter.

The road between Albuquerque and Santa Fe is familiar to many visitors, who vary their route occasionally by heading north on NM 14, or the Turquoise Trail. A longer but largely undiscovered route heads northwest through the Jemez Mountains, with their spectacular panoramas of red rock cliffs, deep, pine-filled canyons, and serene pueblo villages.

Heading out of the hustle and bustle of Albuquerque, the state's largest city, you find the pace slackens and time moves more slowly in the old Hispanic town of Bernalillo. The site of the annual Labor Day New Mexico Wine Festival, the village has a historic main street, once part of the celebrated El Camino Real. Like so many small, quiet villages, Bernalillo's assets are not obvious to the casual passerby. Look closer. In the 900 block of Camino del Pueblo, an old building with a deceptive modern front houses Rose's Pottery House and Art Gallery; the Range Cafe; Home at the Range gift shop; Best Kept Secrets Emporium, with mini shops selling antiques, Santa Fe–style clothing and accessories, and Richard Baca, master jeweler; Wax Poetic, a specialty candlemaker; the studio and gallery of Paula Saville Dimit, woodcarver; and a humble auto service center.

Rose's Pottery House is a treasure trove of Native American art, both classic and current. In this unimposing storefront, Rose Silva, a trader's daughter and granddaughter of a Lebanese immigrant, maintains her father's 37-year collection of Native American art, which rivals anything seen in the West's more sacred repositories. Afficionados of pueblo pottery will be captivated with rare pieces by Maria Martinez, legendary San Ildefonso potter, or prehistoric gems like a snowflake *olla* (pot) from Chaco Canyon or a jug from Mesa Verde. Complementing the museum collection, Rose stocks and sells a variety of Southwestern art from the storytellers of Cochiti's Helen Cordero to the impressive silver concho belts of Navajo silversmiths.

Next to the pottery, Matt DiGregory and Tom Fenton run the Range Cafe, a popular local eatery and bakery specializing in the kind of home cooking Mom would have produced had she been a talented and innovative chef. Daily specials include pasta dishes such as scallop pasta with red chile linguine sauced with cilantro cream and pine nuts, or Tom's meatloaf with roasted-garlic-mashed potatoes and gravy. Breads and confections are available for on-site consumption or takeout.

Adjoining the restaurant, Arlene Thomas stocks her Home at the Range gift shop with "lots of cool stuff you don't really need." There's all sorts of paraphernalia related to the restaurant: T-shirts, sweatshirts, caps, aprons, and Range salsa and salad dressings. Local artists contribute paintings, *santos* and *retablos*, and decorated gourds. A large selection of Navajo folk art sits cheek by jowl with Karl and Mary Hofmann's pottery and Windmill Works frames and mirrors. Arlene acts as the retail outlet for Wax Poetic's unique candles.

If you're interested in discovering how these unusual forms are created, you can mosey over to Jody Isaacson's Wax Poetic Workshop. A common taper is not to be found, but you'll discover many exotic shapes, including knots, branches, braids, and twists.

On NM 313 just a short distance north of its intersection with NM 44, La Hacienda Grande is tucked away down Baros Lane. Shoshana Zimmerman, a naturopathic practitioner, purchased the old adobe in 1993 from the Gallegos and Montoya families, who had settled the area in 1695 after the Pueblo Revolt. She has transformed the old adobe into a gracious bed-and-breakfast with six spacious suites, cozy sitting and reading areas, an intimate dining room, and a large, secluded open-air center courtyard with a covered portico. A near-mystic ambiance pervades, and there are tales of treasure. It is rumored that as the Confederates retreated south after the Civil War battle of Glorietta Pass, they buried their valuables under the hacienda floor. Many have searched for the gold, but none have been successful. Perhaps it is still there, or perhaps this is just a tale.

Leaving Bernalillo, you turn onto NM 44 and cross the Rio Grande. On the river's west bank in the shadow of the *bosque* (cottonwood grove), Coronado State Monument commemorates the ancient Tiwa pueblo Kuaua and the place Francisco Coronado and his men spent the winter of 1540–1541. Today a visitors center traces the history of the site and displays original kiva murals, which deal with the Native American population's complex relationship with the earth and heavens. There are trails through reconstructed ruins, which include a kiva similar to the one that originally housed the images.

As you head north, you pass Santa Ana pueblo's commercial complex and Jackalope, a multi-acre compound that advertises "folk art by the truckload." A Mexican-style market with a plethora of pottery, blankets, baskets, rugs, and tinware from all points south, Jackalope is a diverting place to shop for a piece of cedar and pigskin *equipale* furniture from Guadalajara, a painted terra-cotta figure by Irene Aguilar of Oaxaca, or merely an inexpensive souvenir of your visit.

Route 44 follows the Jemez River valley past Zia pueblo, whose rayed sun sign is the symbol of New Mexico and appears on the state flag. The peaks of the Jemez Mountains rise in shades of red, ochre, and umber to the west, and during the spring, summer, and fall, the sage and juniper-dotted roadsides are carpeted in wildflowers—blue flax, Indian tea, and yellow clover.

At the small farming community of San Ysidro, the route veers onto NM 4. Named for the patron saint of farmers, the somnolent village was the site of a famous dinosaur dig from 1978 to 1980. The large *Camarasaurus* skeleton on display at the New Mexico Museum of Natural History in Albuquerque was discovered there, and another dinosaur, *Seismosaurus*, was uncovered at a nearby site. Your route through town passes a picturesque church and Shirley Powell's Columbine Pottery. A working studio and gallery, the shop carries Joann Barkman-Berndt's Mimbres-inspired ware, masks, and pottery drums, or dumbaks; Marion Ball's sculptured bears and cats; Pat Stalgren's functional dinnerware; Penne Roberts's rabbit pottery; candles by Eileen Tyree; and handblown hummingbirds by Mary Guitierrez, as well as pottery by Shirley, daughter Kellie Powell, and daughter-in-law Debbie Powell.

Following the river into a verdant valley rimmed by red cliffs, you arrive at Jemez Pueblo (say HEM-mus). Among the Jemez, the village traditionally is called Walatowa, a Towa word meaning "this is the place." This is among the most traditional pueblos. The people believe their ancestors originated from an underworld place, *Hua-vu-na-tota*, and migrated from the Four Corners area to the "Cañon de San Diego" region. When Europeans reached the region in 1541, the Jemez had an estimated population of 30,000 and numerous pueblos large and small scattered around Walatowa.

Now a tribe with more than 3,100 members, the Jemez are consummate artisans, best known for their work in clay—bowls, seed pots, sgraffito vessels, wedding vases, and their famous storytellers. They maintain Walatowa Visitors Center, with a gift shop, a photographic exhibit, a reconstructed traditional field house, and on special days, interpretive programs, bread-baking demonstrations, and traditional dances. Spring and fall they mount special arts and crafts shows at the Jemez Red Rocks area, where on off-weekends you may find women selling fresh bread from their beehive-shaped ovens called *hornos*.

When visiting Jemez, the pueblo requests that you check in at the visitors center. Wandering around the village is not permitted, but if you wish to visit a particular artist and make arrangements in advance, allowances generally can be made.

In particular, the Fragua family, whose storytellers are world-famous, welcomes buyers, and Sal and Flo Yepa encourage shoppers to visit their Sun and Fire Pottery House on the main road. Sal, from Jemez, and Flo, part Laguna and part Jemez, specialize in two distinct types of pottery: earthenware, which combines red clay and fine white sand temper, and stoneware, which is temper-free. Their home studio is a warm, friendly place, and they are always willing to spend a few minutes with gringos educating them on the fine points of the potter's art.

Leaving pueblo land, you'll find many shady picnic spots along the Jemez River. If you'd like a cold bottle of wine to accompany your alfresco lunch, be sure to take the turn down NM 290 to the Ponderosa Valley Vineyards & Winery. The vineyards planted by Henry and Mary Street in 1976 have consistently produced award-winning Rieslings as well as exotic local specialties such as Cactus Apple New Mexico Prickly Pear. Mary is usually found pouring for oenophiles at the tasting counter, while Henry is busy in the fields or among the vats. If he's not terribly preoccupied, you might convince him to give you a tour of the winery.

Beyond Ponderosa, the road makes multiple forks and becomes dirt or gravel as it reaches into San Juan and Paliza Canyons. Backtrack to the main road, NM 4, and continue through Cañones toward Jemez Springs. As you enter deeper and deeper into the canyon of the Jemez River, the precipitous walls of Bandelier volcanic tuff rise to the east and west. The tawny pink rock, with its eroded "Swiss cheese" cavities, is the product of the two great eruptions that shaped the Jemez Mountains. "Tent rocks" lining the cliffs are thought to represent cones of hardened ash, which once surrounded volcanic vents. The green of the river valley, the fleetness of the clear, boulder-filled stream, and the glow of the ruddy rock make an unforgettable drive.

Several miles south of Jemez Springs at Mile Marker 11, Shangri-La West Gallery and Trading Post is housed in a lovely adobe compound freshened by a fountain and bursting with flowers, birds, and dragonflies. Owners Rodney and Andrée Moen stock Native American arts and crafts, including a prime selection of the famous storytellers of the region. Through their years as traders, they have developed a rapport with many artists, with whom they deal directly. They showcase the work of many different tribes: Zuni fetish carvings, Hopi silver overlay jewelry, Jemez pots, Oaxaca wood carvings, Casas Grandes pottery, Tarahumara drums, Zia pottery—the list is endless. Both Rod and Andrée are jewelers, and, in addition to the Native American ware, you'll find their unusual handcrafted pieces that include Rod's Egyptian primitive earring designs. Adjoining the gallery, Andrée's The Old Wagon Boutique stocks a wide range of unusual clothing, jewelry, and collectibles.

First-time visitors to Jemez Springs always get a chuckle when they discover that this small resort town was named an "All American City" in 1995. The award was presented in response to the cleanup and beautification of the grassy park at the town center. Although the corporate limits encompass a couple of Catholic retreats, a Zen center, a general store, restaurants, and various accommodations, Jemez Springs's primary draw is its therapeutic hot springs. The bathhouse, which sits on the edge of the park, was built in the 1870s and added to in the 1940s. The cottage-like structure is surrounded by flower beds, and its main room gift shop is filled with a selection of natural health and beauty supplies. Mineral bathtubs are to the rear, with private sections for both men and women. Herbal or sweat wraps and massage are nice additions to the experience, and for those seeking a group encounter, an outdoor cedar tub with a capacity of six is available by reservation.

After a relaxing soak, you'll be ready for some sustenance, and at Deb's Deli and Mercantile you can order up the best lunch in town, a hot espresso or an ice cream parlor delight. Steve and Helen Nichols serve up particularly toothsome burgers, and all their breads, rolls, and pastries are baked on the premises. The side porch with its view of the town's comings and goings is the most popular spot in town on a warm spring or summer afternoon.

Jemez State Monument, a couple miles north of town, embraces the prehistoric ruins of the 13th-century Towa pueblo of Guisewa and the 17th-century Spanish mission of San José de los Jémez, founded in 1622 by Franciscan Fray Alonso de Luga, who came to the New World with Oñate in 1598. Guisewa, meaning "place of boiling waters," was an ancestral home of present-day Jemez pueblo people. Stop at the visitors center to learn more about Jemez history and mythology, and take a few minutes to examine the artifacts recovered from the rubble. A path from the center takes you to the partially excavated pueblo and the impressive church ruins.

As the road climbs beyond the monument, you'll notice cars stopped by the right side of the road. Soda Dam, a calcium carbonate–travertine dike over the river, was formed over the centuries by deposits from a spring surfacing nearby. The colorful formation is 300 feet long, 50 feet high, and 50 feet wide at the base. Kids play in the shallow caves at the base, and photographers burn frame after frame of film on the massive, rust-streaked protuberance.

If you'd like the experience of no-frills natural hot springs where bathing suits are strictly optional, continue up the hill to Battleship Rock picnic area near Mile Marker 23. In the shadow of the prow-like formation, a rather steep trail leads to Battleship Rock hot spring, a 30-by-40-foot pool surrounded by pines.

The trail to perennially popular Spense hot springs is just two miles north of Battleship Rock picnic area, between

Indian Head and Dark Canyon campgrounds. Two rock pools with a series of mini waterfalls are about 100 yards above the river. The water at the top is warmest, cooling as it descends to the lower pool and waterfall.

If your energy starts to sag and you're searching for a place to stay, you could do no better than the Riverdancer Inn, a couple of miles south of town near Mile Marker 16. Owners Linsay Locke and Linda Bedre's quiet oasis on the Jemez River felicitously combines the qualities of a healthful and spiritual retreat with graceful accommodations in the Southwestern style. In an adjoining private century-old refurbished casita, they provide modalities including acupressure, Swedish massage, shiatsu, reflexology, Polarity therapy, cranial sacral balancing, Reiki, Qi-Gong, and aromatherapy in addition to seaweed, aloe, and herbal body wraps and masks. Whatever your needs, Riverdancer has a therapist trained to meet them.

When you leave Jemez Springs, the road climbs consistently upward, past the turnoff to Fenton Lake State Park, Seven Springs Fish Hatchery, and Jemez Falls. Rounding the southern flank of Redondo Peak, you are greeted by an extraordinary sight—a huge grass-covered bowl with dimensions so staggering that buildings, cattle, and ranch vehicles are reduced to microscopic proportions. Once thought to be the site of the world's largest volcano, some 15,000 to 25,000 feet in height, Valle Grande and its sister valleys, Valle San Antonio, Valle Toledo, Valle Jaramillo, and Valle de los Posos, are believed to be a caldera, a basin formed by the collapse of the surface as a result of volcanic activity. Eruptions from this caldera during the Pleistocene period sent a blanket of volcanic ash 1,000 feet thick over a 400-square-mile area, which erosion carved into the mesas and canyons of the Pajarito Plateau. For many decades Valle Grande has been private grazing land with restricted access. There is a move afoot by the federal government to purchase the land and open it for public recreation, but many financial and legislative obstacles remain before this becomes a reality.

The seismic forces that shaped Valle Grande are responsible for creating Frijoles Canyon, home of Bandelier National Monument. As you drive the winding road from the mesa top, you can understand why prehistoric pueblo people called the Anasazi made the canyon home. El Rito de los Frijoles (Little River of Beans) bubbles its way down the canyon floor, bestowing a permanent source of water for man and beast. Along the stream's edge, fertile volcanic soil provides a growing medium, and the canyon's north wall of friable volcanic ash, called tuff, contains natural apertures that were enlarged into cavelike shelters. Unlike Chaco Canyon, which today is a barren, inhospitable place, Bandelier is a haven in the desert.

When you visit, stop at the visitors center, where you will get an orientation to the 50-square-mile park. A 10-minute slide show introduces you to what has been called "one of the largest concentrations of archaeological sites in the Southwest." You'll learn park history and be introduced to Adolph Francis Bandelier, the Colorado rancher and self-trained scholar who was the first to study and report on the ruins. Static exhibits interpret the occupation of the area from about A.D. 1200 to the present, and during the summer, regularly scheduled ranger-led walks originate here.

Stroll the canyon floor along the pretty loop trail bordered in wildflowers. In a quarter mile you'll come to the Tyuonyi pueblo ruins with its big ceremonial chamber, or kiva. Almost immediately to your right, cliff dwellings pock the face of the escarpment. Climb in and around these one- to three-story talus villages that extend along the base of the northern wall for approximately two miles. Many have cave rooms gouged out of the tuff, while others show holes where vigas (wooden support beams) extended the natural shelter. If you have time, say two hours or more, continue to the ceremonial cave.

The cliff dwellings of Bandelier National Monument.

Reached by a 140-foot climb up four steep wooden ladders, the ascent is not for the faint-of-heart or those suffering from vertigo. However, the view from the top is spectacular.

Cottonwood Picnic Area provides shaded bowers for lunch-munchers, and those seeking more extensive hiking trails will discover nearby trailheads to Upper and Lower Falls, the Rio Grande, Frijolito ruins, and the back country.

Leaving Bandelier, you climb Frijoles Mesa and head out NM 4 toward White Rock, where you'll find a winery with a most impressive view. Former Los Alamos nuclear chemist John Balagna's Balagna Winery possesses a splendid overlook of the White Rock Canyon of the Rio Grande River and the Sangre de Cristo Mountains. You can promenade the porch of the tasting room, sipping vintages and gazing down and out at a panorama nonpareil. John's wines are a reflection of his Italian heritage, and he unashamedly displays his "Dago Red" along with other gentler vintages such as zinfandel and chardonnay. "La Bomba Grande," a blend of zinfandel, pinot noir and merlot grapes, is one of John's most popular items. Part *vin ordinare* and part souvenir of the Atomic City, it is bottled with a label depicting a gigantic mushroom cloud.

For directions to the winery, copies of a self-guided walking tour of Los Alamos, a diagram of the buildings of the National Laboratory, and other helpful information, stop at the visitors center on NM 4 at White Rock. Another visitors center is found at the Chamber of Commerce office downtown.

Los Alamos is unlike any other town in New Mexico. One of your first observations might be that the cultural mix, so obvious in the rest of the state, is missing. Instead of Native Americans, Anglos, and Hispanics, you find an international amalgam of highly educated nuclear physicists, chemists, and representatives of other branches of science. At your quarters, you breakfast with a Ph.D. from Helsinki instead of a traveling couple from St. Louis. You also become aware of the absence of typical New Mexico adobe architecture.

If you think back, you'll begin to understand why this place is so different from its sister New Mexico cities. In 1917 in what is now the heart of Los Alamos, a wealthy Detroit businessman with the unlikely name of Ashley Pond purchased the Harold H. Brook homestead. His dream was to create a school dedicated to transforming sheltered boys from wealthy families into robust, learned men through participation in the active, outdoor life. By 1918, Pond's vision was a reality, and for almost 25 years the Los Alamos Ranch School prospered.

During the dark days of World War II, the U.S. government embarked on a highly secret project, headed by General Leslie Groves. His task was to assemble the top minds in physics to tame the power of the atom. In searching for a spot for a clandestine laboratory, he considered five crucial factors: available housing for 30 scientists, land owned by the government or easily acquired in secrecy, an area large and uninhabited enough to permit safe separation of experimental sites, easy control of access for security, and sufficient cleared land so new building could be started immediately.

The school was selected because J. Robert Oppenheimer, the director of scientific research, was intimately familiar with Los Alamos and knew it fit all the criteria. His family's summer home was in the mountains at the headwaters of the Pecos River, and as a boy he'd ridden over the mesas of the Pajarito Plateau on pack trips.

On December 7, 1942, the government gave notice that it was taking over the school, and shortly after, work on the secret laboratories began. By January 1, 1943, the University of California was selected to operate the facility, and a formal nonprofit contract was drawn with the Manhattan Engineer District of the Army. The Manhattan Project, as it became known, was a fact.

Over the next two years, some of the greatest minds in science toiled frantically in the ramshackle town of temporary structures. The old school buildings were pressed into service.

Fuller Hall became a restaurant, the classrooms were turned into the Post Exchange and other shops, and the masters' houses became residences for top project administrators. As these homes were the only houses to offer tubs instead of showers, they were collectively dubbed "Bathtub Row."

On July 16, 1945, the scientists' efforts reached fruition when the first atomic bomb was successfully tested at the Trinity site, a remote spot on White Sands Missile Range. Three weeks after the Trinity test, "Fat Man" was dropped on Hiroshima, and on August 9, a third explosion leveled the city of Nagasaki. Japan gave up five days later with formal surrender ceremonies September 2, 1945.

Although its prime purpose had been accomplished, the city did not die but gradually evolved. Research goes on at the Los Alamos National Laboratory, but now half its effort is devoted to the peaceful uses of atomic energy. The government has turned back commercial and residential properties on the hill to private ownership or to the county of Los Alamos, which was created in 1967. It is almost, but not quite, like any other town.

The best place to begin your visit would be the Los Alamos Historical Museum, housed in what was the Ranch School's infirmary and later guest quarters during the Manhattan Project. Here, more than anywhere else in the city, you get an idea of the flow of time and events. Exhibits deal with area geology and prehistory, homesteading, the Ranch School, and the Manhattan Project. A well-stocked bookstore sells a selection of books dealing with area history.

Some of the museum's most interesting displays depict the Ranch School years with pictures of the boys and masters partaking in vigorous outdoor activities. Since toughening spoiled Easterners was the aim, both teachers and pupils wore shorts and knee socks even during the cold, snowy winters! Two better-known graduates are the author Gore Vidal and Antonio J. Taylor, brother to Lady Bird Johnson.

Fuller Lodge, perhaps the most imposing structure left from Ranch School days, is next to the museum. Listed on the National Historical Register, the jackal log structure with massive front columns originally served as the school's dining and recreation hall. The logs were said to have been hand-selected by the noted architect John Gaw Meem and Ranch School director A. J. Connell.

Today Fuller Lodge is a county-run, multi-use building providing meeting space for laboratory conferences and community events. In addition, the south wing houses the Art Center at Fuller Lodge, which sponsors arts and crafts fairs in August and October and mounts three juried shows throughout the year. Docent tours of the building are available by reservation through the Historical Society headquarters at the museum.

If you've been sightseeing all morning at Los Alamos's 7,400-foot altitude and have developed a ravenous appetite, head for the Hill Diner on Trinity. Originally the "Good Eats Cafe," the Hill, with its knotty pine paneling and camp lodge atmosphere, dishes up a mean platter of chicken-fried steak, bowls of homemade soup, or tasty burgers. Leave room for dessert, however, because their banana cream pie is out of this world. Meltingly ripe chunks of banana rest on a flaky crust, topped with rich cream filling and a halo of whipped cream. The portions are monstrous, so you might want to share with a friend.

Save time in the afternoon for the Bradbury Science Museum, named not for Ray Bradbury of science fiction fame, but for Norris Bradbury, director of research after Oppenheimer's departure at what is now Los Alamos National Laboratory. With more than 130,000 visitors per year, it is easily the most popular attraction in town. The modern structure on the corner of Central Avenue and 15th Street in the heart of downtown has 8,500 feet of exhibit space dedicated to interpreting the role of the laboratory to the lay public.

In all, there are 40 high-tech exhibits on Manhattan Project history and current and historical research projects. Technocrats, students of all ages, and even those who think they are scientifically challenged will enjoy the interactive computer programs, which allow visitors to learn about lasers and light, computer research, and weapon design. The displays of the Fat Man bomb case, a cruise missile, and models of satellites are impressive.

Local, national, and international visitors find the 18-minute film, "The Town that Never Was," a satisfying and comprehensible explanation of the Manhattan Project and life in Los Alamos during the last days of World War II. Historic black-and-white footage graphically portrays world and national events at this critical point in history.

Next to the museum, Otowi Station Science Museum Shop & Bookstore is one of those wonderful stores where you can browse for hours. They stock educational toys and books on area hiking and mountain biking in addition to maps, local histories, and books on atomic history, technical sciences, and computers. Tourist information is graciously dispensed, and if you'd like to spend a couple hours with someone who has the real skinny on Los Alamos, this is where you'll meet Buffalo Tours' Georgia Strickfaden, a Los Alamos native who knows more about the area than any 10 other people combined. Her hour-and-a-half tours feature the historical town site, the National Laboratory, and the Rio Grande overlook at White Rock. She also tailors special-interest tours, ranging from trips to nearby Spanish and Indian villages to excursions to the Jemez Mountains.

Dining in Los Alamos doesn't get any better than the Blue Window, a second-floor bistro at 800 Trinity. Chef Joseph

Griffo presents a varied international cuisine with emphasis on seasonal produce. All pasta, breads, desserts, and ice cream are made on the premises, and the Blue Window is one of the few places in the New Mexican outback where you know you'll get immaculately fresh fish, properly prepared. You might want to start with Chef Joseph's creamy New England clam chowder, followed by pomegranate-glazed quail salad and scallops Provençale, fresh sea scallops sauteed with sweet bell peppers, red onions, and mushrooms served in a garlic-wine sauce. Heavenly! Or perhaps you'd prefer his popular Southwest chicken, a tender chicken breast wrapped in phyllo pastry, stuffed with chipotle-chile pesto and served with a roasted garlic beurre blanc sauce.

After such an exhausting and fulfilling day, you'll want a soft pillow and a welcoming room. Renata's Orange Street Bed & Breakfast is just the place. Originally a duplex home, the simple frame structure belies a gracious interior. The eight rooms (four with private bath) are theme-decorated, and owners Lynda and Mark Hartman have adorned each door frame with clever motifs. "Country Cottage" is a sunny, south-facing room decorated in a bright sunflower motif and features an antique iron bed and wash basin. "Tucson" has Southwestern decor with a handcrafted wardrobe. The other six are as unusual and attractive. A full breakfast is set out in the homelike dining and sitting area overlooking majestic ponderosa pines and flowering apricot trees. Guests are welcome to use the kitchen facilities to either store their snacks or prepare a full meal, if they so desire.

Leaving town, you head out NM 502 and descend a steep hill. If you look sharp, you will see the remains of the original road to your right and prehistoric ruins to your left at the canyon bottom. After the intersection of NM 502 and NM 30, you pass the entrance to San Ildefonso. If you take the first marked road, you encounter Babbitt's Cottonwood Trading Post. Trader Joe Babbitt stocks the Navajo pottery of the

Manygoats family as well as an impressive pottery selection from San Ildefonso, Acoma, Zuni, and San Juan. There are rugs, ribbon shirts, mantas, pelts, and a grocery section where you can buy enamel pots or a cold drink.

Continuing beyond the tree-shaded trading post, you enter the pueblo proper, home of famous potters Maria and Julian Martinez, who revolutionized design with their black-on-black ware. It is still a village of potters and one of the prettier pueblos. Stop at the visitors center to register, pay a fee, and get a map, delineating those areas open to guests. It is pleasant to walk the dusty streets, visit with the potters in their home studios, and examine the duel plazas divided by the giant grandfather cottonwood. Perhaps at journey's end you'll carry home a piece of world-renowned San Ildefonso pottery, a remembrance of hours of enjoyment exploring the Jemez trail.

For More Information

Rose's Pottery House and Art Gallery, 2000 Camino del Pueblo, Bernalillo, NM 87004. Call 505-867-5911. Open Tuesday through Saturday from 8:00 A.M. to 6:00 P.M., Sunday from 10:00 A.M. to 5:00 P.M.

The Range Cafe Restaurant & Bakery, 925 Camino del Pueblo, Bernalillo, NM 87004. Call 505-867-1700. Open daily 7:30 A.M. to 9:00 P.M. in winter, 10:00 P.M. in summer. Website: www.rangecafe.com.

Home at the Range, 925 Camino del Pueblo, Bernalillo, NM 87004. Call 505-867-4755. Open daily from 9:00 A.M. to 9:00 P.M. Website: www.rangecafe.com.

Best Kept Secrets Emporium, The Rose Center, 925 Camino del Pueblo, Bernalillo, NM 87004. Call 505-771-0140. Open Tuesday through Saturday from 10:00 A.M. to 5:00 P.M.

Wax Poetic Workshop, 925 Camino del Pueblo, Bernalillo, NM 87004. Call 505-867-4245. Open Monday through Friday from 9:00 A.M. to 5:00 P.M.

Paula Dimit Studio, 901 Camino del Pueblo, Bernalillo, NM 87004. Call 505-771-1917. Open Wednesday through Sunday from noon to 5:00 P.M.

La Hacienda Grande, 21 Baros Lane, Bernalillo, NM 87004. Call 505-867-1887. Website: www.lahaciendagrande.com.

Coronado State Monument, P.O. Box 95 (one mile west of Bernalillo on NM 44), Bernalillo, NM 87004. Call 505-867-5351. Open daily from 8:00 A.M. to 5:00 P.M.

Jackalope, NM 44, Bernalillo, NM 87004. Call 505-867-9813. Open Monday through Saturday from 9:00 A.M. to 7:00 P.M., Sunday from 9:30 A.M. to 6:00 P.M. Website: www.jackalope.com.

Columbine Pottery, 311 Highway 4, San Ysidro, NM 87053. Call 505-834-7687. Open daily from 9:00 A.M. to 6:00 P.M. Website: www.sulphurcanyon.com/dpowell/columbine.htm.

Walatowa Visitors Center, P.O. Box 100, Jemez Pueblo, NM 87024. Call 505-834-7235. Open daily from 8:00 A.M. to 5:00 P.M.

Sun & Fire Pottery House, 4514 NM 4, Jemez Pueblo, NM 87024. Call 505-834-7717. Open daily from 8:00 A.M. to 6:00 P.M.

Ponderosa Valley Vineyards & Winery, 3171 NM 290, Ponderosa, NM 87044. Call 505-834-7487. Open Tuesday through Saturday from 10:00 A.M. to 5:00 P.M., Sunday from noon to 5:00 P.M.

Shangri-La West Gallery and Trading Post, Mile Marker 11, NM 4, Jemez Pueblo, NM 87024. Call 505-829-3864. Open April–November, daily from 10:00 A.M. to 5:00 P.M.; December–March, daily 11:00 A.M. to 4:00 P.M.

Jemez Springs Bath House, 062 Jemez Springs Plaza, NM 4, Jemez Springs, NM 87025. Call 505-829-3303. Open in winter, daily from 10:00 A.M. to 8:00 P.M.; in summer, daily 9:00 A.M. to 9:00 P.M. Website: www.jemez.com/baths.

Deb's Deli and Mercantile, 17607 NM 4, Jemez Springs, NM 87025. Call 505-829-3829. Open in summer Monday through Friday from 8:00 A.M. to 6:00 P.M., Saturday and Sunday from 8:00 A.M. to 7:00 P.M., in winter daily 8:00 A.M. to 4:00 P.M.

Jemez State Monument, 18160 NM 4, P.O. Box 143, Jemez Springs, NM 87025. Call 505-829-3530. Open daily from 8:30 A.M. to 5:00 P.M.

Riverdancer Inn, 164455 NM 4, Jemez Springs, NM 87025. Call 505-829-3262 or 800-809-3262.

Bandelier National Monument, Los Alamos, NM 87544. Call 505-672-3861, ext. 517. Park open daily from dawn to dusk. Visitors center open daily from 8:00 A.M. to 6:00 P.M. in summer, daily 8:30 A.M. to 4:30 P.M. in winter. Website: www.nps.gov/band.

Balagna Winery, 223 Rio Bravo Drive, Los Alamos (White Rock), NM 87544. Call 505-672-3678. Open daily from noon to 6:00 P.M. Call for hours in January and February.

Los Alamos Visitors Centers, 125 NM 4, White Rock, NM 87544. Call 505-662-8105 or 800-444-0707. Downtown at the Chamber of Commerce, 109 Central Park Square, Los Alamos, NM 87544. Open Monday through Saturday from 9:00 A.M. to 4:00 P.M., Sunday from 10:00 A.M. to 3:00 P.M. Website: www.losalamos.com.

Los Alamos Historical Museum, 1921 Juniper Street, Los Alamos, NM 87544. Call 505-662-6272 or 505-662-4493. Open in summer, Monday through Friday from 9:30 A.M. to 4:30 P.M., Saturday and Sunday from 11:00 A.M. to 5:00 P.M.; winter, Monday through Saturday from 10:00 A.M. to 4:00 P.M., Sunday from 1:00 to 4:00 P.M. Website: www.losalamos.com/Historicalsociety/default.htm.

Art Center and Gallery at Fuller Lodge, 2132 Central Avenue, Los Alamos, NM 87544. Call 505-662-9331. Open Monday through Saturday from 10:00 A.M. to 4:00 P.M.

Hill Diner, 1315 Trinity, Los Alamos, NM 87544. Call 505-662-9745. Open in summer from 11:00 A.M. to 9:00 P.M.; winter, Monday through Sunday from 11:00 A.M. to 8:00 P.M. Website: www.losalamos.com/hilldiner/default.htm.

Bradbury Science Museum, Central Avenue and 15th Street, Los Alamos, NM 87544. Call 505-667-4444. Open Tuesday through Friday from 9:00 A.M. to 5:00 P.M., Saturday through Monday from 1:00 to 5:00 P.M. Website: www.lanl.gov/external/museum.

Otowi Station Science Museum Shop & Bookstore, 1530 Central Avenue, Los Alamos, NM 87544. Call 505-662-9589. Open Monday through Friday from 8:00 A.M. to 8:00 P.M., Saturday from 9:00 A.M. to 6:00 P.M., Sunday from 11:00 A.M. to 6 P.M. Website: www.otowi.com.

Buffalo Tours, P.O. Box 726, Los Alamos, NM 87544. Call 505-662-5711.

Blue Window, 800 Trinity, second floor, Los Alamos, NM 87544. Call 505-662-6305. Open for lunch Monday through Friday from 11:00 A.M. to 2:00 P.M., dinner, Monday through Saturday from 5:00 to 8:30 P.M.

Renata's Orange Street Bed & Breakfast, 3496 Orange Street, Los Alamos, NM 87544. Call 505-662-2651. Website: www.losalamos.com/orangestreetinn.

Babbitt's Cottonwood Trading Post, R.R. 5, Box 320, Santa Fe, NM 87501. Call 505-455-7596 or 800-766-4846. Nine miles west of junction 285/502, San Ildefonso Pueblo. Open Monday through Saturday from 9:00 A.M. to 5:30 P.M.

San Ildefonso Pueblo. Call 505-455-2273. Visitors center open Monday through Friday from 8:00 A.M. to 5:00 P.M. Maria Poveka Martinez Museum open Monday through Friday from 8:00 A.M. to noon and 1:00 to 4:00 P.M. Pottery shops open Monday through Friday from 10:30 A.M. to 5:00 P.M. Fee.

2

Georgia O'Keeffe Country

Getting there: From Albuquerque, take I-25 north 35 miles to St. Francis Drive, exit 282, Santa Fe. North of Santa Fe, connect with U.S. 84/285. Follow St. Francis Drive out of Santa Fe, past the National Cemetery and the turnoff to the opera. Head north on U.S. 84/285, 24 miles to Española, where U.S. 84 divides from 285 and heads northwest 22 miles to Abiquiu, through the small towns of San Pedro, Hernandez, and Chili. Ghost Ranch and the Living Museum are off U.S. 84 north of town.

Leaving Abiquiu, take NM 554 northeast 16 miles to El Rito. Outside of the village, NM 554 meets NM 111, which continues east and south for nine miles. Turn south on U.S. 285 and drive two miles to Ojo Caliente. Leaving the hot springs, continue on 285 south to Española, 25 miles.

Highlights: For a three- or four-day excursion into this region of mystery and color, follow the path of artists and aesthetes to Abiquiu. Visit the Georgia O'Keeffe home and Ghost Ranch, refresh your spirit with the Benedictine monks at Christ in the Desert, discover El Rito, an old community where new and old arts flourish side by side, and bathe in the healing waters of Ojo Caliente hot springs.

When Nature created northern New Mexico, she gathered her forces to shape the spectacular and expanded her color palette to include shades seldom seen in terrestrial forms. Of all the sites in a state known for its colorful scenery, the region around Abiquiu is perhaps the most wondrous and exotic.

The 20th-century American painter Georgia O'Keeffe made the mesas, cliffs, and buttes of Abiquiu famous in her intensely colored paintings, but even for O'Keeffe devotees, a trip to this small Hispanic town on the banks of the Chama River is a revelation. The mystery of "the white place," the vibrancy of the red and yellow cliffs at Ghost Ranch, the imposing form of the flat-topped Pedernal—all are there in shape and shade but not greatly changed from the artist's representation.

It is only a short journey from Santa Fe to Abiquiu. Leaving "the city different," you climb the hill past the National Cemetery and begin a long descent toward Española valley. The four-lane divided highway hums along past the entrance to the Santa Fe Opera and Tesuque Pueblo.

At Pojoaque Pueblo's Poeh Center, you can browse through the small cultural center and museum documenting the struggle of the Pojoaque people to retain their heritage. The adjoining 11,000-square-foot Indian Arts and Crafts Gallery and tourist information center feature a huge selection of northern New Mexican Indian pottery as well as jewelry, sculptures, kachinas, and sand paintings. Seasonal activities include dances and bread baking in the traditional beehive-shaped adobe *hornos* (ovens). Even if you arrive in midwinter, the soft-crumbed pueblo bread is usually available both in the gallery and at Po-suwae-geh, a restaurant specializing in pueblo and regional foods.

A short distance down the pike on Española's outskirts, David Dear's small showroom is the place to shop for elegant silver and gold jewelry. David is a self-taught Anglo jeweler who works in noble metals and draws inspiration from traditional Southwestern designs. Part of the Museum of New Mexico and the Santa Fe Wheelwright Museum's permanent collections, David's jewelry is designed, cast, and hand-finished locally in Arroyo Seco. His concho belts, bolo ties, tip sets, belt buckles, pins, earrings, cuff links, and studs are meticulously cast and exquisitely finished.

Entering Española you cross the Santa Cruz River. A farming and ranching community founded in the middle of the 19th-century, the area served for many years as the shipping point for the produce grown in the Española valley. Today the city's main product appears to be low riders, automobiles that have been specially modified. The basic low rider has had its chassis adapted to accommodate a smaller set of wheels set on a wider axle. The steering wheel is often replaced with welded chain link, and the paint job can be customized to reflect the owner's artistic taste, whether it's a vision of Our Lady of Guadalupe or a space-age scene. Some low riders are equipped with a special hydraulic system, which enables the car to hop, raise up and down, and perform various singular maneuvers. The pride and joy of Hispanic males of all ages, the low rider is mucho macho.

If you have developed an appetite, it's time to divert from the road to Abiquiu and head into town on Riverside Drive. Española has several restaurants specializing in northern New Mexican food. The first place you encounter will be Jo Ann's Ranch O Casados in the Big Rock Shopping Center. The Casados family grows its own red and green chiles and corn products in their nearby valley farm. They serve breakfast all day, and their blue corn tortillas make a wonderful base for enchiladas. A former Kentucky Fried Chicken outlet, the building lacks cachet but more than makes up for it in the flavor and quality of its offerings.

Another modest but genuine purveyor of New Mexican cooking is Matilda's Restaurant, a block off Riverside on Corlett. Matilda and Phillip Guillen have been serving their food to Española's citizens for 44 years. It's a place favored by locals, and you're more likely to encounter families out for dinner than transplants from Santa Fe.

El Paragua, a block off Riverside on Santa Cruz Road (the Taos High Road), is perhaps the most famous of Española restaurants. Larry and Pete Atencio started the business as a taco, tamale, and lemonade stand in 1958. Their dad, Luis, provided them with a beach umbrella to shade them from the hot sun, and it became the stand's namesake, El Paragua, or the umbrella. As good things will, their taco stand flourished, expanded, and matured into a restaurant, enveloping the former tack rooms of the family home and the next-door plumbing shop. Additions continued through the years, making the El Paragua a sprawling complex.

Oddly enough, although the menu runs the gamut from a rib eye steak topped with whole green chiles to lightly breaded, pan-fried trout, the house specialty is still the Tacos Estilo El Paragua, which marries deep-fried tortillas with succulent beef shreds moistened with a reduction of tomato and a hint of cumin.

If you don't want the full restaurant treatment, the Atencios have recently revived the taco stand, renamed El Parasol. You can drive up, place your order, and enjoy your lunch in the shade of the ancient cottonwood trees.

In your meandering around Española, you might encounter individuals robed in white, hair confined by snowy white turbans. They are members of the Sikh Dharma Community, an East Indian religious sect with many non-Indian members. They have an ashram nearby, which draws followers from all parts of the globe, especially during the summer solstice in June.

Before leaving Española, you should spend an hour with Leo Polo-Trujillo and his partner, Beryl D. Steuart, at the Chimayo Trading Post/The Marco Polo Shop. This New Mexico landmark is the quintessential trading post with its solid adobe walls and cavernous, wood-beamed interior. Located where Sandia intersects Riverside Drive, the post originally was founded in the nearby village of Chimayo by Leo's dad, the late Esquipula de Aguero "E. D." Trujillo, a prominent figure in Rio Arriba. Following an unneighborly dispute in 1926, E. D. moved both family and trading post to Española, where he constructed a new compound consisting of the post, the family home, and the Ramona Hotel, named for his wife. In June of 1939 fire destroyed the post and residence. Undeterred, E. D. rebuilt around the baked adobe walls.

The post prospered through the 1930s and '40s as a regular stop on Fred Harvey Tours, but after the death of E. D., the building fell into disrepair. Leo returned to his childhood home in the '80s after a 30-year career as a bursar with Pan American Airlines. The place was a wreck, suffering damage from years of neglect and with many of its unique architectural elements stolen by vandals. Not content to see his heritage destroyed, Leo and his partner, Beryl, who had retired from Air France, dug in and restored the buildings.

Opened in 1983 as the Marco Polo Shop at the Trading Post and named to the state list of cultural properties, the mercantile sells much the same merchandise as the original. There are objects for all pocketbooks. Silver jewelry, old pawn, pueblo pottery, and beautifully carved *santos* fill the antique glass cases. Leo and Beryl's personal collection—marked with NFS (not-for-sale) tags—rests among the New Mexican crafts, baskets from Pakistan, and Zapotec weaving. The partners sit at the entrance, available to anyone interested in a specific item or just wishing to talk about the history of the post and the area. A symbol of their hospitality to travelers is the perennial coffee pot sitting on the burner, free java to anyone in need of a fix.

Leaving the city, you head northwest on the Chama Highway. Passing the small village of Hernandez, you might recall one of photographer Ansel Adam's best-loved and most widely recognized prints, "Moonrise Hernandez," which shows a full moon rising over snowcapped mountains. If you give in to the temptation to search for the scene, chances are you will be disappointed. Modern development has all but obliterated the simple arrangement of church, village, and cemetery. However, if you stop at Romero's Fruit Stand on the west side of the road, Jake or Clarabelle will be happy to point you in the right direction. In addition to information, they stock an incredible supply of New Mexican products: long and short *ristras* (ropes of chiles), *ristras* in the shape of hearts or wreaths, 14 varieties of beans and bean soup mixes, 10 varieties of red and six varieties of green chiles, and corn products like *panocha, chaqueque, atole,* and *harina.*

Heading north and west, you pass the junction of the Rio del Oso, the Rio Ojo Caliente, and the Rio Chama near Chili. Keeping the Rio Chama's waters to the east, you enter the outskirts of Abiquiu. Several commercial services line the highway, but like some medieval fortress, the village itself sits atop a hill.

Abiquiu was first settled around 1744 by a handful of Spaniards and *genizaros*, Christianized Indians freed from slavery. The village, built on top of an old Tewa pueblo on the banks of the Chama River, was a center of trade and the starting point of Fathers Dominguez and Escalante's 2,000-mile trek to California.

For years the village slumbered in relative anonymity. Like many northern New Mexican towns, life centered around home and church. Traditionally, the men supported Los Hermanos de Nuestro Padre Jesus Nazareno, or Penitentes, a clandestine Christian group who, in addition to practicing penance during Lent, also contribute to the welfare of their communities through acts of charity. Their gathering place, or *morada*, occupies a prominent place on Abiquiu's hill.

Before Georgia O'Keeffe bought the ruin overlooking the river and the road to Santa Fe, there was little reason for outsiders to visit the village. O'Keeffe had been living at her home on Ghost Ranch, but the soil was poor and would not support a garden. She wearied of driving to Española or Santa Fe for fresh produce, and the Abiquiu property had both garden space and water.

Suddenly, strangers appeared in the village seeking the famous artist. Both she and the townsfolk grew tired of constant intrusions on their cherished privacy. She is said to have greeted one overardent visitor who wanted to "see" her with four words, "front side," a turn to the rear and "backside," and a slamming door accompanied by "good-bye."

With this history, it is not strange that the town maintains an uneasy truce with guests. No photos are permitted in the village, and should you become disoriented on your way to the O'Keeffe home, your request for directions will be treated courteously but with a distinct touch of reserve.

Administered by the Georgia O'Keeffe Foundation, the artist's home is now open for tours. Formed "to extend and protect the artistic legacy of Georgia O'Keeffe" and "to safeguard her home and studio in Abiquiu," the foundation is compiling a catalogue raisonné of the artist's body of work and is considering transferring the house to the National Trust for Historic Preservation.

The foundation is a faithful watchdog, and they limit the number of visitors and set the rules such as a prohibition on photography, note taking, and recording. Many rooms may be viewed only at a distance to protect the delicate polished dirt floors. The foundation walks the fine line between making the home accessible to O'Keeffe's legion of admirers and maintaining the old adobe property that was never intended to host legions.

Tours are small (a maximum of 12), last approximately an hour, and must be booked in advance through the foundation office. Demand is great, especially during the warm months, so it behooves you to phone ahead as early as possible.

It's all worth it. The gardens are lovingly maintained, even though they are not as extensive as when the artist was in residence. The home, which is kept as it was in 1984, is larger than expected, about 5,000 square feet. O'Keeffe divided the space of the main house into quadrants: storage (books and paintings), living areas, service, and guest quarters.

The house was built around an interior court in the *plazuela* style, and most rooms open onto it, including the sitting room with its ceiling *vigas* (roof beams) and cedar *rajas* (board ceiling lath). A wall of windows, a familiar O'Keeffe signature, overlooks ancient tamarisk trees, and an aged jade plant fills a corner. O'Keeffe's *Yellow Horizon with Clouds* is mounted on the wall. Furniture is minimal. Adobe *bancos* (benches) line the kiva fireplace wall, and a rattlesnake skeleton is seductively displayed under glass at one end. Chairs are by classic designers Charles Eames and Eero Saarinen.

The view from the dining room is extended through "the roofless room," an adjoining outdoor atrium shaded by a screened roof. The table is a model O'Keeffe copied from Rudolf Schindler, a designer for several Frank Lloyd Wright homes. Utilizing hinges, the plywood table opens to accommodate guests, or folds for more intimate dining.

The bright kitchen houses another plywood table, this one supported by sawhorses, and the cabinets are recessed deep into the thick adobe. There is a Chambers gas range and an old Kitchen Aide dishwasher.

The "Indian Room" is a small rectangle off the kitchen. Originally used for visitors of simple status, the chamber features a shepherd's bed elevated above the fireplace so the warmth of the adobe could toast a traveler's bones on cold nights. O'Keeffe used the space mainly to dry herbs and store fruits and vegetables.

The pantry and laundry also adjoin the kitchen. It is interesting to discover how involved O'Keeffe was with the running of her household. Some of the pantry's jars are labeled by her hand, grown somewhat spidery in old age. To those who consider the artist's retreat to New Mexico as the act of an ascetic, it may come as a surprise to discover she had not only a dishwasher but two freezers and a mangle.

The artist's studio and living area were created from the original barn. The studio is breathtaking, with its brilliant light generated by an expanse of windowed wall. From this vantage point, O'Keeffe could view the Sierra Negre, the frequently painted "white place," and the yellow domes of the Dar al Islam mosque. O'Keeffe's collection of stones line the window sills, and *From a Day with Juan* hangs on an opposing wall. The painting celebrated her 1976 visit to Washington, D.C., with Juan Hamilton, an artist, potter, and O'Keeffe's companion in her later years.

The bedroom off the studio is quite small and spare, with two windows at right angles and a small kiva fireplace. "I have a corner," O'Keeffe was known to remark, "you can't have much less than that." The hand of Buddha in the "fear not," or muhdra, position and several of O'Keeffe's ceramic pots are the simple decorations.

After your midday tour, your immediate need will be for bodily fortification. Your best bet both for meals and lodging is the Abiquiu Inn. The dining room has a traditional menu, with specialities in Middle Eastern fare, lamb, and northern New Mexico cuisine. Adjoining the lobby, a gift shop carries selections from around the world as well as work by native and local artisans.

Accommodations vary from plain motel rooms to lovely casitas overlooking the river. With wood stoves, eat-in kitchens, Talavera-tiled baths, and separate bedrooms, the casitas are the best choice, especially in off-season, when you will have to rustle some of your meals.

Bode's General Merchandise is on the main highway at the base of the hill. Founded in 1919, the store once was located in the heart of the village. It carries everything from rabbit feed and fishing lures to a complete line of groceries, including some herbal remedies and natural food items. Prepared food is limited to deli soups, salads, and sandwiches, fresh pastries, rotisserie chickens, or the hot pot full of fresh tamales by the counter.

Most visitors in the know, as well as locals, make the 16-mile drive to El Rito and El Farolito Restaurant. For 15 years Dennis and Carmen Trujillo have been serving up some of the best green chile in New Mexico from their modest café. Dennis goes through over 100 sacks of chile a year, making up his "secret recipe" from three varieties that he selects from crops in Las Cruces and Romero's in Hernandez. All their entrees are excellent, but ah, those green chile burritos! There's just enough heat to leave that little tingle around the lips that chile-heads savor.

A visit to Abiquiu should last more than a single day. Take an afternoon to visit Ghost Ranch, 13 miles northwest of the village. Part of the 1766 21,000-acre Piedra Lumbre (rocks afire) Land Grant, the property and some adjacent parcels were purchased in the 1930s by Mr. and Mrs. Arthur Pack for a guest ranch.

In 1929 Georgia O'Keeffe first visited Taos at the urging of Dorothy Brett and that indomitable patron of the arts,

Mabel Dodge Luhan. Taos and its arts scene were too public for O'Keeffe, and in 1934 she found the spectacular valley of remote Ghost Ranch more to her liking. Renting from the Packs for several summers and returning every winter to New York and her husband, noted photographer Alfred Stieglitz, O'Keeffe finally convinced Arthur Pack to sell her his own residence, Rancho de los Burros, and seven acres of land. She owned this property concurrently with the Abiquiu house, and Ghost Ranch environs are the subjects of much of her best-loved work: the red and gray hills across from the roadside park south of the ranch, Kitchen Mesa's red and yellow cliffs, and flat-topped Pedernal mountain.

In 1955 the Packs donated Ghost Ranch to the Presbyterian Church. Now an adult study center with a variety of programs focusing on the northern New Mexico environment, Ghost Ranch's ties to the O'Keeffe story are largely in the past. The artist's former home is on private land with no public access. There are no Georgia O'Keeffe originals at the ranch, no O'Keeffe museum.

However, guests are welcomed at the center, and with sufficient notice, you can join students of all ages at the cafeteria-style meals or in the simple ranch-style accommodations. There's even an RV area set aside for campers. The center's hiking trails, including the trail to the top of Kitchen Mesa, are open to everyone. A map and sign-in sheet are available at the office reception desk.

In addition, the Florence Hawley Ellis Museum of Anthropology and the Ruth Hall Museum of Paleontology are open to the public. The anthropology museum, constructed on the design of a great kiva, illustrates 12,000 years of life in the Rio Grande–Chama–Gallina valleys. Examples of Indian crafts, both historic and prehistoric, line the displays. The re-created workshop of Max Roybal, *santero* and longtime teacher of wood carving at the ranch, is riveting for lovers of Hispanic arts. Many of his solemn wooden saints keep watch on the foibles of mortals from their *nichos* (niches) by his workbench.

The Museum of Paleontology focuses on the Triassic period, a time when most nearby fossil beds were laid down. Stretching across one wall, "Flora and Fauna of the Triassian Twilight," features *Phytosaur*, a giant lizard. A work-in-progress, the fossilized remains of *Coelophysis*, the earliest known dinosaur, awaits the skilled hands of trained paleontologists commissioned with wresting secrets from its tomb of silt stone.

Ghost Ranch Living Museum is just three miles north of the conference center. Adults and children alike enjoy the exhibits of live native plants and animals. You'll observe fox, deer, elk, raccoon, prairie dog, beaver, badger, striped skunk, bobcat, and mountain lion. All were orphans, pets grown too large and unpredictable, or injured animals unable to return to the wild. At Gateway to the Past Heritage Center, displays focus on area human history.

Teaching people their role in the interdependence of plant, animal, and human life in the land, the museum is pledged to the concept "all life touches other life." Conceived by Arthur Pack, a conservationist, and dedicated to the people of New Mexico, the museum was designed and built by Pack's friend, William H. Carr. Currently it is operated by the U.S. Forest Service.

To visit Christ of the Desert Monastery, you must turn west on Forest Service Road 151, only a couple miles north of the museum. There is no sign, and the first mile is deceptively paved. You will quickly find yourself on a 13-mile dirt track, which can be impassible in a touring car if there has been any recent rain or snow. Check at Bode's for conditions, and give yourself plenty of time to reach the monastery.

You will be traveling through the Chama River Canyon Wilderness Area, with its high polychrome bluffs and riverine habitat. The farther you progress from pavement, the more you understand why Father Aelred Wall and his Benedictine monks founded this sanctuary in 1964 to "sing God's praises in the wilderness" and provide a "place apart" for those seeking prayer and meditation. Currently 23 to 25 brothers from places as diverse as Vietnam and Argentina reside at the monastery, practicing Benedict's precepts of common and individual prayer, reading, study, and manual labor.

Upon reaching the monastery, you should park in the designated area and walk to the foot of the chapel, where there is a large bell. Give the bell rope a good pull or two to summon the guest master, your liaison with the monastic community. Whether you arrive on retreat or as a day visitor, you are welcome to attend any of the seven daily services, walk in those places not considered private by the monks, or visit the gift shop with its cornucopia of religious books and crafts. The wood *santos* from a village near San Miguel de Allende are especially beautiful.

The chapel was designed by George Nakashima, the famous Japanese-American woodworker and architect. The soaring bell tower backs against red rock cliffs, whose fiery tones reflect through chapel windows in the late afternoon. The altar is a five-foot-square block of Colorado granite, and the first monk's choir is graced with a large carving of Our Lady of Guadalupe by Maria Romero Cash.

The second monk's choir contains the tabernacle, also designed by Nakashima. The tabernacle's open doors are painted with representations of a variety of saints, including Gabriel, Benedict, Scholastica, Benedict's twin sister, Francis, and Kateri, the Lily of the Mohawks. A monk from San Juan el Bautista, Mexico, carved the figure of Saint John the Baptist, patron of the monastery, and the large figure of the crucified Christ in back of the lectern.

If you come on retreat, you will be housed in the guest house, which is spare but comfortable. Wood stoves provide heat in cold weather, and light is contributed by kerosene lamps. A common bath has hot and cold running water. Meals are taken in silence in the refectory, and according to the Rule of Benedict, the order's founder, no red meat is served.

Before departing Abiquiu, take time to visit Dar al Islam, an educational organization dedicated to fostering better understanding between the Muslim and non-Muslim worlds. It is two and a half miles down CR 155, a well-maintained dirt road. You turn right about a quarter mile after crossing the Chama River bridge to the northwest of Abiquiu.

The organization's headquarters were designed by Hassam Fathy, the Egyptian architect, and consist of offices, a mosque, and a *madrasa*, or school. The buildings are beautiful—yellow domes punctuated with carved white stucco screen windows. You are welcome to visit, remembering that Muslim law prescribes modesty—no shorts, halter tops, or the like. A head covering for women is appreciated but not required.

Entering the mosque, you'll find benches to remove your shoes and an anteroom to the left containing a tiled tank or fountain for ablutions. A niche, or *mihrab*, in the wall is oriented toward Mecca, and soft rugs carpet the floors. Since religious law prohibits figurative decoration, the mosque's majesty is contained in its series of interlocking arches.

Dar al Islam owns 1,556 acres, including "the white place," one of O'Keeffe's favorite subjects. No special permission is required to hike in the canyon, and you should not miss the opportunity, even if you go but a short distance. It is a moving, you might say disturbing, place. Ghostly columns of gray volcanic tuff rise like spirit sentinels, and sections of the canyon wall resemble giant versions of the drip castles you made of sand on childhood beach outings.

Departing Abiquiu, you head for El Rito, and although it may not be obvious on your first pass through town, it is a community of artists. The second or third weekend in October they hold a studio tour, which includes over 20 stops. If you visit any other time of year, stop at either Martin's General Store, the big white frame building in the center of town, or at El Farolito across the street. They have lists of studios open to the public.

A sampling might include the atelier of Barbara Campbell, who crafts high- and medium-fired stoneware emblazoned with Mimbres characters. Her assistant, Cindy Talamantes, weaves exquisite pine needle baskets.

Nick Herrera, well-known *santero*, has his studio in his residence 1.4 miles out NM 110. Nick does both modern and traditional versions of the saints. You'll see a Penitente death cart driven by the skeletal Doña Sebastiana as well as his humorous 1990s interpretation, which portrays those dry bones perched on a low rider motorcycle.

Kathleen Vanderbrook and her husband, Terry, share a studio to the rear of El Llano Mercantile. He is a potter, and she creates handmade paper, prints, and paintings.

After you've visited El Rito's artist community, drive over to Ojo Caliente hot springs, which have attracted health seekers since prehistoric times. The ruins of three Tewa pueblos rest on the mesa above the resort. Even Cabeza de Vaca, the 16th-century Spanish explorer, is said to have passed by, and it was he who gave the springs its name.

Perhaps the resort's greatest appeal is the variety of its waters: lithia for "depression, sluggish kidneys and excess stomach gas"; iron to fortify the blood; arsenic for "arthritis, rheumatism, stomach, burn relief, excema [sic], and contusions"; and soda springs for "over acidic stomach problems." A selection of treatments awaits the bather: wraps, mineral clay facials, a salt glow rub, and therapeutic massage.

There are three mineral pools: iron, soda, and arsenic. The iron pool, with a temperature of 109 degrees, has a natural sandy bottom ringed with rocks and is open to the air year-round. The arsenic pool at 113 degrees has an attached spa and in cold weather is sheltered by a large tent whose sides can be lowered. The soda pool has a permanent cover to retain heat and steam. All three pools are coed, and bathing suits are the order of the day. If you should go during the cool months, be sure to bring a pair of beach shoes and a warm terry robe for the dash from pool to pool.

A new women's bathhouse replaces the structure destroyed by fire a few years ago. Plush by previous standards, it has heated tile floors, modern showers and locker facilities, treatment rooms, 12 "wrap" tables for sweating out impurities after soaks, and 13 private tubs for arsenic baths. The coed bathhouse also has arsenic tubs in addition to treatment rooms, the men's shower rooms, and locker facilities. Part of the original baths, it retains its slightly funky character.

A resort principal, Gary Mauro, is an artist in bronze and fabric bas-relief works on paper. He has contributed a panel of naked nymphs to the reception area, and his bronze sylphs on their pedestals ornament the pool area.

The old adobe hotel built in the early 1900s has recently been refurbished, although it retains its turn-of-the-century character. Certainly part of Ojo's charm is its laid-back, unpretentious atmosphere. Both rooms and cottages are available, and accommodations are modest but clean. A peculiarity is the lack of showers or tubs in the bathrooms. Bathing, the early owners thought, should be done in the bathhouses, and that hasn't changed.

Poppy's Cafe at the hotel serves three meals a day and specializes in fresh food, prepared to the diner's preference. Vegetarian meals are routine, although the red meat eater won't go hungry.

The Inn at Ojo is an alternative to resort lodging. Once a youth hostel and somewhat seedy bed-and-breakfast, the inn has been purchased by the Wimett family and completely redone. The section containing the original rooms has been torn down and replaced with an attractive adobe building with all the modern amenities. Zemmie, a longtime interior decorator and antique shop proprietor, has furnished the rooms with iron beds and old pine armoires. A full breakfast is served in the cheery common room.

The Shops at the Mercantile are another Wimett family venture. Daughter Leza manages the store, which specializes in unusual natural fiber clothing, much of it designed by her sisters, Claudia and Diana Wimett. In addition, she stocks designer lighting by brother Nicholas Wimett and an eclectic selection of jewelry—some of her own design and constructed of found objects. There're pieces by local artists, knitted ware, and assorted bibelots. Zemmie's collection of antiques for sale occupies one wing of the store. She has an especially fine assortment of old quilts.

Charlie Jordan's Dragon River Herbals in Ojo is a must-see if you're interested in herbal medicine. He specializes in organic, wild-crafted or woods-grown herbs, and his selection runs an encyclopedic range from agrimony to yucca. His nostrums are compounded to treat everything from turista to hay fever.

Before completing your loop of O'Keeffe country, you should make plans to visit the Rancho de San Juan, a member of the prestigious Relais & Chateaux group. Created with an eye to elegance and luxury, the inn rests at the base of Black Mesa with vistas of the San Juan Mountains and the hills of the Ojo Caliente valley.

A bonus to guests of the inn and restaurant is a visit to the "Sandstone Shrine, Windows in the Earth." In the rock formations of the mesa backing the property, owners John H.

Johnson III and David Heath provided artist/sculptor Ra Paulette with the medium required to create a grand opus. Burrowing through the pliant rock, the artist created chambers: a space for performance, an egg-shaped meditation room, and a writing room—all lighted by arched windows overlooking the Jemez Mountains. The general public is welcome to the unusual construction Saturday through Monday by reservation.

Built in 1993, the inn's hacienda and adjoining casitas are arranged around a center courtyard brimming with flowers and native plants. Each casita has distinctive decor that blends the elegance of antiques and Old World fabrics with the charm of the Southwest. Private Talavera-tiled baths, wood-burning fireplaces, and private *portals* (porches) complete the picture.

The hacienda, which is residence to the owners and Johnson's parents, is also home to David and John's extensive collection of art. The first thing that greets you when you enter the foyer is a magnificent Tony Abeyta oil of Navajo *yei* spirits.

The great room is filled with light from a window wall framed with pink and coral geraniums. Everywhere you look, you discover another treasure—a small pair of furred chaps presented to the elder Johnson when he was six by a Sioux lady, the startling mask of the ghost of a drowned whaler carved by a northwestern Maka Indian, and a set of Navajo dance wands.

The adjoining small auxiliary dining room accommodates a carved Balinese mirror against one wall, a breakfront with a collection of carved kachinas and Zuni fetishes, and a high shelf with pueblo pots.

The main dining room, where breakfast and John's gourmet dinners are served, is sun-filled—its antique oak mantel loaded with a throng of kachinas by local artist Duane O'Hagan. A complimentary full breakfast is offered to guests, and dinner is available by reservation to guests and the public Tuesday through Saturday.

To complete your tour of O'Keeffe country, be sure to stop at the Georgia O'Keeffe Museum in Santa Fe. The first art museum in the United States dedicated to the work of a woman artist of international stature, it is housed in an adobe structure renovated by architect Richard Gluckman. The main building houses the majority of the permanent collection in nine large exhibition galleries that wrap around an outdoor courtyard showcasing sculpture by O'Keeffe. With more than 120 paintings, watercolors, drawings, pastels, and sculpture, the holdings represent the largest repository of the artist's work in either public or private hands. Collection highlights include *Autumn Trees—The Maple*, *Abstraction*, *White Rose II*, *Jimson Weed*, and *Kachina*. Founded in 1995 by philanthropists Anne and John Marion, the museum, though entirely private, has a close association with the Museum of New Mexico and its supporting foundation.

For More Information

Pojoaque Pueblo: Poeh Center, Native American Arts and Crafts Gallery/Tourist Information Center, and Po-suwae-geh Restaurant, U.S. 84/285, Box 21GS, Santa Fe, NM 87501. Museum, 505-455-3334; information center, 505-455-2489 or 505-455-3460; store, 505-455-3460; restaurant, 505-455-7493.

David Dear, P.O. Box 1117, San Juan Pueblo, NM 87566. Call 505-753-8141 or 800-753-8141. Open Monday through Saturday from 9:00 A.M. to 5:00 P.M. Website: www.daviddear.com.

Española Chamber of Commerce, 417 Big Rock Center, Española, NM 87532. Call 505-753-2831. Open Monday through Friday from 9:00 A.M. to 5:00 P.M.

Jo Ann's Ranch O Casados, 418 North Riverside, Española, NM 87532. Call 505-753-2837. Open Monday through Saturday from 8:00 A.M. to 8:00 P.M.

Matilda's Restaurant, Box 30107, Corlett Road, Española, NM 87532. Call 505-753-3200. Open Tuesday through Thursday from 10:30 A.M. to 8:00 P.M., Friday from 10:30 A.M. to 9:00 P.M., Saturday and Sunday from 9:00 A.M. to 9:00 P.M.

El Paragua Restaurant and El Parasol Drive-In, 603 Santa Cruz Road, Española, NM 87532. Call 505-753-3211 or 800-929-8226. Serving lunch from 11:00 A.M. to 2:00 P.M. and dinner from 2:00 to 9:00 P.M.

Chimayo Trading Post/The Marco Polo Shop, 110 Sandia Drive, Española, NM 87532. Call 505-753-9414. Open in summer, daily 9:00 A.M. to 5:00 P.M.; winter, daily 9:00 A.M. to 4:30 P.M.

Romero's Fruit Stand (U.S. 84/285, five miles north of Española in Hernandez), Box 179, Española, NM 87532. Call 505-753-4189. Open in summer, daily from 8:00 A.M. to 7:00 P.M.; in winter, daily 8:00 A.M. to 6:00 P.M.

Georgia O'Keeffe Foundation, P.O. Box 40, Abiquiu, NM 87510. Call 505-685-4539. Office open Monday through Friday from 9:00 A.M. to 5:00 P.M. Hour-long tours of Georgia O'Keeffe's home April through last Tuesday before Thanksgiving, Tuesday, Thursday, and Friday 9:30, 11, 2, and 3:30. Call for reservations well in advance. Meet at foundation office off Route 84 next to the Abiquiu Inn. Donation due one month prior to tour.

Abiquiu Inn, Box 120, U.S. 84, Abiquiu, NM 87510. Call 505-685-4378 or 800-447-5621. Restaurant hours vary by season. Call for update.

Bode's General Merchandise, U.S. 84, P.O. Box 100, Abiquiu, NM 87510. Call 505-685-4422. Open Monday through Saturday from 7:00 A.M. to 7:00 P.M., Sunday from 7:00 A.M. to 6:00 P.M.

El Farolito Restaurant, 1212 Main Street, P.O. Box 27, El Rito, NM 87530. Call 505-581-9509. Open in summer, Tuesday through Saturday from 10:00 A.M. to 9:00 P.M.; winter, Tuesday through Saturday from 10:00 A.M. to 7:00 P.M.

Ghost Ranch Conference Center, National Adult Study Center of the Presbyterian Church, Box 11, Abiquiu, NM 87510. Call 505-685-4333. Office open daily from 8:00 A.M. to noon and 1:00 to 5:00 P.M.

Florence Hawley Ellis Museum of Anthropology and Ruth Hall Museum of Paleontology, Ghost Ranch Conference Center, U.S. 84, Abiquiu, NM 87510. Call 505-685-4333. Open mid-June–August, Tuesday through Saturday from 9:00 A.M. to noon and 1:00 to 5:00 P.M.

Ghost Ranch Living Museum, U.S. 84, HCR-77 Box 15, Abiquiu, NM 87510. Call 505-685-4312. Open mid-February–mid-December, daily from 9:00 A.M. to 4:00 P.M. Fee.

Monastery of Christ in the Desert, Guestmaster, P.O. Box 270, Abiquiu, NM 87510. No phone. For retreat accommodations, write well in advance. Do not use Express Mail or Federal Express.

Dar al Islam Foundation, P.O. Box 180, Abiquiu, NM 87510. Call 505-685-4515, ext. 22.

Martin's General Store, NM 554, P.O. Box 9, El Rito, NM 87530. Call 505-581-4567. Open Monday through Saturday from 8:00 A.M. to 6:00 P.M.

Barbara Campbell, 1187 NM 554, P.O. Box 717, El Rito, NM 87530. Call 505-581-4471 or 505-581-4430. By appointment or by chance.

Nicholas Herrera, Canyon Road, P.O. Box 43, El Rito, NM 87530. Call 505-581-4733. By appointment only.

Vanderbrook Studios, No. 2 County Road 246, El Rito, NM 87530. Call 505-581-4597. By chance or by appointment.

Ojo Caliente Mineral Springs Resort, P.O. Box 68, Ojo Caliente, NM 87549. Call 505-583-2233 or 800-222-9162. Baths open in summer Sunday through Thursday from 8:00 A.M. to 9:00 P.M., Friday and Saturday from 8:00 A.M. to 10:00 P.M.; in winter, Sunday through Thursday from 8:00 A.M. to 9:00 P.M. Fee.

Poppy's Cafe & Grill, Ojo Caliente Mineral Springs Resort, P.O. Box 68, Ojo Caliente, NM 87549. Call 505-583-2499. Open from 7:30 A.M. to 8:30 P.M. (9:30 P.M. on Friday and Saturday).

The Inn at Ojo, Hot Springs Road, P.O. Box 215, Ojo Caliente, NM 87549. Call 505-583-9131.

The Mercantile at Ojo, P.O. Box 215, Ojo Caliente, NM 87549. Call 505-583-9153. Open in summer, Monday through Sunday from 10:00 A.M. to 5:00 P.M.; in winter, Saturday and Sunday only from 10:00 A.M. to 5:00 P.M.

Dragon River Herbals, P.O. Box 74, Ojo Caliente, NM 87549. Call 800-813-2118. Open Monday through Friday from 8:00 A.M. to 4:30 P.M. Website: www.DragonRiverHerbals.com.

Rancho de San Juan Country Inn and Restaurant, P.O. Box 4140, Fairview Station, Española, NM 87533-4140. Call 505-753-6818 or 800-726-7121. Office open daily from 8:00 A.M. to 6:00 P.M. Dinner by reservation, Tuesday through Saturday.

Georgia O'Keeffe Museum, 217 Johnson Street, Santa Fe, NM 87501. Call 505-995-0785. Open Tuesday through Thursday, Saturday, and Sunday from 10:00 A.M. to 5:00 P.M., Friday from 10:00 A.M. to 8 P.M.

3

Trading Posts and Ancient Cities

Getting there: From Albuquerque, take I-25 north 20 miles to Bernalillo, exit 242. From Bernalillo head northwest on NM 44 approximately 112 miles to the entrance to Chaco Culture National Historical Park. Take CR 7900 three miles east of Nageezi (paved the first five miles followed by 16 miles of dirt), and turn on CR 7950 and again on CR 7985. When you arrive in the park, you will encounter blacktop. Leaving Chaco, retrace your route to NM 44, and continue on 46 miles to Bloomfield, where you turn north on NM 544 and go seven miles to Aztec. In Aztec follow the signs to Aztec Ruins National Monument. Retrace your steps to NM 64, west three miles to Salmon Ruins, and from there 10 miles to Farmington. Go south 74 miles on NM 371 to Crownpoint. Outside of Crownpoint, head southeast on Navajo 48 10 miles to Borrego Pass. Finish the 19-mile Navajo 48 loop by returning to NM 371. Pass Smith Lake and join I-40 at exit 53, Thoreau. Stauder's Navajo Lodge is eight miles west of Thoreau, off the interstate.

Highlights: On this foray into the heart of Indian country, you'll encounter the ruins of the ancient Anasazi cities of Chaco, Salmon, and Aztec. You'll sojourn in the Navajo Nation, where solitary hogans dot the desert and a few trading posts still fulfill their traditional role of supplying the outback. You'll explore Farmington, a hotbed of sales for *Dine* (Navajo) folk art, and attend a rug auction on the reservation.

This is one of the most challenging and interesting journeys you will make, but before you set out, understand that you will need more preparation than usual if you are to enjoy it to the fullest. Your first consideration should be the extent to which you intend to investigate Chaco Culture National Historical Park. As your delight in this expansive ancient city depends on the amount of time you're willing to devote to its exploration, you should be aware that a quick once-over from the seat of your car is going to leave you longing for more. It's a tease, a come-on, and although it's better than not seeing Chaco at all, it is largely unsatisfying. To really understand the wonder and complexity of the site, you need to stay a day or two—which is possible only by camping. Chaco is a remote and primitive park, and visitors should not expect the comfort and conveniences associated with many other sites. There is no food, gas, lodging, or auto repair. Much of the access road is unpaved, creating access problems after heavy rains. If you have any inkling that the area has received showers, a call to the park is in order before you set out.

Anticipation builds as you set out, bypassing Bernalillo (see Chapter 1) and beginning the northwest trek up NM 44, the main connector between central and northwestern New Mexico. Not too long ago, this route was a dirt strip dotted by trading posts at irregular intervals. Now fully paved, its two lanes are being expanded to four to accommodate heavier traffic between the two points.

Your route takes you through valleys carpeted in wildflowers—Mexican hat, peppergrass, penstemon and clumps of deep purple asters. Soaring red rock mesas capped with gray thrust into the bluer-than-sapphire sky. You increase in elevation and pass into an area of open plains dotted with piñón and juniper. Pale green lines of cottonwoods thread the ditches, and cattle graze in their shade. To the west, Cabezon Peak stands sentinel. The black volcanic plug, visible for miles, is sacred to the Navajos, who believe it is the head of the giant killed by Monster Slayer, one of their twin war gods.

The road takes you in and out of Jemez and Zia Pueblo lands, and eventually leads to Cuba. Travelers passing through town en route to the Four Corners area traditionally have used Cuba as a food and fuel stop. Those in the know beat feet to El Bruno's Resterante [sic] y Cantina on the north side.

Housed in a classic adobe building, El Bruno's has a long history of hospitality. Originally the Silver Star Bar and Cafe, the restaurant was run by Renee Jarimillo for 14 years before being purchased by her brother and sister-in-law, Bruno and Hazel Herrera. For 23 years the Herreras, aided by their children, have honed their classic New Mexican dishes to perfection.

Arriving in time for lunch, you enter the patio through massive old pine doors with their heavy Spanish wrought-iron hinges. In warm weather, diners may enjoy alfresco meals here, in a handsome enclosed area with massive *vigas*,  pots of colorful geraniums, and a kiva fireplace.

Upon entering the restaurant, you pass El Roperito, Hazel's boutique selling Navajo arts and crafts, bottles of the restaurant's special red sauce, and designer clothing. After a quick look around, take a seat in the large, white-walled main dining room. A handsome fireplace in the corner is called into use on cool days, niches are filled with the work of local craftsmen, and paintings by Robert Redbird grace the walls. The atmosphere is restful, with Spanish music playing softly in the background and the teal-tiled tables set with colorful Fiesta ware.

The daily lunch menu is a scaled-down version of the dinner menu, which is also available. Specials, named for towns surrounding Cuba, include Gallina, two shredded chicken tacos with beans, rice, and a side of red chile caribe; the Regina, a sopapilla stuffed with beef and beans and topped with melted cheese, red or green chile, and shredded lettuce and tomato; and the Cuba, one cheese and one beef enchilada topped with red or green chile, melted cheese, and served with rice and beans.

The regular menu is extensive, starting out with appetizers such as chile con queso or Camaron Mexicano, grilled shrimp topped with piñón nuts in chile butter. What follows is a vast list: charbroiled steak specials (El Tampiqueño, a sirloin topped with green chile and cheese sounds especially appetizing), combination plates, chicken specials, enchilada platters, and a section for *niños* (children).

Fully sated, you might take a brisk walk down to Cuba's visitors center. Here you'll find a selection of maps and brochures on the area, friendly service, and advice on the Chaco road conditions. Or drop in on Cleo and Richard Velarde at their store, Richards, where you'll find everything from old pawn to beadwork. The Velardes specialize in Navajo graphic art, and on any day you're likely to find originals by Edie Tsosie, Paul Vigil, and scratch paintings by Sammy Sandoval.

After leaving Cuba, you climb again into upland meadows flecked with clumps of large sage and Ponderosa pine. Passing into a portion of the Jicarilla Apache Indian Reservation, you drive through rolling, largely barren uplands.

Soon you arrive in Counselor, hardly a blip on the screen of life but home to the Counselor Trading Post. If this is your first impression of a post or if you have visited Hubbell's in Ganado, Arizona, you may be disappointed. First glance reveals a general store with shelves of Twinkies, Tide, and motor oil. You have to look harder to see the history here. Founded 65 years ago by Ann and Jim Counselor, the store was sold to Leonard Taft, who later took on Harold and Jane "Turk" McDonald as partners in the 1960s. Taft and the McDonalds additionally acquired the Blanco post, and in the 1960s the McDonalds bought out Taft's interest in both enterprises.

Well-known among the Indians of the Checkerboard section of the Navajo Indian Reservation, Harold and Turk put on a huge Christmas party on the Saturday before Christmas. Hot dogs, doughnuts, and coffee as well as sacks of candy for the children were liberally dispensed. Over 1,200 attended the event some years.

In 1988 a tragedy occurred. As he was closing up shop, Harold was brutally murdered. After his death Turk sold the Blanco post, where the killing occurred, and concentrated her efforts in Counselor. Today their daughter, Kelly Aragon, is post manager, but Turk is still active and continues to live on the premises.

Counselor continues to function as a traditional trading post, buying lambs and raw wool, finished rugs, and a small amount of jewelry from the Navajos. If you show an interest, Kelly will take you in the walk-in safe that functions as their rug room. They carry about 40 quality rugs from weavers such as Eleanor, Arlene, and Louise Johnson, and the selection of patterns is eclectic, ranging from Tree of Life to depictions of Navajo gods, the *yeis*.

Trucking on, you'll pass natural gas wells scattered among the chamisa and blue flax, and at Lybrook, a gas refinery raises its piped and smoke-plumed head. You forge on past eroded hills, red and gray cliffs, and an outcrop of strange brown boulders resting on black sand hills. A scattering of Navajo homes and hogans breaks up the stark landscape before you arrive at the Chaco turnoff.

If you've visited Chaco in years past, you may be surprised to learn the Nageezi and Blanco entrances have been closed and a new entrance created near Mile Marker 112. This was done to route cars to the park visitors center and to protect the Kin Kletso ruin, which was being damaged by traffic passing close by.

You may be perturbed to see Chaco isn't much of a canyon at all—more of a deep wash. And why, you ask, was this unimposing real estate such a center of Anasazi, or pre-Puebloan, culture? With the area's long winters, short growing seasons, and marginal rainfall, it seems an inhospitable place. Yet a sophisticated culture did flourish here a thousand years ago. People farmed the lowlands and built great masonry towns that connected with other towns over a far-reaching network of roads.

By A.D. 1000 Chaco was established as a political and socioeconomic center. It is thought that at one time as many as 5,000 people lived in the surrounding settlements, using Chaco as an administrative and ritual hub. What caused them to abandon this well-developed site? Scientists theorize that a prolonged drought in the San Juan Basin between A.D. 1130 and 1180 combined with a depleted environment led to food shortages that even the Chacoans' clever irrigation systems couldn't overcome. People moved on to better-watered areas, becoming the ancestors to today's Pueblo people.

Your first stop should be the visitors center, which includes a museum, audiovisual programs, publications for sale, and general information. If your time in Chaco is short, you should check in at the desk to determine if a ranger-led walk is scheduled. This is the best method of learning a lot in a short period of time.

If you can't connect with a ranger, drive the eight-mile loop, stopping to explore at the sites that interest you. When hiking, be sure to wear proper footwear, for segments of the paths are uneven and steep. Don a protective hat, and carry water and sunscreen.

There are five major ruins along the loop. Una Vida is closest to the visitors center and can be reached by trail from the parking lot. Only partially excavated, it contains five kivas and about 150 rooms. You'll also encounter Pueblo Bonito, once four stories high and containing 600 rooms and 40 kivas; Chetro Ketl, with 500 rooms and 16 kivas; Pueblo Del Arroyo, with 280 rooms and more than 20 kivas; Kin Kletso, with 100 rooms and five enclosed kivas; and Casa Rinconada on the south side. Casa Rinconada is the only site that is not part of a community structure, and it encompasses the largest of the park's great kivas, 63 ½ feet across at floor level. You may view the kiva from the rim, but entrance is now forbidden. The wear and tear of many feet was damaging the structure.

Hiking trails lead to a number of other sites that require permits, available at the visitors center. Pueblo Alto is on the north rim, and Wijiji is at the canyon's east end. If you tramp the canyon's western end, you will pass Casa Chiquita and come to a large concentration of rock art before reaching the site of Peñasco Blanco. These petroglyphs and pictographs are of great interest to archeo-astronomers, because they contain symbols that have led some to believe they represent the Crab Nebula supernova, recorded in Chinese journals of A.D. 1054.

This is not the only place that interests the scribes of the sky. On a cliff face near the top of Fajada Butte, three large upright slabs of rock stand in front of two spiral petroglyphs. A dagger of light appears on various points of the spirals during spring and fall equinoxes and winter and summer solstices. You can't climb the butte, but the visitors center has an excellent film on its exploration and significance.

Casa Rinconada also is thought to have astronomical/geometrical orientations. The major and minor axes fall along the lines of the four cardinal directions, and there are six irregularly spaced niches placed around the circumference. On the morning of the summer solstice, light from the sun comes through a small window just east of the kiva's north entrance and shines on the opposite wall directly above one of the six niches. As the sun moves higher, the beam sweeps downward and illuminates the niche.

Chaco does not give up its secrets easily, so do plan to camp and enjoy the full experience. The National Park Service operates Gallo campground, with tent and RV sites. It's fairly primitive—there's no shade, power, or potable water. You will find tables, fireplaces (bring your own charcoal), and central toilets. Drinking water is available at the visitors center.

When you finish your inspection of Chaco, retrace your steps to NM 44 and head northwest. You'll soon arrive at the Nageezi Trading Post run by Don and Carol Batchelor, who also operate the Chaco Inn, a small bed-and-breakfast. Nageezi is an old post, opened in 1939 by Jim McKuen and purchased in 1970 by Harry Batchelor, Don's father. The post sells the usual assortment of groceries and necessities plus some interesting Navajo folk art such as wood carvings by the Willito family and sculpture by Lawrence Jacquez.

A few miles farther down the pike, Blanco Trading Post stocks an impressive array of more traditional Navajo work—pitch-lined pottery flecked with mica, jewelry, baskets, and a large selection of rugs. The front of the store stocks groceries and general merchandise, but the handsome back room contains the treasures. The post is owned by Shane and Tiffany Chaffin, who previously managed the post in Crownpoint.

From Blanco you pass through the outskirts of Bloomfield and head north to Aztec. The name of the town was chosen by early settlers to reflect the nearby ruins, which they thought were built by Indians related to the Aztecs of Mexico. Later investigation proved them wrong, as the Anasazi builders were influenced first by Chaco and later by Mesa Verde.

Aztec Ruins National Monument celebrates this cultural mix and was named a World Heritage Site in 1987. Considered a Chacoan outlier by scholars, Aztec was established in A.D. 1111 to 1115 by people who constructed a large, multistory pueblo on rising ground overlooking the Animas River. This huge, D-shaped compound had about 400 rooms on three levels and more than a dozen kivas, including a great kiva in the plaza. The settlement prospered for several decades as an administrative, trade, and ceremonial center, but it declined along with Chaco, for many of the same reasons. Villagers moved away, and the town was deserted until A.D. 1225, when a culture similar to that of Mesa Verde arrived, remodeling the pueblo and adding new structures. Like their predecessors, they flourished for a time and eventually departed.

The first Europeans to view the site in 1776 were Spanish padres Dominguez and Escalante, and their cartographer Bernardo Miera y Pacheco put the location on his map. In a more recent era, the first visitor of record was Dr. John S. Newberry, a geologist. In 1859 he found the pueblo in a fair state of preservation, but in the years following his stay, pot hunters and looters ravaged the ruins. To protect the remnants, they were declared a national monument in 1913. However, it wasn't until 1916, when the American Museum of Natural History began sponsoring excavations, that the site was thoroughly explored. Earl H. Morris headed up the museum's first dig and spent seven years excavating and stabilizing the buildings, and in the 1930s he returned to supervise the reconstruction of the Great Kiva.

Visiting Aztec is a pleasure. The visitors center is located in back of a grove of trees, which provide shade for a picnic area. The center features exhibits and an excellent 25-minute film entitled *Anasazi*, which is shown several times daily. Books, postcards, slides, posters, and videos are for sale, and you can pick up a trail guide booklet for the quarter-mile self-guiding path.

The trail passes through several rooms with intact original roofs as well as the semi-subterranean Great Kiva. Pause a while in the depths of this ceremonial hall and listen while the plaintive notes of a native flute call up the shadows of times past. The dust motes dancing in the rays emanating from the dual entrances call up the whirling ghosts of Anasazi shamans, entreating their gods for favor.

If you're in the shopping mode, stop at Bob and Faith Burnside's Kiva Trading Post at the monument entrance. They have a selection of Navajo rugs, Navajo and Zuni jewelry, and sand paintings, plus the predictable T-shirts and souvenir trinkets.

Skip ahead several centuries, and venture into the town of Aztec, where you'll find the Aztec Museum, Pioneer Village, and Oil Field Exhibit on North Main Avenue. Stroll through a doctor's office, sheriff's post complete with a soft sculpture lawman at his desk, blacksmith shop and foundry, pioneer cabin, general store and post office, and the Cedar Hill Church, all reconstructed from original buildings in the area. From the first weekend in June through the second Saturday of September, museum volunteers reenact a shootout or a melodrama at noon on the Pioneer Village grounds.

Don't miss the 1920 Fort Worth Spudder Drilling rig, with its wooden derrick, and look inside the old "doghouse," a name given to the oilman's office. Traipse through Atwood Annex, with its pictorial history of the equipment and personnel of the San Juan County "oil patch."

Visit the main museum, with its mineral and fossil display, Southwest artifacts, farm and ranch tools, and comprehensive collection of Aztec memorabilia, including a fully equipped barber shop of the era.

At the museum, you can check out their gift shop or pick up a copy of the "Walking Tour of Historic Aztec" brochure, which delineates 24 historic homes, churches, and commercial buildings. Eleven of these are on the National Register of Historic Places and the New Mexico State Register of Cultural Properties.

Leaving Aztec, you retrace your route south, turn west on NM 64, and arrive at Salmon Ruins, San Juan County Archaeological Research Center and Library. A large Chacoan Anasazi apartment complex constructed during the late 11th century, the excavation is located on an alluvial fan at the base of gravel terraces bordering the San Juan River.

Originally a Chaco outlier constructed between A.D. 1088 and 1090, and patterned on the classic "C" shape, the pueblo contained approximately 217 rooms skirting the Great Kiva. The Chacoans abandoned the site around A.D. 1130, and it lay fallow until 1185, when people influenced by the Mesa Verde culture moved in. Their occupation lasted about a century, after which the site was vacant except for a small remnant population.

In the late 1800s, George Salmon homesteaded the area around the ruins and protected it from vandals and treasure hunters for more than 90 years. His homestead and outbuildings remain nearby. In 1969 San Juan County purchased the 22-acre tract, placed the site on the National Register of Historic Places and the New Mexico State Register, and appointed the county Museum Association to administer the property.

Today, in addition to viewing the ruins, you can visit Heritage Park, a series of exhibits displaying traditional habitations of numerous prehistoric and historic groups of the Four Corners area.

The visitors center incorporates the research center and library, a museum of artifacts from the site, and a gift shop well stocked with kachinas, rugs, jewelry, and an excellent selection of regional books. The museum's display area contains a reproduction of a room in the ruins as it might have appeared while still in use by the Anasazi.

If all this inquiry has you fainting with fatigue and panting with hunger, take heart and head off to Farmington. Check into Casa Blanca Bed and Breakfast, where innkeepers Jim and Mary Fabian will make you feel right at home. House philosophy is *"mi casa es su casa"* and "if you ever need anything, don't hesitate to ask."

Casa Blanca is perched on a hill overlooking the town. Its beautifully landscaped grounds, colorful flower beds, and sparkling fountain set the stage for the elegant interior decor. The mission-style house was designed, built, and decorated in the 1950s by Miriam and Merrill Taylor, owners of the Greasewood Trading Post in Lukachukai, Arizona. It still retains that slightly retro air with its classic French and Italian provincial furniture and French-printed wallpaper. The living room, with its softly cooing miniature Australian Diamond doves, is a serene hideaway, and dining room highlights include a fabulous mural of exotic birds. The den, or library, has a fireplace flanked by bookshelves filled with regional tomes, novels, and videotapes. Authentic antique Navajo rugs carpet the floor, and a jigsaw puzzle in progress is usually set up on an *equipale* table.

The four bedrooms and casita are individually decorated. Sequito is an expansive suite with sun porch, tiled double bath, and breakfast room; Aztec has a queen-size, pencil-post folk art bed and patio view; and Chino's navy and white stenciled walls are complemented by a blue and rose Chinese rug. Caballero's hand-carved headboard in the Spanish style was executed by the Merrills, who were students of famous carver Stanley Chittenden. The newest addition, the casita, is detached from the main body of the inn and contains two bedrooms, a Jacuzzi tub, freestanding fireplace, and private fenced courtyard.

All rooms have private baths, telephones, cable television, and VCR. There's a "butler basket" for forgotten necessities in the bath and terry robes in the closets. In summer evaporative coolers and ceiling fans keep the rooms comfortable.

Breakfast is served in the dining room, on the terrace, or in bed, if you prefer. It might include a starter of two fruit juices, apricot and mango yogurt, fresh fruit with walnuts and edible flower garnish, homemade breads and muffins, local jams and jellies, European-blend coffee and an ever-changing menu of entrées, including Southwest specialties. Takeout lunches are available with advance notice.

Afternoon tea is set out between 4:00 and 7:00 P.M. with coffee, a selection of teas, cookies, and a spectacular cake—German Black Forest, if you're lucky. For dinner, Ann, a classically trained chef, will prepare a gourmet meal given 24 hours' notice. There's a choice of three seasonal entrées—perhaps grilled steak, baked salmon fillet with orange-tarragon butter, or roast cornish game hen in mushroom-sage sauce.

If you choose to go out for dinner and you can ignore the usual prejudice of judging all motel chain restaurants as mediocre, try Chatters at the Ramada. It's dining at its finest, and they prepare exceptional game specialties.

If you long for Southwestern food, you won't go wrong at Señor Peppers at the airport. Owned and operated by Greg Hamilton, the restaurant is no terminal taco stand. The softly lighted dining room is a favorite hangout for locals, and they are notoriously picky about their enchiladas, burritos, rellenos, tacos, and huevos rancheros. In addition, there are gringo menu selections ranging from steaks to shrimp and chicken.

After a good meal and a night's rest, you are ready to explore Farmington before setting off to Crownpoint. Your first stop should be Beasley Folk Art on West Main. Jack

Beasley has been called the grandfather of Navajo folk art, and no one in the business knows its history and development as well. As early as 1979 he began encouraging Navajo folk artists such as Mamie Deschillie, Johnson Antonio, the Benally family, the Hathale brothers, and the Willetos. In the simple, primitive cardboard figures, carvings, and mud toys, he saw a market for the pieces that reveal an innocent reflection of Navajo life. Jack says this childish quality appeals to people of all ages, income levels, and sophistication, but especially to the young. "Children really like folk art, because they can relate to it," he says.

Although Jack remains active in the business, son Jason is now managing the store. Navajo folk art has escalated in value in the intervening years, and the Beasleys still have one of the largest stocks from the prominent artists. Have Jack or Jason show you a comparison between two figures by Delbert Buck, a young carver whose work has become immensely popular. One of his earliest efforts sits on top of a display cabinet and other, more recent, work is exhibited throughout the shop. Compare the figures and be amazed at the artist's growth and skill in refining his craft.

If your tastes run to more traditional Indian ware, there are several stores catering to this concern. Russell Foutz Indian Room on West Main has a huge selection of handwoven rugs in all the major patterns. In addition, he carries a wide assortment of Sheila Antonio's miniature beaded Navajo scenes and figures as well as the alabaster carvings of Eugene Pinto and Howard Johnson.

If you're knowledgeable, The Attic on East Main sometimes has bargains, and the Jewel Box Pawn Shop way out on West Main has some of the finest jewelry to be found anywhere. Bob and Carol West have a coterie of craftspeople they support with materials and stones. This makes a huge difference, since many good Navajo smiths don't have the resources to buy fine materials. When they have good elements with which to work, they can produce amazing results.

Be sure to have a bite to eat before venturing down NM 371, a rather barren stretch void of restaurants. The primo lunch spot in Farmington is Something Special Bakery and Tea Room on North Auburn, just a block or two from Main. This attractive restaurant was started 16 years ago by Charliene Barns, and the bakery was added seven years ago by Charliene's son Dean, who eventually took over the burgeoning business from his mother.

Housed in a tidy cottage with outdoor dining on an attached porch, the restaurant serves a different special every day. A month's menus are printed on cards so patrons will be sure not to miss their favorite dishes, which might include roast chicken with apricot stuffing, chile-seared tuna, or "good old meatloaf." There's always one meat and one vegetarian entrée. The ingredients are scrupulously fresh, and all the sauces and dressings are homemade. The desserts are a dieter's downfall. Twelve Old World breads are baked daily by Dean's wife, Deci, in special steam-injection ovens, and delectable cookies and muffins round out the offerings.

Well fortified for your trip, you head south into the Navajo Nation. If you want to see one of the oldest and most authentic trading posts still in existence, take Navajo 48 10 miles to Borrego Pass. This remote post on a dirt road in the heart of the reservation is run by Merle and Rosilla Moore, who manage the place for the heirs of Don and Vern Smouse, the original owners. They do their best to keep the place running, although improvements are hampered by the property being tied up in probate. They sell the usual reservation necessities and some rugs, jewelry, and Navajo-carved kachinas at very reasonable prices.

The post is much as Don Smouse left it when he departed for a nursing home years ago. The stone warehouse is still stocked with full canning jars, dusty, outdated clothing, tires, and a Voss wringer washer, still in its carton. An Edsel and 1968 Cadillac rust in the back, and the orchard's plum, apple, and cherry trees are running wild.

With the afternoon passing, you'll want to repair to Crownpoint, ideally arriving at the elementary school by 4:00 P.M. to watch the Navajo weavers check in their rugs for the rug auction (held on the third Friday of the month). The women in their traditional multitiered skirts, velvet blouses, and massive turquoise jewelry line up patiently in a queue that stretches from the gymnasium through the hall and out the door. At last they arrive at the check-in table, where they register their weaving, receive an identifying number, and tell the helper the minimum price they will accept. All the rugs are tossed on tables, and eager prospective buyers dig right in, checking to see if the weaving is well done—squared sides with even weaving and a good texture. It's a bit of a riot, with wool flying in every direction and guarded comments from the buyers, who range from dealers to wealthy Santa Fe collectors.

At 6:00 P.M. the rugs are moved to the stage, where they will be auctioned. Simultaneously, food service begins. Crownpoint has no restaurant, so to fill demand, the school cafeteria serves a simple meal of Navajo tacos, fry bread, chile and beans, coffee, and punch. In the hall, artisans display jewelry, pottery, crafts, and other art.

The kitchen stops serving at 7 P.M., and auctioneer Wayne Conner promptly starts the auction. There is no set order of sale, and the bidding continues until the last rug is sold, whether that's at 11:00 P.M. or 1:00 A.M. The gym's 240 seats are generally packed with buyers. The weavers and their families sit and stand against the walls, hoping and praying for a good return on their effort. Each auction is different. Sometimes smaller pieces sell well, and other evenings special shapes bring in the big bucks. Prices can range from hundreds to thousands of dollars. Whether or not you buy, it's a wonderful show and one you'll remember.

Leaving Crownpoint, continue south on NM 371, eventually meeting I-25 at Thoreau (pronounced "Throw"). Before hitting the highway, you'll pass the Rainbow Trading Company, owned by David Hayes. He specializes in made-to-order rodeo jewelry but also sells some Indian jewelry, a few rugs taken in trade, and some Navajo kachinas.

The Zuni Mountain Trading Company is next door to the Rainbow. Owner Wayne Harris maintains a more traditional post stocked with general merchandise for the townspeople and a selection of jewelry, baskets, pottery, old pawn, and curios such as bear traps and wagon wheels. Be sure to check out the not-for-sale mounted white buffalo head, taken in trade. Specialties of the house are sterling silver concho belts, which Navajo smiths turn out in a bewildering variety of sizes and shapes.

If you're searching for lodging after such a busy tour, you'll want to reserve a place at Stauder's Navajo Lodge, eight miles west of Thoreau at Coolidge, exit 44 of I-40. The lodge served for many years as a bar, restaurant, motel, and trading post catering to travelers on what is currently a fractured remnant of old Route 66. Times and owners changed, and in 1969 Sherwood and Roberta Stauder purchased the property and transformed it into a red-tile-roofed Spanish-style hacienda with center courtyard. Two comfortable guest cottages line one side of this enclosure, with its shade trees and colorful flower beds.

A continual Continental breakfast is served in the hacienda great room, which boasts a full wall of windows looking out on the grassed backyard, with its full-size heated swimming pool and children's playhouse. In the distance, red rock bluffs shimmer in the clear light.

The Stauders have done an amazing job with the main building. The great room is strewn with exceptional pieces of Southwestern art, some accumulated by Sherwood and Roberta and others part of a collection left to Roberta by her father, an Indian trader who operated the Fort Defiance and Sawmill trading posts in Arizona.

The venerable pool table is draped with a collection of old and rare Navajo rugs, and a woolly sheep, made by the Growler family, guards the floor-to-ceiling stone fireplace. A collection of dolls of all lands looks out from the shelves of an oak server, and a terra-cotta fountain gurgles softly from a corner. Cozy conversational groupings of chairs and settees are scattered around the huge room, and breakfast tables are set with teal mats and pink napkins in sequined boot holders, awaiting the guests soon to arrive for breakfast.

The Stauders encourage their guests to explore the area, and they are knowledgeable about the hiking trails, trading posts, the rug auction, and the shops and special events at Gallup.

However, if you must be on your way and it's mealtime, head a short distance west on I-40 to exit 39, the Giant Refinery at Ciniza, where Executive Chef Dave Dinsmore presides over Baker's Hearth Restaurant. This unlikely pairing of a truck stop and well-prepared food may surprise you, but by now you're doubtless getting used to New Mexico restaurants in improbable places.

The restaurant is open 24 hours a day and serves breakfast, lunch, and dinner. Breakfast might be an omelet, huevos rancheros, French toast, or the hearty trucker's special of three eggs with hash browns, toast, biscuits, or muffins. For lunch, you might order the hot buffet and salad bar, a burger, sandwich combo, Mexican platter, or a meal-in-a-bowl, like the chef's special green chile stew. The dinner menu lists a selection of meat, fish, and poultry. There's broasted chicken, prime ribs, charbroiled salmon steak, grilled pork chops, and the obligatory chicken-fried steak. All baked goods are made on-site, and the pies and portions are exceptional.

For More Information

El Bruno's Resterante y Cantina, Main Street, NM 44, Cuba, NM 87013. Call 505-289-9429. Open daily from 11:00 A.M. to 10:00 P.M.

Richards, P.O. Box 97, NM 44, Cuba, NM 87103. Call 505-289-3284. Open daily from 9:00 A.M. to 3:00 P.M.

Cuba Visitor Center, P.O. Box 56, NM 44, Cuba, NM 87013. Call 505-289-3808. Open April–end of December, Monday through Saturday from 9:00 to 11:15 A.M. and 12:15 to 4:00 P.M.

Counselor Trading Post, 9766 NM 44, General Delivery, Counselor, NM 87018. Call 505-568-4453. Open in summer, Monday through Friday from 8:00 A.M. to 6:00 P.M., Saturday from 8:00 A.M. to noon; in winter, Monday through Friday from 8:00 A.M. to 5:00 P.M., Saturday from 8:00 A.M. to noon.

Chaco Culture National Historical Park, P.O. Box 220, Nageezi, NM 87037. Call 505-786-7014; 24-hour emergency number, 505-786-7060. Visitors center open in summer, daily from 8:00 A.M. to 6:00 P.M.; in winter, daily from 8:00 A.M. to 5:00 P.M. Trails open from sunrise to sunset. Camping limited to seven days. No trailers over 30 feet. Fee. Website: www.nps.gov/chcu.

Nageezi Trading Post, NM 44, P.O. Box 40, Nageezi, NM 87037. Call 505-632-3646 or 800-96-CHACO. Open Monday through Friday from 8:00 A.M. to 4:00 P.M., Saturday from 8:00 A.M. to noon.

Blanco Trading Post, NM 44 (28 miles south of Bloomfield), Bloomfield, NM 87413. Call 505-632-1597. Open Monday through Saturday from 8:00 A.M. to 6:00 P.M.

Aztec Chamber of Commerce, 110 North Ash, Aztec, NM 87410. Call 505-334-9551. Open Monday through Friday from 9:00 A.M. to noon and 1:00 to 5:00 P.M. Website: www.cyberport.com/aztec.

Aztec Ruins National Monument, 84 Ruins Road, P.O. Box 640 (County Road 2900, near junction of U.S. 550 and NM 44), Aztec, NM 87410. Call 505-334-6174. Open in summer, daily from 8:00 A.M. to 6:00 P.M.; in winter, daily from 8:00 A.M. to 5:00 P.M. Fee. Website: www.nps.gov/azru.

Kiva Trading Post, 624 Ruins Road, Aztec, NM 87410. Call 505-334-2949. Open in summer, daily from 9:00 A.M. to 6:00 P.M.; in winter, hours weather-dependent.

Aztec Museum and Pioneer Village, 125 North Main Avenue, Aztec, NM 87410. Call 505-334-9829. Open in summer, Monday through Saturday from 9:00 A.M. to 5:00 P.M.; in winter, Monday through Saturday from 10:00 A.M. to 4:00 P.M. Donation.

Salmon Ruins, 6131 U.S. 64, P.O. Box 125, Bloomfield, NM 87413. Call 505-632-2013. Open Monday through Saturday from 8:00 A.M. to 5:00 P.M.; open Sunday only from noon to 5:00 P.M., November–March. Website: www.more2it.com/salmon.

Casa Blanca, 505 East LaPlata Street, Farmington, NM 87401. Call 505-327-6503 or 800-550-6503. Website: www.cyberport.com/casablanca.

Chatters Restaurant and Lounge, Ramada Inn, 601 East Broadway, Farmington, NM 87401. Call 505-325-1191. Open Monday through Thursday from 6:00 A.M. to 2:00 P.M. and 5:30 to 10:00 P.M., Friday till 10:30 P.M., Saturday from 7:00 A.M. to 2:00 P.M. and 5:30 to 10:30 P.M., Sunday from 7:00 A.M. to 2:00 P.M.

Señor Peppers, Municipal Airport, 1400 West Navajo, Farmington, NM 87401. Call 505-327-0436. Open daily from 6 A.M. to 10:00 P.M.

Beasley Folk Art, 117 West Main, Farmington, NM 87401. Call 505-599-0881. Open in summer, Monday through Saturday from 10:00 A.M. to 6:00 P.M.; in winter, Tuesday through Saturday from 10:00 A.M. to 5:00 P.M.

Foutz Indian Room, 301 West Main, Farmington, NM 87401. Call 505-325-9413. Open Monday through Saturday from 9:00 A.M. to 5:00 P.M.

The Attic, 112 East Main Street, Farmington, NM 87401. Call 505-326-1671. Open Monday through Saturday from 9:00 A.M. to 5:00 P.M.

Jewel Box Pawn Shop, 2400 West Main Street, Farmington, NM 87401. Wholesale and retail. Call 505-325-5693. Open Monday through Friday from 9:00 A.M. to 5:30 P.M., Saturday from 9:00 A.M. to 5:00 P.M.

Something Special Bakery and Tea Room, 116 North Auburn, Farmington, NM 87401. Call 505-325-8183. Open daily from 7:00 A.M. to 2:00 P.M.

Farmington Convention & Visitors Bureau, 3041 East Main Street, Farmington, NM 87402. Call 505-326-7602 or 800-448-1240. Open Memorial Day weekend to Labor Day weekend, Monday through Saturday from 8:00 A.M. to 7:00 P.M.; Labor Day to Memorial Day weekend, Monday through Saturday from 8:00 A.M. to 5:00 P.M., Sunday from noon to 5:00 P.M. Call to confirm. Website: www.farmingtonnm.org.

Borrego Pass Trading Post, 1601 County Road 19, P.O. Box 329, Prewitt, NM 87045. Call 505-786-5396. Open Monday through Friday from 8:00 A.M. to 6:00 P.M., Saturday from 8:00 A.M. to noon.

Crownpoint Rug Auction, Crownpoint Elementary. Crownpoint Rug Weavers Association, P.O. Box 1630, Crownpoint, NM 87313. Call 505-786-7386 or 505-786-5302. Third Friday of month, with some exceptions; call to confirm. Inspection at 4:00 P.M., sale at 7:00 P.M.

Rainbow Trading Company, P.O. Box 395, NM 57 and Aspen, Thoreau, NM 87323. Call 505-862-7119. Open in summer, Monday through Saturday from 7:30 A.M. to 5:00 P.M.; in winter, Monday through Saturday from 7:30 A.M. to 6:00 P.M.

Zuni Mountain Trading Company, 140 NM 371, P.O. Box 780, Thoreau, NM 87323. Call 505-862-7766. Open Monday through Saturday from 8:00 A.M. to 5:00 P.M.

Stauder's Navajo Lodge, HC 32, Box 1 (exit 44, I-40), Continental Divide, NM 87312-9701. Call 505-862-7553.

Baker's Hearth Restaurant, Giant Refinery, I-40, exit 39, (Ciniza) Jamestown, NM 87347. Call 505-863-1116. Open daily 24 hours.

4

From the Mountains to the Plains

Getting there: From Albuquerque, take I-25 123 miles northeast to Las Vegas, exit 345. To detour to Pecos National Historical Park, leave the interstate at exit 307, Rowe, and take NM 63 four miles north to the site. To detour to Fort Union National Monument, leave the interstate at exit 366, Valmora, and take NM 161 eight miles north to the site. From Las Vegas, take NM 518 31 miles north through Sapello and Buena Vista to Mora. In Mora, head north 37 miles on NM 434 through Guadalupita and Angel Fire. Where NM 434 connects with NM 64, go north 10 miles to Eagle Nest, then east 23 miles through Cimarron Canyon and Ute Park to Cimarron. In Cimarron, go south, then east 35 miles on NM 21 through Rayado and Miami to Springer and Interstate 25.

Highlights: When you arrive in Las Vegas, you begin a journey into a New Mexico past attuned to Spanish colonial times and the heritage of the range and the railroad. You'll enjoy wandering the streets of this historic two-part town, half adobe, half Victorian. Take a detour to Pecos National Historical Park.

Head north through the small villages of La Cueva and Mora, and traverse the beautiful Mora and Moreno valleys. In Angel Fire stop at the Vietnam Veteran's Memorial, or enjoy the area's opportunities for skiing in the winter and fishing, golfing, or hiking in the summer.

Leaving Angel Fire, steer northeast to Eagle Nest, a small town in the center of the valley along the shores of Eagle Nest Lake. Rimmed by peaks, including Wheeler on the west, the lake is a fisherman's haven both summer and winter.

Bearing east, you navigate Cimarron Canyon, with its sheer walls and rushing mountain stream. The town of Cimarron is known worldwide as home to Philmont Scout Ranch, and the historic district's St. James Hotel boasts a boisterous history of gunfights, range wars, and bad men.

The two-hour journey between Albuquerque and Las Vegas is enhanced by the beauty and variety of the terrain. Leaving the valley of the Rio Grande, the highway climbs La Bajada Hill's steep escarpment, bypasses Santa Fe, and swings west around the foothills of the Sangre de Cristo Mountains. Joining the path of the old Santa Fe Trail, it crests Glorieta Mesa near the site of the 1862 Union-Confederate battle that crushed the South's attempts to control New Mexico and Colorado. Cutting through the tilted rocks of the hogbacks at the southern end of the range, it crosses steeply sloping beds of multicolored sandstone and shale, finally opening on the vast spaces of the great plains to the east.

Be sure to pause halfway north on your interstate journey, take the short detour at Rowe, and visit Pecos National Historical Park. For more than 10,000 years this site has been the background for human habitation, first for the Pueblo and Plains Indians, then for Spanish conquerors and missionaries, Mexican and Anglo armies, and ultimately for settlers crossing the Santa Fe Trail. Geographically located in a 30-mile-long corridor between mountains and mesa, Pecos was a crossroads for travel and commerce between the upper Rio Grande valley and the plains.

Check in at the attractive visitors center and museum, a gift of the actress Greer Garson and her husband, Colonel E. E. "Buddy" Fogelson. Their donations of money, land from their Forked Lightening Ranch, and key ruins permitted the creation of the monument in 1965.

Walk the paths to the ancient pueblo of Cicuye, where in 1540 the Spanish discovered a city of 2,000 inhabitants, farmers who implemented their wealth with trade between the Apache and Comanche tribes of the plains. Climb a ladder into a reconstructed kiva, a place of ritual and worship where the Pueblo people performed ceremonies to ensure good hunting, plentiful crops, and cures for the sick. View the imposing walls of the great church built by the Franciscan priests arriving with the Spanish. The first church, completed in 1625 and destroyed during the Pueblo Revolt of 1680, was much larger than the second, built in 1717 on the foundations of the original. Look to the wide expanses north and east where the scored ruts of spoked wheels still delineate the passage of the wagon trains along their 800-mile journey from Missouri to Santa Fe.

Leaving Pecos, continue your route to Las Vegas, named not for the Nevada gaming mecca whose birth the New Mexico town predates by more than 150 years, but for the region's "big meadows," part of the 1821 land grant to Luis Maria C. de Baca. Originally a farming and commercial center, the city became an important stop on the Santa Fe Trail and later in 1879 on the Atchinson, Topeka & Santa Fe Railroad. The railroad builders bypassed the old town, or West Las Vegas, and routed the line east of the Rio Gallinas, creating the new Victorian area, East Las Vegas. Once separate communities, the two sections eventually incorporated, although each retains its distinct characteristics to this day—Old Town heavily Hispanic, and West Las Vegas mainly Anglo.

Leaving the interstate at exit 345, take East University Avenue to Grand Avenue. If you arrive on a weekday, turn right on Grand and head for the chamber of commerce to pick up a city guide and copies of the excellent driving and walking guides. Las Vegas has nine historic districts, and the Citizen's Committee for Historic Preservation has designed easy-to-follow tour pamphlets that highlight the more than 900 buildings listed in the National Register of Historic Places. If your journey takes you to town on a weekend, the Plaza Hotel generally has a supply of information.

While at the chamber, go next door to the City of Las Vegas Museum and Rough Riders Collection. The museum was founded after veterans of Teddy Roosevelt's Spanish-American War regiment named Las Vegas their official reunion home. Along with the Rough Riders Memorial Collection, the museum acquired city and county domestic artifacts, from Rio Grande weaving to Spanish colonial furniture.

After securing your maps and brochures and visiting the museum, return to University Avenue. Turn left on Bridge Street, cross the Rio Gallinas, and proceed to the Plaza, the heart of Old Town and the residential historic district. Once a regular stop for ranchers, miners, bankers, bunco artists, card sharks, women of ill repute, and desperados, the Plaza hosted some of the West's most infamous characters—Billy the Kid, Doc Holliday, and Black Jack Ketchem.

The place to start your exploration is the Plaza Hotel, built in the Italianate bracketed style in 1882 and still the site of convivial gatherings today. Restored to Victorian splendor, the second- and third-floor guest rooms are nicely appointed and inviting. The first floor hosts the public areas. The Landmark Grill has an attractive dining room featuring southwestern and Continental cuisine. Or if you're just looking for palaver, wander over to Byron T's Saloon, the local watering hole, where you can rub elbows with cowboys, local businesspeople, and visiting firemen (a slang term for visitors out for a good time).

Stroll the Plaza. From the flat rooftop of the Dice apartments on the north side, Brigadier General Stephen Kearny, Commander of the Army of the West, proclaimed New Mexico for the United States. South and west of the Plaza are the city's oldest homes, early adobe structures built in traditional Spanish style.

Walk down Bridge Street, where you'll find clustered an interesting group of shops: Ray and Barbara Zimmer's Rough Rider Trading Company, with its bounty of New Mexican handcrafted furniture, jewelry, handwoven garments, Western art, weaving, and antiques; Paul Stagner and Dave Ludwig's Meadowland Antiques & Spice Company, a "feast for the senses" with its collectibles, candies, coffees, teas, honey, and spices; Tito's Gallery, with its wide selection of arts and crafts from New Mexican artists; and Tome on the Range, Nancy Colalillo's cozy bookstore. If it's getting on lunchtime, El Rialto's is a Bridge Street institution with its expansive selection of New Mexican cuisine.

In the afternoon, drive out NM 65 to Montezuma, where the United World College of the American West was founded in 1982 by philanthropist Armand Hammer. The educational institution brings together young people from a range of nations, races, and social backgrounds to study in a two-year program and perform wilderness and community services.

Montezuma Castle, the school's landmark, is now in disrepair and closed to visitors. Constructed by the Santa Fe Railroad in 1888 as a multistoried, balconied, 343-room grand spa hotel, it hosted luminaries such as U.S. presidents Theodore Roosevelt, Ulysses S. Grant, and Rutherford B. Hayes. Kaiser Wilhelm and Japan's Emperor Hirohito also were guests.

When the railroad opened its El Tovar Hotel at the Grand Canyon, business for the Montezuma declined, and the railroad closed the property, eventually donating it to the YMCA.

In following years, the structure served many uses, including a Baptist college and a monastery for Mexican priests. Efforts to rehabilitate the building continue.

If you look closely near the base of the hill leading to the campus, you will discover several rustic concrete basins. These modest baths contain hot springs, once used to restore health to soldiers from nearby Fort Union. Still in sporadic use, the springs have a rate of 325 gallons per minute and an average temperature of 130 degrees Fahrenheit.

While you're out this way, stop at tiny Cristo Rey church, approximately two miles beyond the college campus on NM 65. One of the most photographed buildings in the area, its facade is covered with colorful murals depicting the Ascension.

Back in town, it's time to check into your quarters. If you prefer a more intimate setting than the Plaza Hotel, you won't go wrong at Anne and John Bradford's Carriage House Bed and Breakfast in Carnegie Park historic district. The three-story Queen Anne home was built between 1891 and 1893 by Frank Springer, one of territorial New Mexico's leading citizens and founder of the town of Springer, 60 miles northeast of Las Vegas.

Anne bills her decor as "a bit of English countryside in New Mexico," and the warm Victorian ambiance upholds her claim. The public rooms are rich in deep colors and comfortable settees. The five bedrooms are decorated in period furniture, with ruffles and lace in evidence. Floral prints adorn the walls, and a hallway trunk overflows with teddy bears and antique dolls. Old-fashioned hats and gowns festoon a bentwood coat tree, and a glass-fronted case displays a collection of cranberry glass and bone china teacups.

Breakfast is bountiful and includes a selection of sweets and savories. On any one day you might be served a fresh fruit cup, orange juice, carrot and ginger muffins, a loaf of pineapple-zucchini bread, a rich quiche of cheese and bacon, mushroom and onion empañadas, and a melting Bavarian apple torte. You won't go hungry at the Carriage House.

In the late afternoon, go for a stroll in the neighborhood, which contains many beautiful old homes and the Carnegie Library, one of the many the steel king and philanthropist Andrew Carnegie built in small towns all over America. Constructed in 1903 and modeled after Thomas Jefferson's home, Monticello, the library is one of a few Carnegie libraries still operating as a book repository.

Your evening's repast might be at Ronald Romero's Meadows Bar and Grill or Black Jack's Restaurant at the Inn on the Santa Fe Trail. The Meadows specializes in seafood, steaks, and pasta. The house soup is a hearty roast-garlic bisque, and their signature dish, Ale House pasta, marries shrimp, mushrooms, red onions, tomatoes, and beer in a rich, cream-thickened sauce. Black Jack's regulars praise its Black Angus choice beef and its seafood enchiladas made stacked, not rolled, with crab, shrimp, and scallops bound in a green chile–cream sauce.

After retiring to your quarters and a refreshing night's sleep, it's time to finish your tour of Las Vegas. You might want to drive through the campus of New Mexico Highlands University, check out Lincoln Park, with its great brownstone residences, or visit the Railroad Avenue historic district, where you'll discover La Castaneda Hotel. Built in 1898 as one of Fred Harvey's chain of railroad hotels, it is in a state of decline, but an aura of better days still clings to the Mission Revival structure.

Douglas Avenue, which runs through the district, is home to Ken Kimbrel's Twentieth Century Store, located in the old

Masonic Temple. It's chockablock with 25 years' worth of collecting and trading pottery, glassware, furniture, and jewelry.

If antiquing is your thing, you'll want to range farther afield, checking out Plaza Antiques, a 4,000-square-foot, multidealer cooperative on the Plaza's west side. Specialties of the shop include quality antiques, collectibles, primitives, and fine furniture. On the Plaza's south side, Jack Fitch's Antique Accents specializes in fine furniture, Roseville pottery, cut glass, china, and silver. Out Airport Road, Duke Antiques has 75,000 square feet of collectibles housed in two barns. They carry everything from fine furniture to primitives and are open by chance or by appointment.

Stop at Dick's Deli for a quick lunch. Don't be put off by the fact that the deli is housed in a liquor store cum bar. Their "deliciously different" sandwiches include such winners as the "Wild, Wild West," rare roast beef, green chile, pepper cheese, jalapeno relish, lettuce, and tomato on a tortilla, or "Cranky Turkey," oven-roasted turkey breast, cream cheese, and cranberry sauce on sourdough bread. Veggie lovers are accommodated with goodies such as a mushroom melt or hummus, avocado, sprouts, and tomato on whole wheat. Sandwiches are available to go, or you can eat in the lounge to the rear of the store.

Leaving Las Vegas, head north past Storrie Lake State Park, a nice place to picnic if you've taken your order "to go" from the deli. Storrie was created when the waters of the Gallinas River were dammed in 1916. If conditions are right, you'll see water-skiers, windsurfers, and sailboarders plowing the lake's surface.

Forging on, you pass the small village of Sapello before arriving in La Cueva, once a supply ranch for Fort Union, now a National Historic District thanks to the intervention of Colonel William Salman, who purchased the land and buildings between 1942 and 1950. With its old roller mill, settler

Vincente Romero's adobe home, San Rafael Mission Church, and the Mercantile Building, the village would be worth a stop in itself without the added attraction of the Salman Raspberry Ranch.

Open from May through mid- to late October, the ranch and its gardens are a showplace. Their wildflower meadow is a wonder, thick with bachelor buttons, coreopsis, poppies, and lupine. Shoppers flock to the Mercantile, now the ranch store, to stock up on raspberry products, fresh produce, dried flowers, New Mexico products, and unusual gifts. Fresh raspberries are usually available in late August through the first frost, and throughout the growing season you'll find fresh asparagus, sweet corn, pumpkins, onions, garlic, apples, and other fruits, as well as a selection of annuals and perennials. The café serves a variety of excellent sandwiches and daily specials, but you really should try Theresa's tamales, made at the ranch and served with red chile. They are truly scrumptious! If you have room for dessert, Badley's brownie sundae is a rich brownie crowned with vanilla ice cream and raspberry topping.

Outside of La Cueva, you head northwest to Mora, named for the wild berries found in the vicinity. Mora is a county seat and rests at the foot of the beautiful Mora valley, once the breadbasket of the north, its fields filled with wheat. Stretching the length of the Mora River watershed from the Sangre de Cristo Range in the west to the Canadian River in the east, the area is part of an 1835 land grant.

Following the valley north, you pass the village of El Turquillo and shadow Guadalupita Canyon as the road climbs to Coyote Creek State Park, a good place to get out and stretch your legs on a hike to the beaver ponds that dot the creek bed.

Between the park and the road's junction with NM 120, the roadway is narrow and winding, sometimes tapering to a single lane without a center stripe. Although driving commands your attention as you climb the pass between the Mora and Moreno valleys, do sneak a glance at the rushing mountain stream bordered by massive blue spruce and Douglas fir.

Once over the saddle, you encounter a broad mountain meadow with marshes and two small lakes. Passing a group of vacation homes, you face a better highway as you approach Angel Fire, a year-round resort started in the mid-1970s as a ski area. At an elevation of 8,600 feet and with an average annual snowfall of 210 inches, the ski area's 67 slopes and trails attract skiers from instate, Texas, Arizona, and Oklahoma. A nordic center sports a beginner's area and three different loop trails for a total distance of 18 kilometers. Rentals and lessons are available.

In summer Angel Fire attracts golfers, hikers, fishermen, and folks wanting to escape the heat and enjoy the many opportunities for outdoor recreation the region offers. There are summer chairlift rides, an 18-hole PGA-rated championship golf course, tennis courts, horseback riding, mountain biking, and fishing in nearby Eagle Nest Lake.

During any season, the Vietnam Veterans National Memorial is a stop not to be missed. Perched on a hillside with its soaring walls reminiscent of sails, the memorial pays homage to all who served in the war in Southeast Asia. In the chapel, combat boots and notes and letters from Vietnam veterans lie at the foot of a simple cross, and on the wall a list of states and the months scheduled for remembrance is posted. Originally designed and constructed by the family of Dr. Victor Westphall, whose son David was killed in a 1968 enemy ambush in Vietnam, the memorial now is under the aegis of the David Westphall Veterans Foundation.

From Angel Fire, it's a beautiful drive through the Moreno valley to Agua Fria, where you join U.S. 64 to Eagle Nest, a small community on the shores of Eagle Nest Lake. If the appearance of bait shops and marinas is any indication, the lake is fertile ground for Nimrods. The cold waters support a vigorous population of rainbow trout and kokanee and coho salmon. Ice fishing is popular in winter.

From Eagle Nest you head west through Cimarron Canyon, which borders on the 33,116-acre Colin Neblett Wildlife Area. A breathtaking drive any time of year, the sandstone cliffs rise several hundred feet from the canyon floor as the Cimarron River cuts a narrow outlet from the Moreno valley through the mountains. The road parallels the stream, which is dotted with pullouts, picnic areas, and hiking trails.

Passing Ute Park, a small settlement within the canyon, you traverse the western portion of the expansive Philmont Scout Ranch and arrive in Cimarron, a name conjuring up images of the rootin', tootin' Wild West. The sleepy town at the crossroads of U.S. 64, NM 21, and NM 58 comes as a bit of a surprise. The modern part of town, which stretches east to west, is unremarkable. There are several motels, a small city park with a statue of Lucien Maxwell, and Heck's Hungry Traveler restaurant, "home of the original Cimarron Roll." Here you can get the aforementioned sticky bun, New Mexican dishes, or a "Heck of a Burger," a half pound of beef smothered with green chile, cheese, and avocado.

Turn down NM 21 and cross the Cimarron River. In a block or two you're at the St. James Hotel, heart of the historic area. Although the stately hotel is quiet now, it once was the locus of activity for every cowboy, mountain man, and outlaw coming down the mountain branch of the Santa Fe Trail.

The land the St. James occupies, as well as the totality of town properties and beyond, was part of the 1841 Beaubien-Miranda Land Grant, later known as the Maxwell Grant for Lucien Maxwell, who married into the Beaubien family and bought out the other heirs. The Maxwell Grant encompassed 1,714,765 acres and was the largest single landholding in the Western Hemisphere.

Henri Lambert, once a personal chef to presidents Abraham Lincoln and Ulysses S. Grant, bought land from Maxwell and in 1880 built the St. James, a gambling saloon with a reputation for violence. Notorious gunman Clay Allison is said to have danced naked on the bar, and it was usual for cowboys to ride their horses through the wide side door and shoot out the lamps. Twenty-six men were killed within the adobe walls, and when the tin ceiling was first replaced in 1902, there were more than 200 bullet holes imbedded in its surface.

The hotel was carefully restored from 1985 to 1993 by local resident Ed Sitzberger, a retired engineer from Los Alamos and Sandia Laboratories, and in 1993 the Champion family of Seattle purchased the property. The hotel originally had 30 rooms but now is reduced to a more spacious and comfortable 14, all named for the famous and infamous.

Room 18, which is never rented, is said to be haunted by the ghost of T. J. Wright, who in 1881 won the hotel in a poker game and was killed before he could collect his debt. Other ectoplasmic beings that occasionally manifest include a short blonde poltergeist with a pockmarked face who hides things, steals items, and knocks dishes from shelves, and Mary Lambert, the first wife of the original owner, a friendly ghost who leaves the faint scent of perfume.

The hotel's public rooms are a study in Victorian elegance. The lobby settee and chairs are original to the hotel, and many of the transoms and door panels were painted by Harry Miller, a Santa Fe artist who stayed at the St. James. Miller also painted the impressive portraits of the Conqueror Don Diego de Vargas and Father Sera. There are the obligatory mounted heads of deer, elk, bison, pronghorn, mountain lion, and black bear, and in the downstairs hall the gambling saloon's original roulette wheel still stands.

The dining room offers a varied menu of Continental cuisine, with specials such as black bean and green chile soup and bison flank steak. In addition, there is a cozy coffee shop for informal meals and a 10-room motel with redwood sundeck.

Just down the road from the St. James, the Aztec Mill, built by Maxwell in 1864, houses a museum of artifacts from Cimarron and Colfax County. The four floors are filled to the rafters with an eclectic collection, including a model of Maxwell's adobe mansion, Frank Springer's chair, a CS Ranch chuckwagon, Indian artifacts, beadwork, pottery, Philmont memorabilia, the Cimarron Cowboy Hall of Fame, and much more. There's a Will James corner, with books inscribed and illustrated by the writer. James had a riding job on the CS Ranch in 1922 while awaiting a commission for his art. Local ranchers Frank Springer and his associates Jack Nairn and Burton Twitchell recognized the cowboy's talent and funded his education at Yale School of Art. James eventually dropped out but made important contacts in the East that led to publication of his books, which included perennial favorites such as *Smoky*, *Scorpion*, *The Dark Horse*, and *The Lone Cowboy*.

From Cimarron, head south toward Rayado and pass the headquarters of Philmont Scout Ranch. The largest camping operation in the world, it hosts more than 20,000 scouts every summer. The ranch's 137,493 acres (214 square miles) were a gift of Waite Phillips, founder of Phillips Petroleum. Born in Iowa in 1883, Phillips was a twin, one of 10 children from a poor family. At age 16 he and his brother left home, trapped in Montana's Bitterroot Mountains, and worked in logging camps, mines, ranches, and on the railroad. When his twin, Wyiat, died of a burst appendix, he was devastated. To bring him out of his depression, his older brothers enrolled him in business school. A circuit preacher told him of oil opportunities in Oklahoma, and he began the exploration that eventually led to his fortune.

Phillips visited the Cimarron area often to hunt, and in 1922 he began acquiring land in the area. He never had a direct connection with the Scouts but had come to admire their spirit. In 1938 he donated about 35,000 acres and in 1941 another 90,000 acres of the ranch to the organization.

Visitors today can tour his mansion, the Villa Philmonte, and visit the Philmont Museum and Seton Memorial Library. The villa remains pretty much as it was in 1926. The gardens are lush with pools and fountains. The portal walls are decorated with tile from Spain, Italy, and Portugal, and the floor is covered with tiles representing various New Mexican icons—cowboys, Indians, and cattle brands.

Inside the mansion, the formal entry has a Western motif with *horno* fireplace and hand-finished walls. Decorations include a hundred-year-old Zia *olla*, painted *santos*, and a bead- and quill-decorated tepee dew cloth. The living room, with its substantial chairs, painted ceiling beams, Knabe baby grand piano, and a massive fireplace, is opulent but comfortable. The formal dining room has a pullout table seating 16 to 18, Moroccan leather chairs, a fireplace, and a mural of an Indian hunting scene. There is a solarium with a small fountain, where Phillips's daughter is said to have kept goldfish, as well as a library and a New Mexico Room with depictions of Indian and colonial Spanish culture and photographs of ranch visitors such as Will Rogers and Wiley Post. Guided tours, which run 45 minutes, are available throughout the summer and early fall.

The library and museum are in a combined building. The library, named for Ernest Thompson Seton (1860–1946), artist, naturalist, author, and first Chief Scout of the Boy Scouts of America, embraces 5,000 volumes on the religion, culture, history and natural science of the area. It is open to researchers. The museum contains a variety of Seton and Phillips memorabilia. The Plains Room displays include a Sioux tepee and willow backrest, a pipe bag, a beaded woman's dress, a man's porcupine roach, leggings, and moccasins. You'll see Phillips's dress riding gear, a hand-tooled silver and turquoise-trimmed saddle, and many reminders of the ranch days.

Rayado Rancho and the Kit Carson Museum are farther down NM 21. Here from mid-June to mid-August ranch personnel create living history reenactments of the earliest days of the area. The complex is a replica of Carson's home during the period he worked to secure the region from marauding Jicarilla Apaches.

The remainder of your journey takes you through the foothills to the interstate. If your plans call for returning south, stop for a bite to eat at the Santa Clara Cafe in Wagon Mound. A true Western eatery with walls emblazoned with brand marks and mounted deer heads, the Santa Clara is owned and operated by Linda Rankins and her husband. Linda toils behind the counter, chatting up the locals on their coffee breaks or serving her incredible variety of homemade pies. You'll always find apple, cherry, blueberry, peach, buttermilk, egg custard, lemon chess, pecan, raisin walnut, and strawberry rhubarb. Those are just the regulars. Some days she may add pumpkin, sweet potato, prune, or shoo-fly. The food is plentiful, and the prices very reasonable. In addition to standard menu items such as chicken-fried steak, shredded beef and bean burritos, or, incongruous as it may seem, Philly steak sandwiches, there's a daily chalkboard special.

If you have time for one more detour, make it Fort Union National

Monument. Just a few miles off the interstate, the once-proud garrison entrusted with guarding the Santa Fe Trail from Indian attacks now is an adobe shell gradually melting into the earth. Only the walls and a few chimney stacks still stand from what was the largest military installation on the 19th-century Southwestern frontier. Stop at the visitors center to get a map for the self-guided walking tour. As you trace the windblown paths and walk the grass-grown ruts of the old trail, you can understand the feelings of dismay of many of the women who followed their husbands to that lonely, barren, dusty plain.

For More Information

Pecos National Historical Park, P.O. Box 418, Pecos, NM 87552. Call 505-757-6032. Visitors center open Memorial Day–Labor Day, daily from 8:00 A.M. to 6:00 P.M.; Labor Day–Memorial Day, daily from 8:00 A.M. to 5:00 P.M. Fee. Website: www.nps.gov/peco.

Las Vegas–San Miguel Chamber of Commerce, 727 Grand Avenue, P.O. Box 128, Las Vegas, NM 87701. Call 505-425-8631 or 800-832-5947. Open Monday through Thursday from 9:00 A.M. to noon and 1:00 to 5:00 P.M., Friday till 4:00 P.M. Website: www.lasvegasnm.com.

City of Las Vegas Museum and Rough Riders Memorial Collection, 729 Grand Avenue, Las Vegas, NM 87701. Call 505-454-1401, ext. 283. Open Monday through Friday from 9:00 A.M. to noon and 1:00 to 4:00 P.M., Saturday from 10:00 A.M. to 3:00 P.M., or by appointment. Website: www.arco-iris.com/teddy/index.htm.

Plaza Hotel, 230 North Plaza, Las Vegas, NM 87701. Call 505-425-3591 or 800-328-1882. Dining room open from 7:00 A.M. to 2:00 P.M. and 5:00 to 9:00 P.M.; lounge open from 4:00 P.M. to midnight.

Rough Rider Trading Company, 158 Bridge Street, Las Vegas, NM 87701. Call 505-425-0246. Open in summer, Monday through Saturday from 9:30 A.M. to 6:00 P.M., Sunday from 11:00 A.M. to 4:00 P.M.; in winter, Monday through Saturday from 10:00 A.M. to 5:30 P.M.

Meadowland Antiques & Spice Company, 131 Bridge Street, Las Vegas, NM 87701. Call 505-425-9502 or 800-927-5400. Open Monday through Friday from 8:00 A.M. to 5:30 P.M., Saturday from 9:00 A.M. to 5:30 P.M., Sunday during holiday season. Website: www.worldplaces.com/meadowland.

Tito's Gallery, 157 Bridge Street, Las Vegas, NM 87701. Call 505-425-3745. Open Monday through Saturday from 10:00 A.M. to 5:30 P.M., or by appointment.

Tome on the Range, 116 Bridge Street, Las Vegas, NM 87701. Call 505-454-9944. Open Monday through Saturday from 10:00 A.M. to 6:00 P.M.

El Rialto, 141 Bridge Street, Las Vegas, NM 87701. Call 505-454-0037. Open Monday through Saturday from 10:30 A.M. to 9:00 P.M.

Armand Hammer United World College of the American West, P.O. Box 248 (NM 65), Montezuma, NM 87731. Call 505-454-4200.

Carriage House Bed and Breakfast, 925 Sixth Street, Las Vegas, NM 87701. Call 505-454-1784. Website: www.worldplaces.com/carriage.house.b&b.

Meadows Bar and Grill, 500 Douglas Avenue, Las Vegas,
NM 87701. Call 505-426-1604. Open Monday from
5:00 to 9:00 P.M.; open Tuesday through Thursday, lunch
11:00 A.M. to 2:00 P.M., bar menu 2:00 to 5:00 P.M.;
open Friday and Saturday, lunch 11:00 A.M. to 2:00 P.M.,
bar menu 2:00 to 5:00 P.M., dinner 5:00 to 11:00 P.M.
Closed Sunday.

Black Jack's Restaurant, Inn on the Santa Fe Trail, 1133 Grand
Avenue, Las Vegas, NM 87701. Call 505-425-6791. Open
Tuesday through Saturday from 5:00 to 9:00 P.M.

Ken Kimbrel Twentieth Century Store, 514 Douglas Avenue, Las
Vegas, NM 87701. Call 505-425-3180. Open daily from
8:00 A.M. to 4:00 P.M.

Plaza Antiques, 1805 Plaza, Las Vegas, NM 87701. Call 505-454-
9447. Open Thursday through Monday from 10:00 A.M. to
6:00 P.M., Sunday from noon to 4:00 P.M.

Antique Accents, South Plaza, Las Vegas, NM 87701. Open
Tuesday through Saturday from noon to 5:00 P.M.

Duke Antiques & RV Park, 857 Airport Road, Las Vegas, NM
87701. Call 505-425-6978. By chance or by appointment.
Website: www.members.aol.com/dukesmall/.

Dick's Deli, 705 Douglas Avenue, Las Vegas, NM 87701. Call
505-425-8261. Open Monday through Wednesday from
10:00 A.M. to 9:30 P.M., Thursday through Saturday from
10:00 A.M. to 11:30 P.M.

Salman Ranch and La Cueva National Historic Site, junction NM
518 and 442, La Cueva (P.O. Box 1307, Las Vegas, NM
87701). Call 505-387-2900. Open May–October 31, daily.
Abbreviated schedule November–April.

Angel Fire Ski Area, P.O. Drawer B, North Angel Fire Road and
NM 434, Angel Fire, NM 87710. Call 505-377-6401 or 800-
633-7463. Website: www.angelfireresort.com.

Vietnam Veterans National Memorial, P.O. Box 608, Angel Fire, NM 87710. Call 505-377-6900. Open Tuesday through Sunday from 9:00 A.M. to 7:00 P.M.; chapel open 24 hours daily. Website: www.geocities.com/Pentagon/Bunker/2810.

Angel Fire Resort Chamber of Commerce, NM 434, Centro Plaza, P.O. Box 547, Angel Fire, NM 87710. Call 505-377-6661 or 800-446-8117. Open Monday through Friday from 8:00 A.M. to 5:00 P.M.; in winter, open weekends as well.

Eagle Nest Chamber of Commerce, P.O. Box 322, Eagle Nest, NM 87718. Call 505-377-2420.

Cimarron Chamber of Commerce, P.O. Box 604, 104 North Lincoln Avenue, Cimarron, NM 87714. Call 505-376-2417 or 800-700-4298. Open in winter, Monday, Tuesday, and Thursday through Saturday from 9:00 A.M. to 5:00 P.M.; in summer, daily from 9:00 A.M. to 6:00 P.M.

Heck's Hungry Traveler, NM 64, Cimarron, NM 87714. Call 505-376-2574. Open in summer, daily from 6:00 A.M. to 9:00 P.M.; in winter, Monday through Friday from 11:00 A.M. to 7:00 P.M., Saturday and Sunday from 7:00 A.M. to 8:00 P.M.

St. James Hotel, Route 1, Box 2 (17th and Collinson), Cimarron, NM 87714. Call 505-376-2664 and 800-748-2694. Coffee shop open Tuesday through Sunday from 7:00 A.M. to 8:00 P.M. Dining room hours vary by season.

Aztec Mill, 220 West 17th Street, Cimarron, NM 87714. Call Cimarron Chamber of Commerce, above. Open first weekend in May to Memorial Day weekend, Saturday from 9:00 A.M. to 5:00 P.M., Sunday from 1:00 to 5:00 P.M.; Memorial Day–Labor Day, Friday through Tuesday from 9:00 A.M. to 5:00 P.M.; from first weekend in May, Saturday from 9:00 A.M. to 5:00 P.M., Sunday from 1:00 to 5:00 P.M.; after Labor Day to end of September, Saturday from 9:00 A.M. to 5:00 P.M., Sunday from 1:00 to 5:00 P.M. Closed from October to the first weekend in May. Fee.

Philmont Scout Ranch (four miles south of Cimarron on NM 21), Cimarron, NM 87714. Call 505-376-2281.

Villa Philmonte, NM 21 Cimarron, NM 87714. Forty-five-minute tours, first week in June–end of August, every 30 minutes from 8:00 A.M. to 4:30 P.M.; May, September, and first week of October, 10:30 A.M. and 2:30 P.M. Tickets available at museum. Tours are limited to 25 people.

Philmont Museum and Seton Memorial Library, NM 21, Cimarron, NM 87714. Open in summer, daily from 8:00 A.M. to 5:00 P.M.; September 1–May 31, Monday through Friday from 9:00 A.M. to 5:00 P.M.

Kit Carson Rayado Rancho, NM 21, Cimarron, NM 87714. Open summer only, daily from 8:00 A.M. to 5:00 P.M.

Santa Clara Cafe, P.O. Box 113, Wagon Mound, NM 87752. Call 505-666-2011. Open Monday through Saturday from 8:00 A.M. to 8:00 p.m., Sunday from 9:00 A.M. to 6:00 P.M.; may close early in winter.

Fort Union National Monument, P.O. Box 127, Watrous (eight miles north from I-25, exit 366), NM 87753. Call 505-425-8025. Open Memorial Day–Labor Day, daily from 8:00 A.M. to 6:00 P.M.; Labor Day–Memorial Day, daily from 8:00 A.M. to 5:00 P.M. Website: www.nps.gov/foun.

5

The Turquoise Trail

Getting there: From Albuquerque, take I-40 east to exit 175, Cedar Crest/Tijeras. From the interstate, take NM 14 northeast six miles through Cedar Crest to San Antonito, where Sandia Crest Scenic Byway, NM 536, detours approximately eight miles through Sandia Park to Sandia Ski Area and Sandia Crest. If you continue on NM 14, you travel 12 miles to Golden. Madrid is 11 miles beyond Golden, and Cerrillos, three miles beyond Madrid. Cerrillos to the NM 586 turnoff west is seven miles. Head west on NM 586 eight miles and cross the interstate at exit 271. Turn right on the Frontage Road, and go approximately four miles, passing Santa Fe Downs Racetrack. Turn left on Los Pinos Road. The museum, El Rancho del las Golondrinas, is three miles from the intersection.

Highlights: Although the interstate route from Albuquerque to Santa Fe is fast and fairly scenic, the Turquoise Trail, or NM 14, does so much more than just get you there. Cedar Crest is home to eccentric Tinkertown Museum, and San Antonito provides a gateway to the wooded eastern slopes of the Sandia Mountains. The trail leads northeast through the old gold-mining town of Golden and coal-producer Madrid, now an artists' enclave and village of shops. South of San Marcos, you intersect the Cerrillos hills, cross the interstate, and stop at El Rancho de las Golondrinas, a living history museum of rural Spanish colonial culture.

For Albuquerque visitors accustomed to the view of the Sandia (Watermelon) Mountains from the west, a trip up the Turquoise Trail is a revelation. The Sandias run approximately 20 miles between Tijeras Canyon and the northern foothills. The western edge of the range is a precipitous array of Precambrian granite peaks and canyons, transformed nightly by alpenglow into the mellow rose tints that gave the pinnacles their name.

The eastern side presents a different story with its gradual wooded slopes of Pennsylvanian limestone. Here the desert falls away, and you're faced with a change not only of altitude but also of climate. "East Mountain," as it is dubbed by Albuquerque residents, often is colder, rainier, and snowier than the city or West Mesa areas. Although it can provide treacherous road conditions in winter when city streets are bare, its weather is a blessing in summer for residents seeking to escape the desert heat.

As you leave boulder-ridden Tijeras Canyon and begin your ascent, you pass through Cedar Crest, a typical mountain community with its small shops and stores providing essential services to residents not wanting to take the trek into Albuquerque.

High on a ridge, Elaine O'Neil's bed-and-breakfast provides a montane retreat for travelers. The cozy stone-and-log chalet sits on four acres overlooking the Ortiz and Manzano (Apple) Mountains. If you wander out on the balcony in the morning, you're likely to see mule deer or a racoon making an early foray through the cherry, plum, and peach trees. A great getaway for those shunning the city life, Elaine's location still provides an easy commute to Albuquerque or Santa Fe.

Continuing up the trail, you pass Cañoncito, a small settlement and arrive at the outskirts of San Antonito, where you connect with Sandia Crest Scenic Byway. In the era of Disney, just another roadside attraction might elicit gigantic ho-hums.

These generally eccentric creations of a fertile imagination can't compete with Space Mountain, nor do they try. Most originated with a hobby, a dream, or an obsession. Tinkertown Museum on the Sandia Crest Highway is a perfect illustration. Creator Ross Ward has placed a prominent sign saying:

> Tinkertown began as a hobby more than 30 years ago and slowly evolved into the museum collection you will enjoy. No taxpayer's money, no government funds and no public grants have been used in building or maintaining this display. We still believe in free enterprise and determination. You can do it, too, no matter what your project may be.

Back in the 1940s and '50s, Ross was growing up in the Midwest and learning to carve from a Boy Scout handbook. His first opus was a miniature circus, which he set up in his garage for the amusement of his buddies. His diminutive world was the casualty of a fire, but his drive to create did not abate. In the 1960s he began to develop his Western town, which today consists of 23 buildings peopled by all sorts of characters, from the politician hopping out of the bed of a woman of ill repute to the blacksmith at his forge.

During the mid- to late '60s, Tinkertown was housed in a medicine-show wagon parked in front of the New Mexico State Fair's Indian Arts Building, and Ross dressed as the slick hustler. When the collection grew to greater proportions, Ross and his wife, Carla, decided to find it a permanent home, and today's Tinkertown was born.

Tinkertown's walls are a combination of stone, cement, and wood scrounged from old buildings, and bottles—more than 40,000 of them. Before recycling was fashionable, Ross met Simi Valley's Grandma Prisby, who had created a bottle village from discards. Her philosophy was:

> I took the things you threw away
> And put them together night and day;
> A million pieces all in one,
> Washed by the rain and dried by the sun.

This intrepid, independent spirit is carried on by Ross and Carla at Tinkertown.

Take time to really inspect the scenes when you stop at this remarkable one-man creation, with more than 1,000 figures and 20,000 miniatures. Notice the detail in both the village and the equally impressive circus, with a side show, menagerie tent, and three-ring big top. Buttons animate certain figures such as the aerial acrobats or the town elder in a rocker.

In addition to the circus and Western town, Tinkertown houses a variety of collections, such as wedding cake couples, antique tools, dolls, toys, bullet pencils, and the *Queen Theodora*, a full-size, 42-foot English sailing ship Ross's brother-in-law employed to traverse the Seven Seas. You'll discover two animated music machines, "Rusty Wyer and the Turquoise Trail Riders," and the amazing "Otto, the One-Man Band," a six-foot contraption that consists of fully functioning accordion, drums, and xylophone—all controlled by a music box roll. Perhaps you'll see what the future holds by dropping a coin in the Esmeralda Fortune Telling Machine, made in 1940 by the Munves Company, New York, and for years a feature at Riverview Park in Chicago.

After leaving Tinkertown, continue on the Crest Highway. You'll pass Sandia Peak Ski Area, where 25 slopes and trails tempt downhill and cross-country skiers and snowboarders from mid-December to mid-March. On summer weekends the scenic chairlift ride transports sightseers or mountain bikers to the summit, where both hiking and biking trails await.

The drive terminates at 10,678 feet. From the observation deck, the city of Albuquerque is spread like a blanket below, and on most days you can see well beyond the escarpment containing Petrogylph National Monument and West Mesa's five volcanic cones to Mount Taylor, 60 miles to the west. Sandia Crest House, a gift shop and snack bar, is open daily.

If you want to see more, portions of the Crest Trail (TR 130) provide a short but bracing hike. Remember, it's not the distance, it's the altitude. This 1.3-mile one-way scenic path begins at the south end of the parking lot. Meandering through aspen glades and across flowering meadows, it leads to the Rock House at Vista Point, built by the Kiwanis, once used to house weather forecasting teams, and now vacant. Continuing at a gradual downhill angle, your walk ends at the terminal of the Sandia Peak Aerial Tramway, which climbs 2.7 miles up the western face of the mountains. In addition to a visitors center for Cibola National Forest, the tram summit houses the High Finance Restaurant and Tavern, with a varied lunch and dinner menu and a fantastic view. On days when the winds are right, you're likely to see hang gliders soaring like colorful, wide-winged birds after launching into thermals rising off the Rio Grande valley.

Descending from the crest, you again join NM 14 as it winds northeast. You pass the Gallery of the Sandias, modestly ensconced in double-wide manufactured housing. Don't let the simple exterior fool you. Iris Horlick stocks an impressive range of arts and crafts from the four corners of the world. There are Hmong jackets from Thailand, Daniel Hutchinson's whimsical animal masks, Linda Brewer's imaginative ceramic animals, Australian aborigine Dreamtime artwork, Southwestern jewelry, and more.

Continuing down the trail through grasslands dotted with juniper and piñón, you approach Golden. Aptly named, Golden sprang up as the result of a short-lived gold rush. The deposits proved scanty, and shortage of water made mining attempts difficult. Today a few homes, a church, and Beatriz Galaviz's La Casita gift shop make up the town. La Casita (little house) is a rewarding stop. Beatriz's family has lived in Golden for generations, and the shop once was home to her aunt. She stocks an eclectic assortment of Indian crafts, including storyteller necklaces from Santo Domingo's Marie Coriz, jewelry by Navajo silversmiths Jefferson James and Robert Largo, and unusual bone carvings of Navajo maidens by Dwayne and Ron Upshaw.

From Golden, it's a scant 11 miles to Madrid (pronounced MAD-rid), once a vigorous coal-mining town and currently undergoing a rebirth as a colony for artists and craftspeople. Tucked in a valley on the north side of the Ortiz Mountains, Madrid's anthracite fueled area gold smelters as early as 1835. With the 1880s' arrival in New Mexico of the railroad, demand for this high-quality coal increased, and a short branch of the Santa Fe Railroad was built into town. At one time the town produced 250,000 tons of coal yearly and was larger than Albuquerque.

The company built rows of housing, some of which have been restored. A golf course and tennis courts entertained the workers, and the town's Christmas light displays were so famous that TWA made detours to fly over the town. With the advent of diesel, coal demand dropped and the mines closed, as they had all over the country. Its economic base destroyed, the town went into decline, and in 1975 the owners sold the whole town—residences, shops, and all.

As you arrive in town, you will see everywhere evidence of Madrid's past—the weathered residences, the culm heaps, the mine ruins. As depressed as the town was in the 1970s, it hums with vitality today. The old buildings have been converted into galleries, shops, and restaurants. Getting a parking place on weekends can be an exercise in patience.

An abandoned house in Madrid—evidence of its rocky past.

If you'd like to learn more about the town, stop at the Old Coal Mine Museum, Engine House Theatre & Mine Shaft Tavern. You can browse through the museum (which has an actual seam of coal and a 1900 steam locomotive), attend a melodrama, or have a bite to eat.

Shops run the gamut from souvenir joints to fine-art galleries, but several deserve special mention. The Company Stores Building, with the shaded porch, houses Primitiva, Cambio, and Maya Jones. Primitiva specializes in imports, mainly from Mexico and South America, in addition to showcasing the work of regional artists. Their two floors contain tin lanterns, a huge selection of Mexican furniture, rugs, lacquerware paintings, Huichol beadwork, Casas Grandes pottery, and much more. Maya Jones specializes in Guatemalan clothing and crafts. They stock a comprehensive collection of Guatemalan yard goods—a bonanza for anyone with a sewing project in mind. Cambio has a selection of natural fiber clothing and accessories.

The Gifted Hand showcases several outstanding artists: Jaqui Stevens, an Indian Market Master of pottery who works in a contemporary style; Patricia Naylor, who creates smoked ceramic wall art; Ricardo Tarango, working in hand-tooled silver and gold jewelry; Michael Kluck, a talented woodcarver (check out his life-size ravens); and Seri Hollander of Madrid, who executes contemporary metal sculptures. Both Judy Mohr, the owner, and Tate Zeniceros, the gallery director, are very knowledgeable and can help you select the perfect piece for your collection.

Before you head to Linda Dunnill's Java Junction for a home-baked pastry and a cup of latte, or to shop for a hot sauce and unusual T-shirt among her encyclopedic selection, stop in at the Turquoise Trail Trading Post. This Madrid fixture stocks everything from rocks to rugs. Doren Bird will show you special items from Santo Domingo, her pueblo, and you will be hard-pressed to find a finer selection of jewelry from the well-known Coriz family, who produce tufa-cast silver masterpieces. Of special note is the custom inlaid jewelry, much designed and crafted by Randy, the post manager.

For a total change of pace, head on up the road to Cerrillos (Little Hills). Before 1680, Indians mined the beautiful green turquoise that streaks the nearby peaks, and when the Spanish arrived, they continued to work the mines. Turquoise from Cerrillos was part of the crown jewels of Spain. Gold and silver were discovered in 1879, and when the supply of precious metals was depleted, the town still had its veins of coal needed by the Atchison, Topeka & Santa Fe Railroad. At its prime in the 1880s, Cerrillos supported 21 saloons and four hotels catering to miners and railroad workers.

The sleepy, picturesque town has retained none of its boisterous past, but the dusty streets have a really timeless quality. Several movie companies have elected to film here because of the town's ambiance. You may be surprised to see "Wortley Hotel" and other reminders of the Lincoln County War painted on the two-story structure housing Simonis store. This anomaly was created during the filming of *Young Guns*. Walt Disney filmed *The Nine Lives of Elfego Baca* here in 1968.

E. J. Mitchell's What Not Shop has seen many guises—a grocery, post office, pool hall, and meat market, to name a few. However, for 45 years the 1892 quarry stone building has served as repository and sales center for E. J.'s love of the deal. Originally from North Carolina, this former schoolteacher is as weathered and crusty as his building's exterior. From a chair down by the iron stove, he presides over his collection of minerals, Navajo rugs, Indian jewelry, Zuni fetishes, and American antiques. He's democratic in his wares. Carnival, cut, and pressed glass, old campaign buttons, and other curios keep company with the native crafts. There's an eclectic jumble guaranteed to keep you poking in corners for longer than you'd anticipated.

Other Cerrillos attractions include Carine LaPointe's workshop and gallery, where she sells her traditional and modern jewelry. A student of Santo Domingo's Leo Coriz, she specializes in tufa-cast silver designs.

A third stop of note is Art Space. In this fine new adobe gallery and atelier, husband and wife team Barbara Harnack and NJ Lancaster showcase Barbara's ceramic sculpture pieces, NJ's raku pottery, and works by Hawthorne, Hensche, Warren, Goetz, and Christoffersen. NJ's grandfather was Jack Warren, cocreator of the 1929–1942 comic strip "Pecos Bill." If you remember this character, you'll get a kick out of the gallery's memorabilia.

Off a well-marked side street on the town's western edge, Todd and Patricia Brown built their Casa Grande Trading Post, Cerrillos Turquoise Mining Museum, and petting zoo. The post and museum of local memorabilia occupy 31 rooms, all constructed by Todd over the years. The well-tended petting zoo houses a supercilious white llama, several goats, and a bevy of fancy fowl. Food for the animals is available in the post.

Leaving Cerrillos, you head east and north to San Marcos. This area was home to a large Tano pueblo at the time of the Spanish Entrada. There is a folk tale that the Spanish in Santa Fe were warned by an Indian from San Marcos when the Rio Grande pueblos rose in revolt in 1680. This so greatly enraged the collaborating pueblos that they destroyed the town, sending some to live with the Hopis and others to exile with different tribes.

The ruins are there still, with nothing else to designate the district but a large feed and supply store fronted by the San Marcos Cafe, Tom and Susan MacDonell's creation and one of the finest eating establishments south of Santa Fe. Open for breakfast, lunch, and weekend dinners, the café serves an eclectic cuisine—mostly New Mexican but peppered with daily specials such as osso buco, pork and spätzle, and catfish jambalaya. There's always a couple of made-from-scratch soups, a quiche of the day, and a fiery green-chile stew. Save room for dessert. The selection is extensive, but the bourbon apple pie is a sellout favorite.

Just south of the café, your route swings west on NM 586, traverses the Cerrillos hills, and crosses the interstate. After a short stint on the Frontage Road, you pass the Downs at Santa Fe and head toward La Cienega (The Marsh) and El Rancho de las Golondrinas (The Ranch of the Swallows).

A major *paraje* (stopping place) on El Camino Real, Las Golondrinas was acquired by Miguel Vega y Coca in about 1710 and is one of the most historic ranches in the Southwest. The family intermarried with the Bacas, and the property was passed to their descendants, who in turn sold it to the Curtin family in 1932.

In 1939 Leonora Curtin visited the New York World's Fair and met Finnish diplomat Y. A. Paloheimo. They married and developed a vision to restore the old ranch as a living history museum dedicated to the language, culture, and history of Spanish colonial New Mexico. They salvaged the remaining buildings, erected authentic structures on existing foundations, and brought in related buildings from other sites. The museum was opened in 1972, and in 1982 title was transferred to a charitable trust.

The sprawling 200-acre site is a town unto itself, with an 18th-century *placita* house, a 19th-century home replete with outbuildings, a molasses mill, a threshing ground, several early water mills, a blacksmith shop, a wheelwright shop, a winery, and vineyards. A separate section portraying a mountain village has a *descanso* (resting place) with hilltop crosses; a *campo santo*, or cemetery; and a *morada*, the meetinghouse of Los Hermanos de Nuestro Padre Jesus Nazareno, or Penitentes. Dedicated to Our Lady of Peace, it is a replica of the south *morada* at Abiquiu.

If you can plan your trip to include one of the special events, so much the better. A Civil War Weekend starts off the season, followed by the Spring Festival and Spanish Renaissance Fair, Santa Fe Wine Festival, Summer Festival and Frontier Market, and Harvest Festival. Theme weekends such as "Arts, Crafts, Textiles, and Adobe" and "Faith, Santos, and Santeros" are scattered through the summer months. Costumed villagers portray life in the village, operating the mills and doing the farm and domestic chores. Entertainers perform the old music, dances, and plays, and craftspeople demonstrate and sell their traditional art. It is a colorful, entertaining experience.

Don't neglect the gift shop, which stocks a wonderful assortment of Spanish colonial crafts. You'll find *retablos* (figures of saints painted on a flat surface), *bultos* (three-dimensional carvings of saints), tinware, jewelry, and other items, all very reasonably priced.

Several caveats if you plan to visit Las Golondrinas: self-guided tours are open to walk-ins only June through September, Wednesday through Sunday from 10:00 A.M. to 4:00 P.M. In April, May, and October, you may phone for an appointment for a guided tour. Since you will be visiting during the warm months, it is important that you bring sunscreen, a hat, water, and sturdy shoes. The paths are a bit rough, and you will be covering a lot of territory.

As you leave Las Golondrinas and return to the interstate for your journey to Albuquerque or Santa Fe, you reenter today's New Mexico, a land shaped by the many elements encountered on your sortie up the Turquoise Trail. Perhaps you feel a bit of nostalgia for those earlier days. Not to fear. The trail awaits further exploration another day.

For More Information

Turquoise Trail Association, P.O. Box 1335, Cedar Crest, NM 87008. Call 505-281-2467. Website: www.turquoisetrail.org.

Elaine's: A Bed and Breakfast, P.O. Box 444, 72 Snowline Estates, Cedar Crest, NM 87008. Call 505-281-2467 or 800-821-3092. Website: www.elainesbnb.com.

Tinkertown Museum, P.O. Box 303, 121 Sandia Crest Road, Sandia Park, NM 87047. Call 505-281-5233. Open April–October, daily from 9:00 A.M. to 6:00 P.M. Fee.

Sandia Peak Ski Area, 10 Tramway Loop NE, Albuquerque, NM 87122. Call 505-242-9133 or 505-856-6419. Open for skiing mid-December to mid-March. Summer chairlift rides on holidays, Memorial Day weekend through the Balloon Fiesta (early October), Thursday through Sunday from 10:00 A.M. to 4:00 P.M. and holidays. Website: www.sandiapeak.com.

Sandia Peak Aerial Tramway, 10 Tramway Loop NE, Albuquerque, NM 87122. Call 505-856-7325. Fee.

High Finance Restaurant and Tavern, Sandia Tram summit. Call 505-243-9742. Reservations required.

Gallery of the Sandias, P.O. Box 311, 12540 North NM 14, Sandia Park, NM 87047. Call 505-281-4333. Open in summer, daily from noon to 8:00 P.M.; in winter, Friday through Wednesday from noon to 7:00 P.M.

La Casita, 1759 North NM 14, Sandia Park (Golden), NM 87047. Call 505-281-3896. Open Monday through Saturday from 10:00 A.M. to 4:30 P.M.

Old Coal Mine Museum, Engine House Theatre & Mine Shaft Tavern, 2846 NM 14, Madrid, NM 87010. Museum and theater, call 505-438-3780; tavern, call 505-473-0743. Melodrama held Memorial Day–after Labor Day, Saturday at 3:00 and 8:00 P.M., Sunday and holidays at 3:00 P.M. Museum open daily from 9:00 A.M. to 5:00 P.M. Tavern open for lunch Monday through Thursday from 11:00 A.M. to 4:00 P.M.; for dinner Wednesday, Friday through Sunday from 5:00 to 8:00 P.M.

Primitiva, 2860 Main Street, Madrid, NM 87010. Mail: P.O. Box 161, Cerrillos, NM 87010. Call 505-471-7904. Open daily from 10:00 A.M. to 5:30 P.M.

Maya Jones Imports, Company Stores Building, Madrid, NM 87010. Call 505-473-3641. Open in summer, daily from 10:00 A.M. to 5:30 P.M. Winter hours vary.

Cambio, Company Stores Building, NM 14, Madrid, NM 87010. Call 505-424-9722. Open in summer, daily from 10:00 A.M. to 5:30 P.M. Hours vary in winter.

The Gifted Hand Gallery, 2851 NM 14, Madrid, NM 87010. Call 505-471-5943 or 800-471-5943. Open daily from 9:30 A.M. to 5:00 P.M.

Java Junction, 2855 NM 14, Madrid, NM 87010. Call 505-438-2772. Open daily from 8:00 A.M. to 5:00 P.M. Winter hours vary. Website: www.java-junction.com/java-junction.

Turquoise Trail Trading Post, 2864 NM 14, Madrid, NM 87010. Call 505-471-0629. Open in summer, daily from 9:00 A.M. to 6:00 P.M.; in winter, from 10:00 A.M. to 5:00 P.M.

What Not Shop, Cerrillos, NM 87010. Call 505-471-2744. Open daily from 10:00 A.M. to 5:00 P.M.

Carine's Jewelry, P.O. Box 29, Cerrillos, NM 89010. Call 505-474-4072 for hours.

Art Space, 98 B Gold Mine Road, Cerrillos, NM 87010. Call 505-474-7564. Open by appointment.

Casa Grande Trading Post, Museum and Petting Zoo, Waldo Street, Box 131, Cerrillos, NM 87010. Call 505-438-3008. Open daily. Fee for museum.

San Marcos Cafe, 3877 NM 14 (San Marcos), Santa Fe, NM 87505. Call 505-471-9298. Open Monday through Wednesday from 8:00 A.M. to 2:00 P.M., Thursday through Saturday from 8:00 A.M. to 2:00 P.M. and 5:30 to 8:00 P.M., Sunday brunch from 8:00 A.M. to 2:00 P.M.

El Rancho de las Golondrinas, 334 Los Pinos Road, Santa Fe, NM 87505. Call 505-471-2261. Open April–May, self-guided tours by reservation; June–September, Wednesday through Sunday from 10:00 A.M. to 4:00 P.M. Fee. Website: www.golondrinas.org.

6

Savoring the Salt Missions Trail

Getting there: From Albuquerque's I-40/I-25 interchange, take I-25 south 9.8 miles to exit 220, Rio Bravo. Take Rio Bravo west 4.2 miles to Coors Boulevard/NM 45. Go south on Coors 8.8 miles to NM 314. A short dogleg to the left on NM 314 is followed by a quick right on NM 147. Isleta Pueblo is 1.3 miles over a dirt road.

Leaving the pueblo, retrace your steps and return to NM 314 south for 6.7 miles until you reach NM 6 in Los Lunas. Turn right for Luna Mansion or Teofilo's or left to continue. Follow NM 6 for three miles to NM 47 south. After 8.5 miles, turn right on NM 309 and follow the route across the river (1.9 miles).

Turn left on Main Street, Belen, and left .2 miles on Becker Street. Follow Becker to the end. Pete's Cafe is on the right. Turn left onto First Street. The Harvey House museum is straight ahead.

From the museum, take First Street to Dalies and follow Dalies to Main. Turn right on Main and right on NM 309. Follow NM 309 .7 miles. Take a right on NM 109 (Jarales Road). The P & M Farm Museum is 2.8 miles on the right, the mill 3.5 miles, also on the right.

Continue on Jarales Road 3.5 miles, and turn left on NM 346, crossing the river. Turn right on NM 304 after 1.5 miles and continue south through Veguita, Las Nutrias, and Boys Ranch, nine miles.

Take U.S. 60 east to Abó, 29 miles, and Mountainair, nine miles. Detour south on NM 55 for 25 miles to Gran Quivera. Retracing your route to Mountainair, continue on NM 55 north to Punta de Agua and Quarai, eight miles. Follow NM 55 north 16 miles to NM 337 through Manzano, Torreon, and Tajique. Go north 30 miles through Chilili to Escobosa, Ponderosa, Cedro, and Tijeras. Exit Tijeras at I-40.

Highlights: If you're in Albuquerque for several days, do the unexpected and head south. You'll visit Isleta Pueblo and its ancient church, dine at historic Luna Mansion or Teofilo's in Los Lunas, visit the Harvey House Museum, a farm museum and a working roller mill in Belen and Jarales, follow the Rio Grande through old Hispanic villages of Veguita and Las Nutrias, and roam the ruins of the great Indian pueblo and Spanish mission complexes of Abó, Quarai, and Gran Quivera.

For visitors to New Mexico, a sojourn in Albuquerque may be brief before heading north to the charisma of Santa Fe or the celebrated mountains of the Taos. These locales exert a siren call, hard to ignore. But for the traveler seeking the uncommon, the path less taken, a venture south along the great river will transport you to a land steeped in history, its roots deep in the *bosque* soil of the Rio Grande.

As you leave the city on Interstate 25, take a minute to look around you. The Sandia Mountains rise 10,000 feet to the east, a tilted fault block of 1.4-billion-year-old granite topped with 300-million-year-old sedimentary rock. To the west of the city, the land rises to the mesa, the Llano de Albuquerque, 5,800 to 6,000 feet above sea level. Five small volcanic cones, extinct for 250,000 years, define the horizon along a north-south fault. Few cities in the world have as many extinct volcanoes nearby as Albuquerque—about 270 within 65 miles!

Dividing the city proper from West Mesa, the Rio Grande flows along, yearly adding to the layer of sediment, which through the ages has filled the great rift containing the river. A muddy torrent when spring snowmelt courses from the northern mountains, the river seems placid enough during the balance of the year as it winds its way from its source in Colorado to its mouth in the Gulf of Mexico.

Leaving the hustle and bustle of the state's largest city, you head south on Coors Boulevard, which runs parallel to the river through gradually diminishing commercial development. Approaching the Isleta Reservation, you enter a wetland where hawks patrol the sky and sandhill cranes browse for forage in the fields. Your route passes under the interstate, intersecting Black Mesa, a basalt lava flow.

Unlike some pueblos, Isleta has never been forced to relocate. It has occupied the same location since Captain Hernando de Alvarado, a soldier in Coronado's expedition, came through in 1540. The Spaniards named the place Isleta after their word for a small delta or island, but the Indians named their village Tsugwevaga, or "kick flint," after a popular kicking race played with a piece of obsidian. Since it is located so near to Albuquerque, many of today's residents work in the city. But this brush with modern life seems hardly to have affected the pueblo's guardians. Once within the dusty plaza, the centuries fall away.

St. Augustine mission church was built about 1613, and although it was almost completely destroyed in the Pueblo Revolt of 1680, it was rebuilt when the Spanish returned. It is one of the oldest, if not the oldest, church in New Mexico, and its stained-glass windows portray various scenes of pueblo life. The altar is crowned with a carved image of the crucified Christ encrypted with the credo "I Am the Bread of Life." The church gardens are scented islands of meditation, and a special grotto celebrates Kateri Tekakwitha, the "Lily of the Mohawks," the United States's only beatified Native American.

Several entrepreneurs have small gift shops on the plaza's perimeter, and frequently you can purchase crusty loaves of pueblo bread fresh from the beehive-shaped adobe ovens called *hornos*.

To forestall disappointment, call the tribal office prior to visiting Isleta. During times of sacred ceremonies, non-Indians are prohibited from entering the pueblo. And remember, this is home to the residents, not a tourist attraction. Courtesy and respect go a long way to making your visit memorable.

Not long after leaving Isleta, you arrive in Los Lunas, named for the Luna family, early settlers who laid claim to the San Clemente Grant of 1716 originally awarded to Don Felix Candelaria. The union of the Luna and Otero families developed into a powerful political force in Valencia County, and in 1880, when the Santa Fe Railroad approached Don Antonio José Luna to purchase a right-of-way that included the family hacienda, he agreed, with the stipulation that a new home would be built to his specifications. What emerged is a curious but gracious estate, Southern colonial in style but built of adobe—a stately Southwestern Tara.

Today the elegant white columns and expansive bay windows enclose a fine restaurant, the Luna Mansion. Restored to the 1920s opulence created by doyenne Josefita Manderfield Otero and designated a State Historic Site, the facility is owned by Earl Whittemore. The various rooms of the house have been converted into charming dining quarters graced with many family treasures and photos from years gone by. The menu is "classic" with a Southwestern touch, and the restaurant is famous for its fine wine cellar, which boasts many rare vintages. Reasonable daily specials include such home-style favorites as green-chile chicken pot pie and thinly sliced top sirloin au jus.

Although the Luna Mansion is open for dinner only, you won't go hungry if you arrive in the area at lunchtime. Across the street from the mansion's iron gates, Teofilo's offers classic New Mexican cooking with some of the finest red chile in the state. The restaurant, a registered State Landmark, is housed in the home of an early Los Lunas doctor. Acclaimed by local businesspeople and travelers alike, the restaurant really hums at noon as plates of carne adovada and tamales fly out of the kitchen. Owners Pete T. (Teofile) and Tenci Torres use many of the family recipes developed by Pete's mother, Eligia, who runs a well-known cafe in Belen. Do try anything with the "red," a sauce with the complex blend of flavors found in the best chile. With a sufficient bite to satisfy chile heads, it is mellow enough for the tourist.

A serendipitous means of sampling the specialties is ordering the combination platter: a chile relleno, beef taco, and cheese enchilada. Leave room for dessert. The natillas are what angels would have for pudding—rich, light as air, and flavored with vanilla, cinnamon, and nutmeg.

Thoroughly sated, you may not be thinking of food again—until say, dinner hour. However, do stop a short distance out of town at Sunset Foods, purveyors of truly great jerky under the brand name Carne Seca de Santa Fe. Thinly sliced inside round of beef is dried and flavored with a variety of seasonings: red chile, green chile, pepper, teriyaki, mesquite, hickory, country style, or natural. If you can't decide, ask for a sample. They will oblige. Then try to eat just one piece.

Continuing south through fields watered by irrigation ditches called *acequias*, you pass many small farms and the small village of Tome. To the northeast you can see El Cerro de Tome, a hill crowned with three crosses. This dormant volcano is the scene of an annual Good Friday pilgrimage climb for many local people. A park with an entrada arch and iron sculptures of the region's three founding races, Indian, Spanish, and Anglo, is located at the base.

Your next destination, Belen, originally was a sleepy Spanish farming community. Recipient of an economic boost when the Santa Fe Railroad came through in 1880, the town was touted as the "Hub City." The convergence of the north-south line and the Belen cutoff from the east relays both freight and Amtrak cars northwest toward Gallup and Los Angeles.

Located next to the still-busy railroad yards, the Valencia County Historical Society Museum is situated in an original Harvey House, one of a series of elegant railside hotels built by Fred Harvey throughout the Southwest. The museum houses a permanent collection of material on the Santa Fe Railroad and serves as a repository of memorabilia and mementos of Valencia County history. There is a representative Harvey Girl's room—a white iron bed, a steamer trunk, washstand, and primitive rocker. Recruited for a year's contract to work as waitresses, these women of good reputation discovered the West while serving the traveling public.

Before leaving Belen, you might want to visit Pete's Cafe across the street from the museum. Owned by Eligia Torres, this restaurant is the gastronomic incubator for many of the fine New Mexican dishes served at Teofilo's in Los Lunas.

Heading out of town toward Jarales, you will discover the P & M Farm Museum. Housed in the barn and the hacienda with its L-shaped adobe wing, the collection gives new meaning to the word eclectic. Garnered by Pablo and Manuela Chavez from estate, yard, and garage sales throughout Valencia County, the 50-year collection of objects ranges from antique cars to Barbie dolls. You may be astounded to see two six-foot wooden kachinas dancing amid a life-size Victorian party scene, but Manuela is not bound by tradition in her displays. As she accompanies you on your tour, you learn much about family history as well as the provenance of the exhibits. The museum rooms are unheated, so dress warmly during cool months, and leave time to enjoy the encyclopedic collection.

A quarter-mile south on Jarales Road, Jose and Kathy Cordova operate the Valencia Flour Mill, the last family-owned steel-roller mill in the state. This commercial operation, which is certified organic, turns out tortilla and sopapilla mixes and low-gluten pastry flour from New Mexico red winter wheat.

Although Jose comes from an old Valencia County family, both he and Kathy were working in Minnesota when a visit to New Mexico took them to El Rancho de las Golondrinas, a re-creation of an early Spanish settlement south of Santa Fe. The museum's restored mills captivated them, and when they discovered that the mill Jose's grandfather established was for sale, they purchased it from the family estate and set about becoming millers. Actually, they are reviving a tradition. Before flood control changed the nature of the area, Belen was a wheat-growing and milling center. Now the Cordovas must purchase most of their supplies from the northern and eastern part of the state.

There are no tours as such, but if you come at a slack time, Kathy might break away from her books to show you the 1920 Decatur milling machine, which Jose has beautifully restored to working condition.

The next miles of your journey take you through the tiny Hispanic river towns of Veguita (Little Meadow) and Las Nutrias (The Beavers). Before joining U.S. 60, you pass the gates of New Mexico Boys Ranch, a residential facility for boys operated by a Christian nonprofit organization. A working cattle ranch with 2,400 acres, the property occupies a site on the old Camino Real that was once a watering hole and salt reservoir.

You now are heading north into the Estancia Basin. Once long ago in prehistory, the area was covered by a vast lake, which gradually dried up as the climate became more arid. The salts left behind condensed into salt flats and salt "lakes" a few inches deep. The Spanish named the place Salinas Jurisdiction. They used Indian labor to carry the salt down to the Rio Grande, where it was transported to the silver mines in Chihuahua, Mexico. Salt was a necessary part of the "patio" process of smelting silver.

However, even before the Entrada, there were settlements in the Estancia Basin. Archaeologists differ as to the exact date Paleo-Indians occupied the region, but estimates range anywhere from 19,000 to 10,000 years ago. At first, the people were nomads, hunter-gatherers. Later two great ancient cultural traditions overlapped in the Salinas—the Anasazi and Mogollon. They produced settled societies that at first built clusters of pit houses and eventually mastered the art of above-ground masonry structures. Villages grew up and flourished. The area became a major trade center between the Rio Grande pueblos and the Plains tribes to the east.

Today the once prosperous villages and the missions the Spanish built to serve them are in ruins. The wind sweeps through both pueblo and church, piling little drifts of sand against walls that witnessed the comings and goings of gray-robed friars and the everyday life of the people. Now the only sign of life is the whip-tailed lizard warming itself in the sun, or the voice of the occasional visitor.

What happened? A clash of cultures was partly to blame. The Spanish brought a new set of values and a new religion to the pueblos. Famine and European diseases played their roles.

Compounding these elements was the dependence of a very large population on rainfall for agriculture, more than usual reliance on hunting, and high exposure to the depredations of the Apache. Over a period of time, these factors led to a gradual migration of the people to join other native groups along the edge of the Rio Grande. The final disintegration occurred during the 1680 Pueblo Revolt, when the remnants of the Salinas people fled with the Spanish to the El Paso area.

Today Salinas Pueblo Missions National Monument consists of the ruins of three separated pueblos/missions: Abó and

The ruins of Abó pueblo and mission, Salinas Pueblo Mission National Monument.

Quarai to the north and Gran Quivera to the south. Your first stop is Abó, a favorite of many for its splendid isolation and the ruins of the mission church of San Gregorio de Abó. Built between 1629 and 1659, the church and *convento* have a design that combines European form with Indian construction materials and techniques. The walls are of sandstone rock and mud mortar, with two exterior buttresses and a bell tower supporting the west wall to a height of 40 feet. The *convento* walls act as east-side buttresses, and the crenelated roof gives a fortress-like appearance to the church and mission compound. In the morning sun, the buildings glow with an almost incandescent light. An unexcavated Tampiro Indian pueblo lies south of the mission and is connected to it by a half-mile-long, handicapped-accessible trail. There is a small visitors center with a display area, books for sale, and rest room facilities.

To reach the second of the Salinas Missions, you must detour south 25 miles to Gran Quivera, a modern designation for the village known originally by the name Cueloze. The Spanish renamed it Pueblo de las Humanas, which means a town of Indians with stripes painted or tattooed over their noses, a characteristic of Plains Indians appearing in many pictographs in this region.

The site encompasses the excavation of a large pueblo with plazas, homes, storage rooms, and ceremonial kivas; the ruins of the old mission church, San Buenaventura; and the Chapel of San Isidro, the first Christian church built on the site by Father Letrado, who was later killed at Zuni during the Pueblo Revolt. Here, too, there are a half-mile-long trail that wanders among the ruins, a visitors center, books for sale, and rest room facilities.

The farming and ranching town of Mountainair is the headquarters for Salinas Pueblo Missions National Monument, where you may secure additional information or request the ranger to screen the 40-minute film, *The Excavation of*

Mound Seven, written and narrated by archaeologist Alden Hayes, the supervisor of the 1965–1967 excavation.

Mountainair is a good place to pause for a meal or overnight stay. Founded in 1903 by three Kansas men in anticipation of the construction of the Santa Fe Railroad's Belen cutoff, the town is at the highest point on the railroad's southern transcontinental route. Once known as the "Pinto Bean Capital of the World," the area was hit by a severe drought in the 1950s, which forced a change in the economic focus to ranching.

One of the early settlers, Clem "Pop" Shaffer, was a bit of a frontier hippie. An acclaimed merchant, horse trader, land speculator, philanthropist, and folk artist, he built his idiosyncratic hotel over his hardware and implement store in 1923. You'll be happy to learn that the hotel with all its eccentricities has survived and is open for business under the management of Axel Kayser. The bed-and-breakfast rooms are simple but adequate, and meals are available at the hotel dining room, which specializes in New Mexican cuisine. The food is fine, but it's the ambiance that attracts. Pop was a decorating fiend, with every possible surface painted or carved with a combination of whimsical forms and Native American symbols. The chairs alone are painted in five colors.

Both the hotel and Rancho Bonito, where Pop grew much of the produce for the dining room, are on the National and State Registers of Historic Places. Pop's eccentric art forms, his wooden zoo at the Rancho and his hotel decor, are classified as Folk Art Environmentalist, a style in which "expression often takes the form of a lifetime, single project . . . guided by the desire to form an environment over which the artist has complete control."

Eight miles beyond Mountainair, the red walls of Quarai's church, La Purísima Concepción de Cuarac, rise above the small valley. The smallest of the three missions, it is thought to have been constructed around 1630 under Fray Juan Gutierrez de la Chica, who came to minister to the Tiwa-speaking Indian pueblo. Like the other pueblos, it was abandoned in the late 1600s. The visitors center contains a museum with a model of the original mission, as well as Indian and missionary artifacts.

Heading north, you pass a series of small Hispanic towns. Manzano was named for the apples grown in orchards thought to have been planted by Franciscan friars in the 17th century. Torreon, Tajique, and Chilili were all built on the sites of Indian pueblos. Torreon was named for the fortified towers the Spanish built to the south, and Tajique is a corruption of the Tiwa pueblo name. Chilili is from a pueblo word for "very weak spring" or "sound of water barely trickling." It is one of the oldest place names in New Mexico, having been recorded as the site of a pueblo in 1581. The present Hispanic settlement was established as part of a land grant in 1841.

The small settlement of Escabosa is home to Carmen and Val Sanchez's Sierra Farms. Their fine goat cheese is popular throughout the Albuquerque area and may be found in gourmet delis and natural food emporiums. Products include a mild white farm cheese; queso fuego spiced with green chile and jalapeños; feta; two robust hard-textured cheeses, sabroso and sabroso herb; and Carmen's cheesecake. In addition, they package their chevre in virgin olive oil with a variety of condiments: Italian or Southwestern spices; a combination of basil, sun-dried tomato, and garlic; and baby dill. These are all for sale in their cheese house, provided the goats have been productive and the supply hasn't been gutted by overenthusiastic customers.

In addition to providing an outlet for their fine cheese, Sierra Farms is a wonderful place to visit, especially for youngsters. A six-acre site, The Children's Field, is dedicated to agricultural education and is geared for grades three and up with information on crop growth, food preparation, farm animals, and production of fiber for clothing. For the younger children, there is the farm itself. Carmen loves to show kids around, giving tidbits of information on each animal's habits and attributes. Her enthusiasm and ebullient personality easily charm all who meet her.

Your last stop on the Salt Mission Trail is the Sandia Ranger station in Tijeras. To the rear of the station, the ruins of another old pueblo lie under the sighing grasses. In the mid-1300s it was a settlement with 200 rooms, a dozen or so smaller buildings, and a great kiva. Although a second phase of growth occurred in 1390, by 1425 the people had moved on. Today a large mound of earth marks the remnants of the pueblo, but illustrated trail signs and a scale model bring the scene to life. If you are resourceful and imaginative, you may be able to pierce the veil of time and hear in the wind the whisper of the past—the spirits of a departed but not forgotten people.

For More Information

Isleta Pueblo, P.O. Box 1270, Isleta, NM 87022. Call 505-869-3111 or 505-869-6333. Open Monday through Friday from 8:00 A.M. to 4:30 P.M.

Los Lunas Chamber of Commerce, 3447 Lambros, P.O. Box 13, Los Lunas, NM 87031. Call 505-865-1581. Open Monday through Friday from 8:00 A.M. to 5:00 P.M.

Luna Mansion, P.O. Box 789, Main Street, Los Lunas, NM 87031. Call 505-865-7333. Open Friday and Saturday from 5:00 to 9:30 P.M., Sunday through Thursday from 5:00 to 9:00 P.M.

Teofilo's, 130 Main Street, Los Lunas, NM 87301. Call 505-865-5511. Open in summer, Friday and Saturday from 11:00 A.M. to 9:00 P.M., Sunday through Thursday from 11:00 A.M. to 8:30 P.M.; in winter, Friday and Saturday from 11:00 A.M. to 9:00 P.M., Sunday through Thursday from 11:00 A.M. to 8:00 P.M.

Sunset Foods, 3072 NM 47 (Tome), Los Lunas, NM 87031. Call 505-865-9202. Open Tuesday through Saturday from 10:00 A.M. to 6:00 P.M., Sunday from 11:00 A.M. to 5:00 P.M. Closed Monday.

Greater Belen Chamber of Commerce, 712 Dalies, Belen, NM 87002. Call 505-864-8091. Open Monday through Wednesday from 10:00 A.M. to 4:00 P.M., Thursday and Friday from 10:00 A.M. to 2:00 P.M. Website: www.belennm.com.

The Harvey House Museum, Valencia County Historical Society, 104 North First Street, Belen, NM 87002. Call 505-861-0581. Open Tuesday through Saturday from 12:30 to 3:30 P.M.

Pete's Cafe, 105 North First Street, Belen, NM 87002. Call 505-864-4811. Open Monday through Thursday from 11:00 A.M. to 8:00 P.M., Friday and Saturday from 11:00 A.M. to 8:30 P.M.

P & M Farm Museum, 478 Jarales Road, Belen, NM 87002. Call 505-864-8354 for appointment. Fee.

Valencia Flour Mill, P.O. Box 210, 74 Mill Road, Jarales, NM 87023. Call 505-864-0305. No formal tours.

Salinas Pueblo Missions National Monument, P.O. Box 517, corner of Ripley and Broadway, Mountainair, NM 87036-0517. Monument headquarters, call 505-847-2585; Gran Quivera, 505-847-2770; Abó, 505-847-2400; Quarai, 505-847-2290. Headquarters open daily from 8:00 A.M. to 5:00 P.M.; sites open from 9:00 A.M. to 5:00 P.M. Website: www.nps.gov/sapu.

Mountainair Chamber of Commerce, 217 Broadway, P.O. Box 595, Mountainair, NM 87036. Call 505-847-2795. Open daily from 10:00 A.M. to 5:00 P.M.

Shaffer Hotel and Dining Room, P.O. Box 459, Mountainair, NM 87036. Call 505-847-0628. Open in summer, daily from 7:00 A.M. to 9:00 P.M.; in winter, open daily from 7:00 A.M. to 8:00 P.M.

Sierra Farms, Inc., P.O. Box 790 (Escabosa), Tijeras, NM 87059. Call 505-281-5061. Open March–October, Tuesday through Sunday from 10:00 A.M. to 5:00 P.M.; November–February, Tuesday through Sunday from 10:00 A.M. to 5:00 P.M. Closed Monday. Mail brochure available.

Tijeras Pueblo Archaeological Site, Sandia Ranger District, Cibola National Forest, 11776 NM 337, Tijeras, NM 87059. Call 505-281-3304. Trail open Monday through Friday from 8:00 A.M. to 5:00 P.M., Saturday and Sunday from 8:30 A.M. to 5:00 P.M.

7

Billy the Kid Territory

Getting there: From Albuquerque, take I-25 south to San Acacia, exit 163. From San Acacia, take NM 408, which runs 10 miles through the villages of Chamizal and Polvadera to the outskirts of Lemitar. Your option here is to continue on to San Antonio on NM 408 or leave the pavement and drive Quebradas Scenic Byway, a well-maintained dirt and gravel road that is navigable by touring car in dry weather. The road leaves Lemitar and traces east and south approximately 27 miles before joining U.S. 380 11 miles east of San Antonio.

To visit Bosque del Apache National Wildlife Refuge, drive south from San Antonio eight miles on NM 1. Retracing the route on your return, go north to U.S. 380. The exit to Trinity Site is 12 miles beyond San Antonio, and Carrizozo is 53 miles.

Continue east on U.S. 380. The distance between Carrizozo and Capitan is 20 miles, Capitan and Lincoln, 12 miles, and Lincoln and Hondo, 10 miles. Turn west on U.S. 70 at Hondo, passing through San Patricio and Glencoe. Take the Hollywood exit to detour into Ruidoso, 24 miles from Hondo.

Leaving Ruidoso, resume the journey southwest 12 miles on U.S. 70 through Apache Summit to the junction of NM 244, which winds 29 miles to Cloudcroft. From Cloudcroft, take U.S. 82 west through Mountain Park and High Rolls to U.S. 70/54, 20 miles south to Alamogordo. The turnoff to White Sands National Monument is 14 miles southwest of Alamogordo on U.S. 70.

Returning to Alamogordo, drive north 30 miles to Three Rivers, and take Forest Service Road 579 five miles to the Petroglyph Site. Carrizozo is 28 miles beyond Three Rivers on U.S. 54.

Highlights: While in the Rio Grande valley, visit Bosque del Apache National Wildlife Refuge, home of thousands of wintering waterfowl and sandhill cranes. From the green of the riverine environment, cross the notorious Jornada del Muerto and pass the site of the first atomic explosion (open to the public only the first Saturdays of April and October).

Explore deep into the Sacramento Mountains, stopping at the tiny towns of Capitan, home of Smokey Bear, and Lincoln, site of the infamous Lincoln County War. Drop into the beautiful Hondo valley, made famous by the Hurd-Wyeth family of artists. Stop for a while in the busy four-season resort of Ruidoso before ascending to the lofty heights at Cloudcroft, with its shops and restaurants.

Leaving the mountains, descend into the Tularosa Valley, where a short detour will take you to the gleaming gypsum dunes of White Sands National Monument. Heading north and passing the ridge containing thousands of petroglyphs near Three Rivers, you end your tour in Carrizozo.

Many small farming and ranching communities doze in relative obscurity between the interstate and the Rio Grande River, where the soil is rich, and water for irrigation is plentiful. San Acacia is one such community. Named for a Roman soldier martyred for his Christian faith, the community once boasted a fine church and a school. The original mission was built in the 1800s. A proud structure of adobe three times the size of the present building, it contained massive *vigas*, wooden pews, and hand-carved *santos*. The land on which it stood was donated by a rancher, and the village provided the construction labor. Before the era of dams, dikes, and levees, the region was susceptible to occasional rampages of the Rio Grande, and in 1929, a flood claimed the church. Some material was saved, and the parishioners rebuilt the current sanctuary on a smaller scale. Through the years the building has fallen into disrepair, and only a shell remains.

The other prominent town structure, the old schoolhouse, has had a resurrection as Gay Dwyre's San Acacia Gallery. Gay's family goes back many generations in San Acacia. She had been living in Santa Fe with regular homecomings to the family ranch, and the abandoned schoolhouse tugged at her heart. Wanting to do something to give the village back its pride, she hit upon the idea of a country gallery.

The old adobe has adapted well to its new use. Featuring regional artists with exhibits changing on a monthly basis, it showcases work ranging from traditional *santos* to pottery and painting. Fernando Mercado is the resident artist, and twice yearly, at the gallery's birthday Easter weekend and during Socorro's Festival of the Cranes, Gay plans special events featuring artists and their works, music, and a bountiful buffet.

Leaving San Acacia, you pass through the small villages of Chamizal and Polvadera, arriving in Lemitar, where Quebradas Scenic Byway originates. Las Quebradas means "the breaks" in Spanish, and the drama of the land's desolation, broken here and there with the green punctuation of juniper, creates a haunting beauty. The journey is one that internationally known Taos artist Doug West has portrayed many times in his exquisite serigraphs.

Head back west on the highway to San Antonio, now just a crossroads but once a bustling town and popular stop on the Atchison, Topeka & Santa Fe Railroad. Conrad Hilton, famed hotelier, was born here in 1887 and got his start in the family business hustling bags and directing travelers from the train station to his father's store and hotel.

Currently, you'll find a store, gas station, and the venerable Owl Bar and Cafe, where Adolfo and Rowena Baca are celebrated for serving scrumptious green-chile cheeseburgers. Although the cheeseburgers are best known (the Owl serves between 400 and 500 a day on busy weekends), the restaurant also features steak dinners. Decor is minimal, with the walls of the dimly lit interior plastered with dollar bills and business cards. There's a rumor that the expansive front bar originally came from the Hilton's store.

After a good solid burger chased down with chili cheese fries, take the south road to Bosque del Apache National Wildlife Refuge. The "Woods of the Apache" is managed and maintained by the U.S. Fish and Wildlife Service and is one of the nation's most successful wildlife refuges. Stretching nine miles along the Rio Grande, the 57,191-acre tract was purchased by the government beginning in 1936, with the refuge formally established in 1939. Even with years of heavy grazing, it still supported a rich wildlife population. This changed in 1941, when a river flood destroyed the cottonwood savannah and buried the marshlands under more than 30 feet of silt.

The following years were ones of rebuilding. Dikes were constructed and water diverted to develop forests and marshes. Today there are 325 species of birds: 15,000 sandhill cranes, 40,000 snow geese, 400 Canada geese, and 60,000 ducks make the refuge their fall and winter home, flying in from nesting grounds a thousand miles away. Mornings and evenings are the most spectacular, when the immense population takes to the sky creating a whirling, wheeling, honking snowstorm of birds sometimes stretching a mile in length.

During the third week of November, the refuge, U.S. Fish and Wildlife Service, the city of Socorro, and the Socorro County Chamber of Commerce sponsor the immensely popular Festival of the Cranes. Visitors may choose from seminars, workshops, and tours to birding sites, including sites not generally open to the public. In addition, there are other featured events, such as an arts and crafts show, concerts, and special exhibits. Events fill up fast, so if you're planning to visit at this time, try to preregister by October 31. You can buy tickets at the Socorro Chamber of Commerce office through mid-November or at the refuge front desk on a first-come, first-served basis after November 15.

If you're not anticipating an in-depth experience such as a seminar or tour, you can visit the refuge anytime. The refuge is at its prime in the winter, with thousands of snow geese, waterfowl, eagles, sandhill cranes, and a small contingent of whooping cranes. During spring and fall, you can see migrant warblers, flycatchers, and shorebirds. The summer months are prime for nesting songbirds, waders, shorebirds, and ducks. Year-round residents include mule deer, coyote, porcupine, muskrat, Canada goose, coot, pheasant, turkey, quail, and roadrunner.

Your first stop should be the visitors center, where you can pick up a brochure with a map of the hiking trails and a self-guided, 15-mile auto tour. There are displays, videos, a bookstore, and current information on sightings. A limited number of binoculars are available for rent, in case you've forgotten to bring them. Picnic tables wait under shade trees for visitors savvy enough to have packed their lunch—a good move especially on busy fall and winter weekends, when local restaurants are busy. Don't forget a water bottle, and bring insect repellent if you come during the warm months. Remember, these wetlands are marshes, and that means mosquitos!

Leaving the refuge, retrace your steps to San Antonio and head east through the Jornada del Muerto (Journey of the Dead Man). This expanse of sun and sand was named not for its inhospitable nature, but for Bernardo Gruber, who escaped from the local arm of the Inquisition and attempted to cross the desert. His desiccated corpse was discovered at a place called El Alemán (the German).

A short distance into the region you pass Range Road 7, which is the northern entrance to the Trinity Site and is open to the public only the first Saturdays of April and October. If you've timed your visit to coincide with these dates, you can visit the site of the first atomic test operation, known as Project Trinity. Here on Monday, July 16, 1945, U.S. scientists successfully detonated the device that would power the bombs dropped on Hiroshima on August 6 and Nagasaki on August 9.

Today the site bears little evidence of that massive explosion, which shattered windows 120 miles away. You enter the restricted area from the north by way of the Stallion Gate or from the south on a tour departing from the Otero County Fair Grounds in Alamogordo. The surrounding landscape is otherworldly, with the Oscura–San Andres Mountains to the east, and to the south a series of hills rising like the backbone of some prehistoric beast. Checking through security, you join a line of cars directed to a parking site, where a festive atmosphere prevails, with food vendors selling "Atomic Burgers" and souvenir stands purveying T-shirts, books, and knickknacks.

You must walk a quarter-mile to Ground Zero, where a large fenced enclosure contains a monument, historical photos fastened to the wire barrier, a shelter protecting a portion of the original crater, a replica of the "Fatman" bomb casing, and a sample of the footing from the test tower.

If you wish to visit the McDonald Ranch, where the plutonium core of the bomb was assembled, you must return to the parking lot and use army tour buses provided. The ranch house was built in 1913 by Franz Schmidt, a German immigrant, and an addition was constructed on the north side in the 1930s by the McDonald family. Abandoned in 1942, when the

Alamogordo Bombing and Gunnery Range took over the land to use in training World War II bombing crews, the house stood empty until the Manhattan Project support personnel arrived in early 1945. The U.S. Army, working with the National Park Service, restored the building in 1984, and the exterior appears as it did in 1945. The interior is empty except for the World War II–era photos that line the walls.

Leaving the Missile Range, Route 380 crosses the foothills of the Oscura Mountains and climbs the edge of Chupadera Mesa. On the outskirts of Carrizozo, you encounter the massive lava flow that dominates the views of the Tularosa Valley. Originating from a small extinct volcano to the north named Little Black Peak, this flow covers more than 125 square miles. Amazing as it seems, plants and animal life make the region home. Mule deer, a small band of Barbary sheep, coyotes, kit foxes, bobcats, and ringtail cats prowl its expanse. Pockets of soil harbor the white waxy spire of yucca flowers and the scarlet bloom of hedgehog cactuses.

The portion of the lava flow that frames the highway and borders the town is a national recreational area named Valley of Fires. The U.S. Bureau of Land Management maintains campground sites, a pavilion, a three-quarter-mile nature trail, and a visitor information station. If you decide to explore the trail, wear sturdy shoes, carry water, and try to hike in early morning or late afternoon to beat the heat.

Carrizozo is just four miles to the southeast. Named for the abundance of reeds (*carrizos*) growing at springs north of town, Carrizozo grew to a city of respectable size when the El Paso and Northeastern Railroad built a roundhouse and repair yards there, bypassing the mining town of White Oaks. With the decline of railroading, the need for maintenance yards diminished, and Carrizozo's economy suffered.

As the seat of Lincoln County, the town is still a regional hub, with a few stores, county offices, and a library. The Outpost restaurant is a good example of an old Western saloon, with its expansive bar, mounted animal heads, jukebox, pool table, and small dance floor. The menu is predictable, running heavily to staples such as burgers and chicken-fried steak.

If you have an interest in old ghost towns, take a detour north to White Oaks, where three prospectors discovered gold in 1879. By 1884 White Oaks had 1,000 residents, but the mines played out and most of the population departed. A few buildings from the 1890s remain standing, and the town is still home to a handful of residents and artists.

West of Carrizozo, you enter the Sacramento Mountains, the road running between Nogal Peak to the south and Vera Cruz Mountain to the north. As you ascend into Lincoln National Forest, you pass through different climatic zones: the Lower Sonoran at 3,000 to 5,000 feet, with its grama grass, mesquite, creosote bush, opuntia, and yucca; the Upper Sonoran at 5,000 to 7,000, feet with its piñón pine and buffalo grass; the transition zone, with forests of ponderosa pine and hardwoods; and finally, in the upper elevations of 8,000 to 10,000 feet, the Canadian zone, with Douglas fir and quaking aspen.

Arriving in Capitan, you can't miss the town's best-known attraction, Smokey Bear Historical Park. It was in the nearby mountains on May 9, 1950, that a crew fighting the Los Tablos forest fire found a badly singed black bear cub clinging tenaciously to the side of a burnt pine tree.

While most people believe this was the start of the Smokey Bear Fire Prevention Program, the truth is that in 1944 artist Albert Staehle produced a bear wearing Levis and a ranger hat for an original poster. The bear was called "Smokey" after New York City fire chief Joe Martin. The little cub became the embodiment of the artist's concept.

As the real Smokey grew, he was moved to quarters at the National Zoo in Washington, D.C. Upon his death, his body was returned to his birthplace and buried in Capitan, where a whole complex is devoted to his memory. You can visit his grave in a pretty garden at the park, or you can spend time at the visitors center, where there are exhibits about forest fires, a history of the fire prevention campaign, and a theater. Next to the park, a small log cabin was built by volunteers with local funds and is operated as a museum and gift shop.

Capitan's second big attraction is what many have called the finest restaurant in New Mexico. The Hotel Chango Restaurant and Art Gallery is the brainchild of Jerrold Donti Flores, a native New Mexican. Jerrold, whose family has been in the restaurant business for three generations, was born at Fort Stanton and reared in San Francisco. An artist, bon vivant, and creative genius, his touch is evident in the innovative menu and in the warm, eclectic decor.

Never predictable, always original, the menu is a collaboration between Jerrold and chef Robert Pascuzzi, who trained in major hotels in southwest Florida. Robert classifies their cuisine as "New American—fusing many nations' disciplines with a decidedly Chango twist."

The menu for a summer evening might begin with an appetizer of bruschetta, toasts salved with fresh tomato relish constructed with fresh basil, balsamic vinegar, and piñón nuts. Follow this with a chilled soup of diced cantaloupe, honeydew, and watermelon, accented with minced mint and chilled, fresh juices. The third course could be their signature dish "Waves," Chinese pastry layered with herbed chicken and seasoned with black sesame, herb, and garlic paste; Thai chiles fused with walnut oil, cilantro, and mango puree; and extracts of beet, cilantro, mango, and Washington apple. Add to this a dessert selection that would make the angels sing, and you have an incomparable dining experience.

Many travelers have been known to plan their trips around the Chango's hours, which are Tuesday through Sunday evenings. Needless to say, reservations are requested.

After a meal of such proportions, you won't want to venture far, and the Casa de Patrón in Lincoln is a short 12 miles down the pike. Although Jerry and Cleis Jordan's warm hospitality is not the only reason to visit Lincoln, it is a sure incentive. These two former Texans have adopted the old adobe home of former politico and territorial merchant Juan Patrón and converted it into a snug harbor where good food, good music, and fine art are all part of the ambiance. The gourmet breakfasts are legend, and both public and guest rooms in the main house, the Trail House, and the Casita Cottage are engagingly decorated in a Southwest territorial motif. There's homemade soap in the baths and a saucer of homemade candy on the night tables. The collection of old washboards is somewhat of a trademark, with antiquing guests frequently adding to the assortment.

Lincoln evenings are quiet, and to entertain guests, Cleis can orchestrate a sing-along or a themed salon evening of music, food, and conversation. She has a master's degree in organ performance, an accomplishment that is verified when she takes time from her busy schedule to play the handmade tracker pipe organ in the dining room or the grand piano in the parlor. Of course, everyone who comes to Lincoln wants to know about the town's connection with the famous outlaw, Billy the Kid. Yes, Billy did spend a night or two at Juan Patrón's home while awaiting trial.

When William Bonney first came to the little town in the Rio Bonito valley, Lincoln was in the midst of a clash between two factions trying to wrest political and economic control of the region. Englishman John Tunstall and his partners, Alexander McSween and cattle baron John Chisum, took on the established powers, led by James Dolan and L. G. Murphy. The 1878 murder of Tunstall was the fuse that ignited the hostilities and led to the creation of "the Regulators," a vigilante group vowed to avenge the murder. The climactic gun battle between the two sides lasted five days, but hostilities continued for nearly a year.

One of the Regulators was teenage ranch hand William Bonney, also known as "Kid" Antrim and later as Billy the Kid. Billy eventually was captured near Fort Sumner by Sheriff Pat Garrett, but not before he shot his way out of the Lincoln jail, where he was to hang for the murder of Sheriff William Brady. During his escape, he killed Deputy Robert Ollinger; a marker outside the courthouse designates where Ollinger fell.

Lincoln's place in history does not depend on its association with Bonney. Other players as famous were part of its legacy: New Mexico governor Lew Wallace (author of *Ben Hur*), Black Jack Pershing and the Buffalo Soldiers, Indian scout Kit Carson, Pat Garrett, and Apache Chief Victorio.

Today the properties on both sides of the road look much as they did at the turn of the century. When you tour the courthouse, you will still see the bullet hole from the Kid's escape. The building has been restored and is now operated by New Mexico State Monuments, which also owns other historic buildings in Lincoln such as the Tunstall Store, the José Montaño Store, the Convento, and the San Juan Church.

The Hubbard Foundation administers the Dr. Woods House and Annex, two houses, and a store, in addition to the Anderson-Freeman Museum, where you can watch a video capturing Lincoln's tumultuous past or examine exhibits highlighting the various forces influencing its history. Across the courtyard from the museum, a well-stocked store carries gifts, souvenirs, and a large selection of regional narratives.

Guests at Casa de Patrón often find their way to Tinnie's Silver Dollar Saloon and Restaurant for dinner. Tinnie is just a couple of miles beyond the intersection of U.S. 380 and U.S. 70 and well worth the trip. The building is an old mercantile and post office, built in the 1870s. Purchased by Robert

Anderson of Roswell in 1959, it was renovated and its landmark tower and pavilion added. Photographs from Tinnie's past as well as 13 paintings from artist Peter Hurd grace the walls. The elegant decor is a legacy of San Patricio artist John Meigs, who scoured the countryside for the ornate doors, stained-glass windows, furniture, and artwork. The old store houses the banquet room, and the former stables are now a gift shop. Currently owned by Salem Sager, the Silver Dollar is not all surface glitter. The menu, which runs to steak, seafood, and pasta, is well balanced, and the food preparation pleasing.

From the Rio Bonito (Beautiful River) valley, you head southeast into the Hondo valley. The Hondo is one of New Mexico's most beautiful, with its river, fruit orchards, and small farms. It is no small wonder that through the years famous people have settled there—Helen Hayes, author Paul Horgan, and the Hurd-Wyeth family.

The village of San Patricio is the locus of present-day artistic activity. In its confines are Fort Meigs, John Meigs's home, and the Hurd La Rinconada Gallery, which exhibits major pieces by Peter Hurd and Henriette Wyeth Hurd, as well as work from other notable family members Michael Hurd, Jamie Wyeth, Carol Hurd Rogers, and Peter de la Fuente.

La Rinconada is located on Sentinel Ranch property, the New Mexico home of Peter Hurd and his wife, Henriette, daughter of famous illustrator N. C. Wyeth. The gallery is a work of art unto itself. Designed by Michael, its steeply pitched copper roof, dormers, and tiered brick terrace complement the pastoral surroundings.

For those wanting more than a brief visit, the Hurd Ranch Guest Homes on the property provide an in-depth San Patricio experience. The gallery guest wing has a large bedroom, kitchen, bath, and living area opening onto the terrace. Orchard House and Apple House are cozy renovated old adobes, and La Helenita, named for Helen Hayes, who was often a guest, is the jewel in the crown. The elegant two-bedroom, two-bath, fully equipped casita has three fireplaces and a Jacuzzi, and it is decorated and furnished with antiques.

With the Rio Ruidoso to your left, you travel southeast toward Ruidoso Downs, home of Ruidoso Downs Race Track, the Billy the Kid Casino, and the Hubbard Museum of the American West. If you like to watch the ponies run, the Downs schedules Thoroughbred and quarter horse races from Memorial Day to Labor Day weekend.

Whether you're a track fan or not, be sure to stop at the museum, where you'll find not only exhibits on horse lore but a special collection of art, sculpture, and historical pieces. The core of the collection came as a legacy from Anne C. Stradling, who started her accumulation of horse-related artifacts at age six when she hung a bit and worn-out stirrup on the wall in the family's New Jersey barn. Her encyclopedic accumulation grew to more than 10,000 horse-related items: carriages, wagons, saddles, bits, and bridles. Fine art, furniture, and silver came from her family estate, and a distinguished group of Indian artifacts is the result of her Arizona days. The museum complements the permanent assembly with changing exhibits.

An imposing sculpture fronts the museum. Ruidoso's well-known master of bronze, Dave McGary, created *Free Spirits at Noisy Water*, a grouping of eight larger-than-life-size horses depicting the seven classic breeds. The scope of the project is monumental—three stories tall at its highest point and stretching nearly the length of a football field. A Thoroughbred leads the procession, followed by the quarter horse, the Appaloosa, the Paint mare and her foal, the Arabian, the Morgan, and the Standardbred.

Ruidoso evenings are enhanced by a visit to the $20 million-dollar Spencer Theater for the Performing Arts. A short distance northeast of town near the Sierra Blanca Regional Airport, the center was designed by Albuquerque architect Antoine Predock, and its modern lines make a striking presence on the mesa. A gift to the region by Alto resident Jackie Spencer and her husband A. N., the cultural center books musicals, drama, concerts, dance, and children's programs.

When you venture into the village of Ruidoso, you'll find a variety of restaurants and shops along Sudderth Drive. Marilyn Patterson's Galleria West has Native American jewelry in gold and silver, artifacts, and occasionally old estate jewelry. Her helpful sales people are a bonus.

Shirley Kostka's White Dove carries downtown's best assortment of Indian crafts, and White Mountain Pottery stocks a large selection of work by regional clay artists. The Kenyon Thomas Gallery at the corner of Paradise Canyon and Sudderth inventories Kenyon's award-winning pottery and wife Marcia's handsome weaving.

If you enjoyed Dave McGary's *Free Spirits at Noisy Water*, you'll be dazzled by his McGary Studios: Expressions in Bronze on Sudderth Street. Considered a master of realism depicting Native American Indians of the past, McGary showcases two decades of his sculpture in his gallery.

Cafe Rio could be the best restaurant in Ruidoso, although you'd never guess it from the pizza parlor exterior. Neil and Mary Jo Germain serve up all the traditional Italian favorites, pizza and calzones, but good as these are, it's the Portuguese/Mediterranean café menu that shines. A head of garlic slow-roasted in olive oil or Portuguese kale soup are robust starters. Entrées include delectables such as Cajun jambalaya; herbed polenta with Portuguese *molho* sauce; and finally Greek *spanakopita*, a spinach and feta cheese pie baked in flaky phyllo dough. If you've room for dessert, their double layer chocolate cake with chocolate espresso frosting is superb. Two other places worth mentioning are Michelena's Italian Restaurant and La Lorraine, classic French cuisine in an elegant setting.

Heading south from Ruidoso, you pass through the Mescalero Apache Indian Reservation en route to Cloudcroft. The reservation, established in 1872, consists of 460,177 acres between the Sacramento and White Mountains. The tribe manages hunting and fishing preserves; the Inn of the Mountain Gods, a luxury resort and casino; and Ski Apache, a downhill ski area on the slopes of Sierra Blanca.

Cloudcroft can leave you breathless, literally. At 8,640 feet, the little town often tops the cumulus. Founded in 1898, when a group of surveyors for the railroad reached the summit of the Sacramento Mountains and established a camp for logging operations, Cloudcroft's cool summer weather made it a popular retreat for Alamogordo and El Paso residents. The main street, Burro Avenue, is filled with the usual tourist lures— knickknack shops, restaurants, and a small archive, the Sacramento Mountains Historical Museum, which is loaded with photographs and artifacts of early days.

Cloudcroft's most distinguished destination is The Lodge. Constructed of logs in 1899, the original structure burned in 1909, but by 1911 the new building had been completed on its current, more scenic site. The Lodge is a complete four-season resort. Warm season guests enjoy a nine-hole Scottish links golf course, an outdoor pool, hot tub, and sauna. Winter visitors downhill ski at nearby Ski Cloudcroft, or cross-country ski, inner tube, or snowmobile at The Lodge.

The Lodge public rooms are adorned in rich wood moldings, turn-of-the-century furniture, antique fixtures, mounted game, and paddle fans. Breakfast, lunch, and dinner are served in the Fireside Room Terrace and the Conservatory of Rebecca's Restaurant, named for the resident ghost, a red-headed chambermaid who met her end at the hand of a jealous lover. The 61 rooms have been completely renovated and each is individually decorated.

As you leave Cloudcroft and descend from its lofty summit, watch for the old railroad trestle on your left. The road twists and turns as it plunges down through the peach, pear, cherry, and apple orchards of High Rolls and Mountain Park. By the time you reach the Tularosa Basin and U.S. 54, you will have gone from fir and aspen of the high mountains to the mesquite and creosote of the Chihuahuan desert.

No journey to this area is complete without a visit to Alamogordo and White Sands National Monument, 15 miles southwest of the city. This quirk of nature is not comprised of sand particles as we commonly recognize them, but of fine particles of gypsum, a hydrous form of calcium sulfate.

It is not too far beyond human ken to imagine the shallow sea that covered this area 250 million years ago. The gypsum-bearing marine deposits that form the sands were deposited at the bottom of this body of water, and the whole area was uplifted into a giant dome 70 million years ago. The dome collapsed approximately 10 million years ago, and the Tularosa Basin was created. The sides of the original dome now comprise the San Andres and Sacramento Mountain ranges.

The dunes developed—and continue to form—when mountain rains dissolve gypsum from the rocks and carry it into the basin. Since the area has no outlet for drainage, water and its sediments are trapped. As the fluids evaporate, the crystalline gypsum is deposited on the surface. Winds blowing across the low-lying depressions carry gypsum particles downwind. These accumulate, creating dunes.

If you plan to visit, be prepared for road delays en route. White Sands National Monument's 275 square miles are completely surrounded by White Sands Missile Range. When tests are conducted on the range, U.S. 70 between the park and Las Cruces may be closed. These closures occur about twice a week and last from one to two hours.

Upon arrival, your first stop at the monument should be the visitors center, a historic adobe building with geology exhibits and a diorama explaining the formation of the dunes. Rangers can help you plan the best use of your time, whether you expect to hike the one-mile, self-guided Big Dune nature trail or drive the eight-mile scenic road into the heart of the dunes. At the center, you can also browse their book selections or check out the adjoining gift shop.

There is an art to experiencing this land so inhospitable to all but a few plants and animals. The glistening, highly reflective sands become downright uncomfortable during the heat of the day, so plan your explorations for early morning or evening. If you're hiking, carry water, wear a hat, and use a sunscreen.

After the majesty of those eye-dazzling dunes, almost anything else is an anticlimax. However, if you have space fans in your entourage (perhaps if you're old enough to remember Sputnik), you'll enjoy stopping at the Space Center's International Space Hall of Fame, the IMAX theater and planetarium, the Stapp Air & Space Park, and the Astronaut Memorial Garden.

The Hall of Fame displays space-related artifacts, models, and memorabilia. There are pictures and biographical sketches of such space pioneers as Neil Armstrong, the first man to walk on the moon, and Alexei Leonov, of the former USSR, the first man to walk in space.

Exhibits include the always popular moon rock; the primate capsule and space suit for Ham, first chimpanzee in space; a Mercury capsule model; a Gemini spacecraft model; a Lunar Module model; and many others. The memorial garden commemorates the seven American astronauts who died in the January 28, 1986, explosion of the *Challenger* space shuttle.

The Air and Space Park displays articles too massive for an indoor exhibit, such as a Nike Ajax missile and the Lance surface-to-surface combat missile. The planetarium and theater feature IMAX films, star shows, special multimedia presentations, and laser light concerts.

As you head north leaving Alamogordo, you pass the outskirts of Tularosa, named for the red reeds that grew along the banks of Tularosa Creek when settlers first arrived in the area. The town was established in 1863 with the mapping of the 49 original blocks and the recording of water rights. Those 49 blocks are now on the National Register of Historic Places, and the original ditch irrigation continues to water the town's lush gardens, yards, and tree-lined streets. The valley surrounding the city is a major growing area for pecans, pistachios, and alfalfa.

Tularosa celebrates two major yearly festivals: the Rose Festival the first weekend in May, with an old-timer picnic, carnival, arts and crafts festival, and crowning of the Rose Queen, and on the following weekend, the St. Francis de Paula Fiesta, featuring Spanish dancers, a carnival, and regional foods.

The scenery along the route to Three Rivers and Carrizozo is typical of the Chihuahuan desert, with its expanses of creosote bushes, cholla and prickly pear cactus, yucca, and sotol. Before heading out to the interstate, take a detour on County Road B30 to Three Rivers Petroglyph National Recreation Site. A rocky ridge of basalt is the stage for the parade of more than 20,000 human figures, animals, and esoteric symbols scratched in the rock by generations of prehistoric Jornada Mogollon Indians. Positioned on an open plain with the San Andres Mountains on the eastern horizon, it is a lonely place, with the wind whipping through the scrub and howling over the boulders. In such a great enormity, man needed the reassurance of his gods and totems to keep the wild spirits at bay. At the same place today, the weight of the wilderness is intense, the road and car a modern assurance.

For More Information

San Acacia Gallery, Box 1-A, San Acacia, NM 87831. Call 505-835-1007. Open Wednesday through Sunday from 10:00 A.M. to 5:00 P.M.

Owl Bar and Cafe, P.O. Box 215, San Antonio, NM 87832. Call 505-835-9946. Open Monday through Saturday from 8:00 A.M. to 9:30 P.M.

Bosque del Apache National Wildlife Refuge, P.O. Box 1246, Socorro, NM 87801. Call 505-835-1828. Visitors center open Monday through Friday from 7:30 A.M. to 4:00 P.M., Saturday and Sunday from 8:00 A.M. to 4:30 P.M. Tour route one hour before sunrise to one hour after sunset. Seasonal tour road, April–September. Websites: hanksville.phast.umass.edu/misc/bosque.html or www.pbs.org/audubon/wildwings/bosque.html.

Festival of the Cranes, P.O. Box 743, Socorro, NM 87801. Website: www.nmt.edu/mainpage/festival/homepage.html.

Socorro County Chamber of Commerce, 103 Francisco de Avondo, Socorro, NM 87801. Call 505-835-0424. Open Monday through Friday from 9:00 A.M. to 5:00 P.M., Saturday from 9:00 A.M. to noon. Website: www.socorro.com or www.nmt.edu/socorro/homepage.html.

Trinity Site (see Alamogordo Chamber of Commerce for tour information), Public Affairs Office, Building 122, White Sands Missile Range, NM 88002. Call 505-678-1134. Site open first Saturday of April and October; Stallion gate, from 8:00 A.M. to 2:00 P.M.; caravan from Alamogordo departs at 8:00 A.M. Website: www.wsmr.army.mil.paopage/Pages/Trinst.htm.

Carrizozo Chamber of Commerce (in the train caboose at the corner of Routes 54 and 380), P.O. Box 567, Carrizozo, NM, 88301. Call 505-648-2732.

Valley of Fires (four miles northwest of Carrizozo on U.S. 380), Bureau of Land Management, Roswell Resource Area, Fifth and Richardson, P.O. Drawer 1857, Roswell, NM 88292. Call 505-627-0272.

The Outpost, 415 Central Avenue, P.O. Box 811, Carrizozo, NM 88301. Call 505-648-9994. Open Monday through Thursday from 11:00 A.M. to 10:00 P.M., Friday and Saturday from 11:00 A.M. to 11:00 P.M., Sunday from noon to 10:00 P.M.

White Oaks: see Carrizozo Chamber of Commerce, above.

Smokey Bear Historical Park, 118 Smokey Bear Boulevard, Capitan, NM 88316. Call 505-354-2748. Open daily from 9:00 A.M. to 5:00 P.M. Fee. Website: www.emnrd.state.nm.us/forestry.

Smokey Bear Museum, 102 Smokey Bear Boulevard, Box 729, Capitan, NM 88316. Open Memorial Day–Labor Day, daily from 8:00 A.M. to 5:00 P.M.; in winter, daily from 9:00 A.M. to 4:00 P.M.

Hotel Chango Restaurant and Art Gallery, 103 South Lincoln Avenue, Capitan, NM 88316. Call 505-354-4213. Open Wednesday through Saturday from 5:00 P.M. to closing. Reservations suggested.

Capitan Chamber of Commerce, 102 West
Second Street, P.O. Box 441, Capitan, NM
88316. Call 505-354-2273. Open daily from
8:00 A.M. to 5:00 P.M.

Casa de Patrón, P.O. Box 27, Lincoln, NM
88338. Call 505-653-4676 or 800-524-5202. Website:
www.casapatron.com.

Lincoln Historic District (one ticket for all properties), fee:
Historic Lincoln, a subsidiary of the Hubbard Museum of the
American West, P.O. Box 98, Lincoln, NM 88338. Call 505-
653-4025. Open daily from 8:30 A.M. to 5:00 P.M.

Lincoln State Monument (Old Lincoln County Courthouse
Museum, Tunstall Store, Torreon, San Juan Church, Montaño
Store), Route 380, P.O. Box 36, Lincoln, NM 88338. Call 555-
653-4372. Open daily from 8:30 A.M. to 5:00 P.M.

Silver Dollar Saloon and Restaurant, P.O. Box 299, Tinnie, NM
88351. Call 505-653-4425. Open daily from 11:00 A.M. to
11:00 P.M.

Fort Meigs, P.O. Box 107, San Patricio, NM 88348. Call 505-653-
4320. Says John Meigs, "For your survival, let us know of your
arrival."

Hurd-Wyeth La Rinconada Gallery and Hurd Ranch Guest Homes,
P.O. Box 100, San Patricio, NM 88348. Call 800-658-6912.
Gallery open Monday through Saturday from 9:00 A.M. to
5:00 P.M., Sunday June 1–Labor Day only, from 11:00 A.M. to
4:00 P.M.

Ruidoso Valley Chamber of Commerce, 720 Sudderth Drive,
P.O. Box 698, Ruidoso, NM 88355. Call 505-257-7395. Open
Monday through Friday from 8:30 A.M. to 5:00 P.M., Saturday
from 9:00 A.M. to 3:00 P.M., Sunday from 9:00 A.M. to 1:00 P.M.

Ruidoso Downs and Billy the Kid Casino, 1461 Highway 70W, P.O. Box 449, Ruidoso Downs, NM 88346. Call 505-378-4431. Downs open daily Memorial Day–Labor Day; casino open Sunday through Thursday from 11:00 A.M. to 11:00 P.M.; Friday and Saturday from noon to midnight.

Hubbard Museum of the American West, 841 U.S. 70W, Ruidoso Downs, NM 88346. Call 505-378-4142. Open May–Labor Day, daily from 9:00 A.M. to 5:30 P.M.; Labor Day–April, daily from 10:00 A.M. to 5:00 P.M. Fee. Website: www.zianet.com/museum.

Spencer Theater for the Performing Arts, Route 220, Box 140, Alto, NM 88312. Information, call 888-818-7872; tickets, 800-905-3315. Website: www.spencertheater.com.

Galleria West, 2538 Sudderth, Ruidoso, NM 88345. Call 505-257-4560. Open daily from 10:00 A.M. to 6:00 P.M.

White Dove, 2318 Sudderth, Ruidoso, NM 88345. Call 505-257-6609 or 505-258-5859. Open daily from 10:00 A.M. to 6:00 P.M.

White Mountain Pottery, 2328 Sudderth, Ruidoso, NM 88345. Call 505-257-3644. Open Monday through Saturday from 10:00 A.M. to 5:00 P.M.

Kenyon Thomas Gallery, 546 Sudderth Drive, Ruidoso, NM 88345. Call 505-257-1056. Open Monday through Saturday from 10:00 A.M. to 5:00 P.M.

McGary Studios: Expressions in Bronze, 2002 Sudderth, Ruidoso, NM 88345. Call 505-257-1000 or 800-687-3424. Open Monday through Saturday from 10:00 A.M. to 5:00 P.M.

Cafe Rio, 2547 Sudderth, P.O. Box 1004, Ruidoso, NM 88345. Call 505-257-7746. Open daily from 11:30 A.M. to 8:00 P.M.

Michelenas Italian Restaurant, 2703 Sudderth, Ruidoso, NM 88345. Call 505-257-5753. Open Tuesday through Sunday from 11:00 A.M. to 9:30 P.M. Closed Monday.

La Lorraine, 2523 Sudderth, Ruidoso, NM 88345. Call 505-257-2954. Open Monday from 5:30 to 9:00 P.M., Tuesday through Thursday from 11:30 A.M. to 2:00 P.M. and 5:30 to 9:00 P.M., Friday and Saturday from 11:30 A.M. to 2:00 P.M. and 5:30 to 9:30 P.M.

Inn of the Mountain Gods, Route 4, Carrizo Canyon Road, P.O. Box 269, Mescalero, NM 88340. Call 505-257-5141 or 800-545-9011.

Sacramento Mountains Historical Museum, P.O. Box 125, Cloudcroft, NM 88317. Call 505-682-2932. Open Monday, Tuesday, Friday, and Saturday from 10:00 A.M. to 4:00 P.M., Sunday from 1:00 to 4:00 P.M. Closed Wednesday and Thursday. Website same as Cloudcroft Chamber of Commerce, below.

The Lodge, One Corona Place, P.O. Box 497, Cloudcroft, NM 88317. Call 505-682-2566 or 800-395-6343. Website: www.thelodge.com.

Cloudcroft Chamber of Commerce, 1 Zenith Park, P.O. Box 1290, Cloudcroft, NM 88317. Call 505-682-2733. Open daily from 10:00 A.M. to 5:00 P.M. Website: www.cloudcroft.net.

Alamogordo Chamber of Commerce, 1301 White Sands Boulevard, P.O. Box 2828, Alamogordo, NM 88311. Call 505-437-6120 or 800-826-0294. Website: www.alamagordo.com.

White Sands National Monument (off U.S. 70), P.O. Box 1086, Holloman AFB, NM 88330-6124. Call 505-479-6124. Open in summer, daily from 7:00 A.M. to 9:00 P.M.; in winter, daily from 7:00 A.M. to 6:00 P.M. Fee. Website: www.nps.gov/whsa.

The Space Center, P.O. Box 533, Alamogordo, NM 88311. Call 505-437-2840 or 800-545-4021. Fee. International Space Hall of Fame, open daily from 9:00 A.M. to 5:00 P.M. Tombaugh IMAX Dome Theater, open in winter, Monday through Friday at 10:00 A.M., noon, 2:00, and 4:00 P.M.; Saturday and Sunday at 10:00 A.M., 11:00 A.M., noon, 2:00, 3:00, and 4:00 P.M.; in summer, hourly between 10:00 A.M. and 4:00 P.M. Evening IMAX feature, daily at 7:00 P.M. Website: www.zianet.com/space.

Tularosa Chamber of Commerce, 301 Central, Tularosa, NM 88352. Call 505-585-9858. Hours vary.

Three Rivers Petroglyph National Recreation Site, County Road B30, five miles off NM 54, 17 miles north of Tularosa. Bureau of Land Management, Caballo Resource Area, 1800 Marquess Street, Las Cruces, NM 88005. Call 505-525-4300. Campsites, picnic shelters, interpretive trail.

8

Mining Towns and Mountains

Getting there: From Albuquerque, take I-25 south 77 miles to Socorro, exit 150. From Socorro, follow U.S. 60 west 27 miles to Magdalena, where you take a marked road south three miles to the ghost town of Kelly. Retrace your steps to Magdalena, and continue west on U.S. 60, 23 miles to NM 166, the turnoff for the VLA visitors center. Leaving the center, return to U.S. 60 and drive 11 miles to Datil, where you turn south on NM 12. Staying on NM 12 through Old and New Horse Springs, Aragon, Apache Creek, and Reserve, go south on U.S. 180 29 miles to Glenwood.

If the weather has been dry, you're feeling adventurous, and you've secured an excellent map showing Forest Service roads, you can leave civilization in Reserve and head south on NM 435, which joins Forest Service Road 141 before turning to gravel at Negrito Fire Base. From here, you follow dirt and gravel roads—Forest Service Roads 28 and 159 to the mining ghost town of Mogollon. This is definitely the long way around and should not be attempted in the rain or late in the day.

From Glenwood, retrace your steps 29 miles on U.S. 180 to its junction with NM 12 north, which passes Reserve and joins NM 32 at Apache Creek. Stay on NM 32 north 41 miles to Quemado, where you take NM 36, 74 miles to NM 53. Zuni Pueblo is 10 miles west on NM 53. East of the junction of NM 36 and 53, El Morro National Monument is 25 miles, Bandera Volcano and Ice Caves 41 miles, and Grants a total of 75 miles.

Highlights: After exploring old Socorro, with its mission church and leafy plaza, you head into the neighboring peaks, where you investigate the dusty little town of Magdalena and explore the nearby ghost town of Kelly, once center for silver and zinc mining. The vast open Plains of San Agustin beckon, and coasting along through this vast sea of grass, you spy the multiple antennae of the Very Large Array (VLA) Radio Telescope marching in formation to the horizon.

Taking a southerly turn through Apache Creek, you wend your way to Glenwood. After a foray into Whitewater Canyon, with its famous Catwalk National Recreational Trail, retrace your steps north through Reserve and Quemado, finally arriving at Zuni Pueblo for a visit to the old mission church, with its murals depicting the pueblo kachinas and the cycle of the seasons. Browse the shops for inlay jewelry in turquoise, jet, and shell, or check out the fetish carvings.

Leaving Zuni, you range east through the Zuni Mountains, pausing at the Ramah Navajo Indian Reservation to observe the native weavers. Farther on you scale the heights of El Morro National Monument and stop at Bandera Volcano and Ice Caves. Journey's end is Grants, crowned by Mount Taylor.

Long before the Europeans came to New Mexico, the Piro, early ancestors of today's Pueblo people, built the town of Pilabo, where fertile fields stretched east to the Rio Grande and an evergreen spring provided water for drinking and agriculture. In 1598, the weary explorers of the Juan de Oñate expedition arrived at the Piro village on their way to establishing a colony near Santa Fe. The villagers gave the wanderers food and shelter, and the Spanish left behind two Franciscan priests, who established the mission of San Miguel and named the place Nuestra Senora de Perpetua Socorro. Later it was simplified to Socorro, which means "help" or "aid" in Spanish.

During the Pueblo Revolt of 1680, the Piros were one of the few Rio Grande tribes to side with the Spanish, and to escape the wrath of their brethren, the tribe fled south, where their descendants still reside near El Paso.

Socorro lay in ruins for many years. By the late 18th century officials in Santa Fe began to see the wisdom of resettling the area to protect wayfarers on the El Camino Real, which ran right through the old plaza. However, it wasn't until 1815 that the governor of New Mexico ordered the area resettled.

The Atchison, Topeka & Santa Fe Railroad arrived in 1880, and what followed was both an explosion in population and mining activity. The nearby mountains were rich in ore, which was ferried to Socorro for smelting. In 1889 the New Mexico School of Mines (currently New Mexico Institute of Mining and Technology) was established. In the 1890s the price of silver and other metals declined, ending the mining boom, and Socorro's economy once more became dependent on agriculture.

During World War II, the village played host to many of the scientists from nearby White Sands Missile Range, and today scientists and astronomers from the Very Large Array Radio Telescope make Socorro their post in civilization.

Don't be dismayed by the commercial strip that greets you as you exit the interstate. This amalgam of fast-food joints and motels serves the needs of busy travelers. One shop on this stretch of road warrants a stop by discriminating crafts buyers. Sundance Gallery stocks a wide assortment of regional crafts, including the distinctive Mimbres-inspired pottery of Karlene Voepel. Be sure to check out her Little Critters, miniature animals in sufficient abundance to fill a tiny Noah's Ark. Silversmiths Donald and Della Baca's sandhill crane jewelry and St.

Miguel pendant and earring sets are other standouts, as are the stained-glass pieces created by shop owner James Klinglesmith.

To see the heart of Socorro, you must traverse California Street's commercial district, turn right at the Manzanares light, and go one block west. The San Miguel Historic Area is crowned by Kittrel Park or the Plaza, as it is more commonly known. Kittrel is a green oasis highlighted by a cooper-roofed bandstand and ornate cast-iron benches, where the town's *viejos* (senior citizens) gather to discuss politics or the weather.

An army field in the 1850s and one of the village's original six Spanish colonial plazas, the park was named for Dr. L. W. Kittrel, a local dentist. Kittrel was instrumental in beautifying the area, and he is buried there.

Surrounding the square is a scattering of shops, a gallery, and many historic buildings. The Abeytia Building on one corner houses the Hilton Drugstore, opened in the 1890s by relatives of Conrad Hilton and one of the oldest continuously operating pharmacies in the state. On the south side, the historic (some say notorious) Capitol Saloon sits cheek by jowl with Doug West's upscale gallery, where you can inspect both Doug's luminous serigraphs and the work of artists working in other media.

From the Plaza, you'll want to head down Bernard Street toward the old mission. The present church was constructed between 1819 and 1821 and is estimated to have been built on the ruins of the earlier mission burned during the Pueblo Revolt. There is a legend that when the priests heard of the impending trouble, they had the Indians disassemble the solid silver communion rail, which was buried along with other valuables. Many have searched for the treasure, but none have met with success.

Another legend concerns the name of the church. It is said that during a raid by Apaches around 1880, the Indians withdrew when they saw a man with wings and a shining sword poised above the door to the church. The parishioners sent a petition to their bishop in Durango, Mexico, requesting the name of the church be changed to San Miguel in honor of Saint Michael, God's warrior archangel. The church has born his name ever since.

The church has undergone several restorations since then, and its current adobe bell towers are typical of California Mission style. There are four subfloors under the present church where early dignitaries and former pastors are entombed. The main doors are generally open, but if you wish to see the interior, a courtesy stop at the parish office would be seemly.

Socorro's Hammel Brewery and Museum houses exhibits on the brewing industry but is open only the first Saturday of the month. Built by the Hammel brothers during the boom years, the brewery produced Illinois Beer until shut down by prohibition. The plant operated as an ice house and soft drink bottling plant until it closed in the 1950s.

Not only rock hounds but anyone with more than a passing interest in geology will enjoy visiting the New Mexico Bureau of Mines and Mineral Resources' Mineral Museum on the second floor of the Workman Addition (Gold Building). The collection of more than 10,000 specimens began with an assortment from the college and was augmented by contributions from the prominent mining speculator C. T. Brown and others. Perhaps the most interesting samples are the fluorescent minerals illuminated by ultraviolet light, or the minerals from New Mexico—aquamarine smithsonite from Kelly, Silver City copper, gold from White Oaks, and uranium from Grants.

If you wish to further investigate the town, the chamber of commerce at 103 Francisco de Avondo has a free walking-tour brochure detailing the various quarters and their historic structures.

Famished explorers should walk back toward the plaza. On Manzanares West, you'll find Martha's Black Dog Coffeehouse, owned by Martha Rimmel, who received her training under Albuquerque's famous chef Rosa Rajkovic. The decor is simple—lots of plants and sun-drenched windows—but the food is artful. More than a place for a cup of joe and a muffin, the Black Dog features New Mexican products prepared in inventive ways. On any afternoon you might find a freshly made soup, a fortifying quiche, or pasta dishes such as fettuccini with zucchini and tomatoes in garlic sauce or penne in artichoke sauce.

If you have your heart set on classic New Mexican food, go where the locals go, La Pasadita at 230 Garfield. Probably not found on any list of officially recommended restaurants, this tiny café would not be out of place in a Mexican border town. You'll find oilcloth-topped tables, families with children chattering away in Spanish, and basic corn, beans, and chile cooking. The enchilada plate is especially recommended, its red or green chile topping crowned with a poached egg.

Another restaurant worthy of mention is the Val Verde Steak House in the historic Val Verde Hotel. Built in 1919, the main body of the Spanish Mission Revival–style hotel has fallen into disrepair, but the section occupied by the restaurant has been refurbished.

Bibliophiles will relish the Dana Book Store, also located in the Val Verde. Owner Gladys Dana is a fund of local lore, and her stock of regional and Southwestern books is extraordinary.

Leaving Socorro, you head out into the Magdalena Mountains, clothed in the greens of mesquite and creosote bush. Soon the vegetation changes to tracts of grass, apache plume, and juniper. Eventually, you arrive at the old mining town of Magdalena. It's hard to believe that this quiet village once was one of the largest cattle-shipping centers in the Southwest. With the demise of mining and the abandonment of the railroad spur that hauled both ore and livestock, the town settled into its current somnolent state.

If you stop at city hall, you can pick up the key for a self-guided tour of the Box Car Museum, with its artifacts of Magdalena's glory days. The old railroad car sits on a section of track to the rear of the building housing both the government and the library.

Magdalena Cafe is a good place to eat in town. Owner Alanna Van Winkle boasts "home-cooked meals since 1986." The usual fare runs to hot roast-beef sandwiches, chicken-fried steak, burritos, and homemade pies and cakes. You'll be dining with the locals, which on any day could include a state cop, high school students, Navajos from the Ramah Reservation, or bona fide cowboys.

From Magdalena it's 3.5 miles on a part-paved, part-gravel road to the ghost town of Kelly. Kelly was an active silver and zinc mining area, that had a population of 3,000 at one time. The ore played out, the people departed, and what remains are ruins, a cemetery, and St. John Baptist Church.

The old mine up the hill operates from mid-May to mid-October for rock hounds, who pay an entrance fee and prospect for any of the 80 minerals found on the site. Five shafts lead to 24 tunnels with a total length of 42 miles. Traylor Shaft still sports its famous head frame, designed by Alexandre-Gustave Eiffel (who also designed the Eiffel Tower) and constructed by Gustav Billing in the 1880s. Many of the tunnels are flooded and all are closed, but the four stockpiles contain a wealth of malachite, Smithsonite, fossils, pyrite, quartz, and other minerals.

Departing Magdalena, you climb out of the mountain valley and enter the Plains of San Agustin, a prehistoric lake basin 45 miles long and 12 miles wide. Juniper and piñón punctuate the vast grasslands as the road scribes a straight line to the horizon. Finally, the Very Large Array dishes materialize. The 27 giant antennae, which capture radio photographs of the heavens, appear like white sails upon an ocean of brush. A three-armed railroad track provides a movable base, with each arm 13 miles in length. When packed together, the dishes operate like a wide-angle lens on a camera. When far apart, they function like a zoom lens.

Radio waves are a form of low-frequency light. The Very Large Array collects these faint waves emitted by celestial objects and sends them to the control building, where the by-products are combined to form a single image. In truth, all the dishes function as one giant radio telescope.

The VLA visitors center has displays that help you understand both the nature of radio waves and the functioning of the VLA. A 20-minute slide show entitled "Star Trails" further amplifies the work done here. A short walking tour takes you outside and up close and personal with the 94-foot dishes, measuring 82 feet in diameter. Standing by one of these behemoths, you are startled to discover it is moving, constantly focusing on those beams from space.

Leaving the VLA, you head toward the far distant foothills of the Mangas Mountains. Reaching New Horse Springs, you exit the Plains of San Agustin, and crossing the Continental Divide, approach the Apache and Gila National Forests. At Reserve, determine whether you want to follow NM 12 west or brave the dirt and gravel Forest Service roads.

If you take this tack, you will go through the ghost town of Mogollon, not truly deserted but home for a scattering of artisans. You should have no problem negotiating this route in a touring car as long as weather has been dry and you have a good, detailed map. Your reward for valor is a beautiful drive and the possibility of sighting an elk herd. The drawback is the extra time it takes and the possibility of chancy road conditions.

If you choose the highway, you will head south near Rancho Grande Estates and follow U.S. 180 south, through Alma to Glenwood, a good spot to stop for the night. Los Olmos Guest Ranch was built in the mid-1940s and survived a series of owners until Jerry and Tiffany Hagemeier took it on in 1991. The main lodge exudes Western hospitality, but don't expect the typical dude ranch. Los Olmos is basically a bed-and-breakfast. Worn brown-and-white cowhides are tossed on the wood floor, an artfully decorated player piano sits in a corner, and bearskins and six-point buck heads hang on the walls. One side room houses a pool table and a neon blue jukebox, and another wing has a library and television. Movies are shown every night.

There's a pool for summer swims and a Jacuzzi for relief of sore muscles. Fourteen rustic, green-trimmed rock cabins are scattered around the 10-acre grounds, which are shaded by cottonwoods and the giant elms for which Los Olmos is named.

Breakfast is served in the dining room with wraparound windows. On any day it could include your choice of pancakes or hash browns, eggs, and bacon or sausage. Dinner is available Wednesday through Sunday by special reservation of two or more, or you can try one of Glenwood's restaurants. The Blue Front has a bar in front and an eating establishment in the back that is known for its burgers, fries, and homemade pies.

The road bordering Los Olmos leads to Whitewater Canyon, site of one of the most unique hikes in New Mexico, the Catwalk National Recreation Trail. During the mining era of the late 1890s, deposits of gold and silver were discovered in the mountains high above the canyon. The Helen Mining Company had 13 claims in this area. To process the ore, in 1893 John T. Graham built a mill at the head of the wash, and eventually the town of Graham, or Whitewater, grew up around the works. The mill could not have been constructed closer to the mines due to the rough, narrow canyon.

Water was not always available at the town, although the creek ran almost continuously farther up. To remedy the situation, a four-inch pipeline was built that followed the west wall of the canyon. In 1897 a larger amount of water was needed to power a new generator, and an 18-inch pipeline was built parallel to the old line.

It was quite a feat of construction. Brace holes were drilled into the solid rock walls to hold the timbers and iron bars supporting the water line along its course. Repairs often were necessary, and the workmen who had to walk the line to repair damage dubbed it "The Catwalk."

When Graham mill closed in 1913, most of the construction material, including the pipelines, was salvaged and sold. All that remains of the mill is a section of wall near The Catwalk's entrance.

In the 1930s the Civilian Conservation Corps (CCC) was assigned the task of rebuilding The Catwalk as an attraction in Gila National Forest. The CCC Catwalk served until 1961, when the present metal structure was constructed by the National Forest Service. Floods roaring down the canyon wreaked havoc with the trail, and in 1986 the portion past the steel span was relocated out of the flood path.

To visit The Catwalk, take NM 174 (Catwalk Road) about five miles to the paved road's end at the Whitewater picnic ground. A short uphill walk takes you to the start of the steel walkway, which hangs 20 to 30 feet above the waters of the creek. This section is easily negotiated and less than a mile in length. More ambitious hikers can continue on Trail 207, a strenuous journey to the junction of Whitewater and South Fork Creeks. Here ruins of the power plant that supplied electricity for the mines and Mogollon can still be seen.

After your foray into the wilds, depart Glenwood, passing the expansive WS Ranch, where Butch Cassidy and his Wild Bunch were employed as honest wranglers. You'll drive through

Alma, site of many raids by Indians and Mexicans, and follow your earlier route to Apache Creek, an excellent place to stop, gas up, and get a cold drink or a snack. There's not much in the way of civilization between here and Zuni.

The one exception is Quemado, where Jim and Irene Jaramillo run El Sarape Cafe, a snug little eatery decorated with multicolored Mexican serapes, deer and antelope heads, and an original tin ceiling. Irene prepares daily specials, "authentic New Mexican food," and her taco salad may be the best you'll find anywhere.

After the long haul between Glenwood and the junction of NM 53 and 36, you'll welcome the short detour to the west to Zuni. If you've visited Acoma's Sky City or the Taos Pueblo, your first impression of Zuni might be less than propitious. Although there's the beautiful Corn Mesa, a silver stream, and acres of green fields, Zuni is not located on a soaring mesa, nor are its stone buildings comparable to Taos's twin adobe apartments. The highway cuts through the modern village, and the route to the old plaza and its mission church is not readily apparent. However, Zuni is very old, and its history is intrinsically woven with the Southwest. It was in the old village of Háwikuh that the Spanish first encountered the Pueblo people.

In the spring of 1536 four survivors of a shipwreck near present-day Galveston arrived in Culicán, Mexico, after five years of Indian captivity and a weary foot journey through western Texas and northern Mexico. En route they heard tales of the incredible riches to be found in the "Seven Cities of Cibola," somewhere to the north.

Eventually arriving in Mexico City, they petitioned the viceroy, Antonio de Mendoza, to mount an expedition to these unknown lands. Mendoza was unwilling to commit a large force, but agreed to dispatch a Franciscan friar, Marcos de Niza, along with Estevan, a black Moorish slave and shipwreck survivor, as guide. They traveled north through Arizona, and Estevan was sent ahead to scout the terrain. Instead of discovering the "seven gold cities," he came upon the Zuni village of Háwikuh. Zuni history relates that when Estevan arrived, he demanded women and turquoise. This did not sit well with the Zuni, and he was summarily executed. Good Fray Marcos fled back to Mexico City, where he compounded the "cities of gold" fiction to defend his participation in the unsuccessful venture.

Responding to these wild tales, the young Francisco Vásques de Coronado, governor of Nueva Galicia, led 300 soldiers and 800 Indians from Compostela to Háwikuh in 1540. Coronado was deeply disappointed at finding only a simple agricultural community instead of a golden hoard. The Zuni did not welcome his presence. Initially, they defended their city with vigor, but compared to the Spanish force of arms, they were badly outclassed and forced to surrender.

Throughout the remainder of the 16th and early 17th centuries, the Spanish were a periodic manifestation in the Zuni villages. In 1629 the first Catholic mission was established in Háwikuh, and the priests were well received at first.

Unrest followed as the Spanish made more and more excessive demands on the pueblos for food and slaves. This culminated in the 1680 Pueblo Revolt, when all the priests were killed and the mission at Halona:wa burned. The Spanish were absent for 12 years, and in 1692 Don Diego de Vargas led an army out of Mexico to negotiate peace with the pueblos.

With a population of around 8,500, Zuni today is the largest of New Mexico pueblos and has all the conveniences of a modern town—restaurants, grocery stores, gas stations, and especially jewelry stores. Zuni jewelers are known worldwide for their exuberant use of colored stones in their inlay jewelry. Zuni carvers craft fetish stone animals with meticulous attention to detail. Bead workers make *koshares* (clowns), turkeys, and dancers in sizes ranging from one to six inches. It seems as if the whole community is one gigantic band of artists.

Your first stop should be the A:shiwi A:wan Museum and Heritage Center. The tribal museum has rotating exhibits on Zuni history and culture, in addition to acting as a visitors center. Adjoining the museum, Pueblo of Zuni Arts and Crafts stocks a wide array of jewelry, paintings, fetishes, and pottery.

If you're searching for beadwork, the Pueblo Trading Post has one of the best selections in town. In addition, they have an exhaustive line of pottery, fetishes, and jewelry. Stop by and watch their silversmiths at work. Of course, if the piece you seek isn't available in either of these locations, you surely will find it at one of the other multiple shops and trading posts along the highway.

You should not leave Zuni before visiting its old mission church, noted not just for beauty and historic value, but especially for the spectacular murals decorating its walls. The mission has a long history. After the Pueblo Revolt, all outlying Zuni villages were abandoned, and most of the inhabitants moved into the old village of Hálona on the banks of the Zuni River. Hálona became modern Zuni. Although a church existed there since about 1629, there are no ruins or descriptions of the building, which was destroyed during the insurrection.

Over the remnants of the old structure, in 1706 Fray Juan Alvarez constructed a new church, which was dedicated to Our Lady of Guadalupe. After the Mexican Independence in 1821, many Franciscans returned to Spain, leaving only a handful of priests to serve the missions of northern New Mexico. By the 1840s, when the region came under control of the United States, missionary work ceased and the buildings fell into ruins.

In 1966 and 1967 the National Park Service excavated the mission and parts of the *convento* for the tribe and the

Our Lady of Guadalupe Church, Zuni.

Roman Catholic Diocese of Gallup. A Gallup contractor and stonemason undertook the reconstruction, which was completed in 1970.

During the restoration, several elders spoke of the murals that adorned the interior walls before the mission was abandoned. The school's pastor contacted Alex Seowtewa, a noted local artist, and asked him if he would take on the project of re-creating those murals. The project began in 1970 and involved not only Alex but his sons Gerald and Kenneth.

Creating a stunning dramatic impact, 24 life-size kachinas or *kokos* run the length of the two side walls. These images portray the supernatural beings that the Zuni believe bring rain, successful hunting, prosperity, and all good things. In traditional ceremonies they are impersonated by village men, and their actions are directed by the elders at specific times of the year. The Zuni believe that the spirit of the kachina actually enters the form of the dancer, transforming him into the being he represents.

The figures on the south wall of the nave represent kachinas associated with summer ceremonies, while the northern wall displays kachinas seen in winter rituals. Traditional plants and local wildlife accompany the dancers, and even the sky mirrors the seasonal change. Seowtewa warrants the figures are authentic in every detail, down to the clacking bill of the great Sha'lako kachina and the antic figure of the Mudhead. What makes this masterpiece so extraordinary is both its location, tucked away in a dusty little New Mexico town, and its accepted presence in a Catholic mission.

Heading east out of the village, you pass Towayálane, the sacred Corn Mesa, rising 1,000 feet above the valley floor. The Zuni Mountains in colorful striations of buff, ochre, and gray crest to the north. The next hamlet is Ramah (RAY-mah), a town settled by Mormons in 1876.

Before reaching El Morro, you'll pass the cutoff to the Ramah Navajo Indian Reservation. Pine Hill is headquarters of the Ramah Navajo Weavers Association, a grassroots cooperative made up of more than 40 traditional weavers. These artisans work to increase family self-reliance using indigenous resources and native skills. Leaders in restoring *churro* stock, a traditional breed believed to be the ancestral sheep of the Navajo people, the association operates in four areas: improving weaving techniques, breeding better wool sheep, restoring and protecting the land, and developing leadership.

Each weaver raises her own sheep, cards and spins the wool, hand-dyes the yarn using native plants, and weaves on the traditional upright loom. If you phone ahead, a weaver will meet you at the cooperative. There you can view or purchase the weavings, which range in size from miniatures to full-size rugs.

Just down the highway from the Ramah turnoff, El Morro National Monument rises from the valley floor like some great gray ship. The technical term for the formation is a cuesta, a long formation with a gentle upward slope that drops off abruptly at one end.

El Morro is a historic registry of those who passed by. The Zuni gave it the name A'ts'ina, or "place of writings on the rock," the Spaniards called it El Morro, "the headland," and Anglo-Americans dubbed it Inscription Rock because the generations of travelers who carved symbols, names, dates, and fragments of their histories. Here in one place are Anasazi petroglyphs keeping company with the scratching of explorer Don Juan de Oñate. Farther on you'll find the inscriptions "Beale" and "Breckinridge," two soldiers in the army's 1857 camel corps.

The walk to Inscription Rock is agreeable, passing the evergreen spring where travelers through the ages knew they could secure water. The trail covers about a half-mile and takes 45 minutes to an hour, depending on how long you linger to decipher the imprints.

The ruins of two Anasazi pueblos top the cuesta, one cloaked in sand and vegetation, the other, A'ts'ina, partially unearthed and stabilized by archaeologists in the 1950s. The path to the top is a two-mile loop with an increase in elevation of 200 feet. Allow one and a half to two hours, and be sure to take water, which is available at the visitors center, the origin of all trails. The center also stocks books, posters, slides, tapes, and CDs. A small but comprehensive museum deals with the El Morro region from prehistoric times, and a 15-minute video is screened regularly.

When searching for accommodations, you have two alternatives. Twelve miles east of El Morro and three miles west of the ice caves, Sheri McWethy operates Cimarron Rose Bed & Breakfast on 20 ponderosa pine–covered acres. Cimarron Suite is reminiscent of a mountain cabin, with its pine plank floor, wood-burning parlor stove, and claw-footed bathtub. Bandera Suite is decorated in traditional Southwestern style and has a private patio. Suites have their own entrances and full kitchens. Sheri's breakfasts of homemade foodstuffs are delivered to guests' doorsteps to consume at their leisure.

If Cimarron Rose is full, you won't go wrong stopping at El Morro RV Park and Cafe, near the national monument. If the idea of cabins in an RV park conjures up images of a dilapidated, unheated tourist court, have no fear. In the eight years they've owned the property, Lou and Billie Gross have completely redone the two existing cabins and constructed two more. The cottages are heated, clean and comfortable, and all have refrigerators for guests' convenience. The café is open for breakfast, lunch, and dinner and features New Mexican food, burgers, soup, and sandwiches.

As you head east, you enter El Malpais National Monument, a mammoth lava flow originating from several volcanos over 2,000 to 113,000 years ago. El Malpais means "badlands" in Spanish, and the area features jagged spatter cones, a lava tube cave system extending at least 17 miles, and fragile ice caves.

On the highway, you skirt the northern section of the monument. There are two trailheads accessible from the road, the mile-and-a-half round-trip Junction Cave Trail in the Calderon area and the seven-mile, one-way Zuni-Acoma Trail. These are not casual hikes, and should not be attempted without proper preparation. The lava is rugged, sharp, and exceedingly hot in warm weather. Wear *very* sturdy hiking boots, a hat, and leather work gloves, and carry a ration of one gallon of water per person per day. Trails are marked with rock cairns, which may be illusive due to their small size and the rocky terrain which camouflages them.

If you want a kinder, gentler introduction to the region's geography, take the turnoff to Bandera Volcano and Ice Caves. This small area is privately owned and more accessible to the casual visitor. The cave is a collapsed lava tube where the year-round temperature never rises above 31 degrees Fahrenheit.

As you approach Grants, you will be popping in and out of monument land. Before exiting onto Interstate 40, you might want to spend an hour or two in Grants, originally settled in 1872, when Don Jesus Blea homesteaded on the south side of San Jose Creek. The advent of the railroad, lumber from the Zuni Mountains, and mining for copper, fluorspar, and pumice all contributed to the city's early growth. After the completion of the Bluewater Dam in 1929, the nearby fertile valley was a utopia for truck gardens (gardens whose produce was trucked to market), and the quality of the vegetables earned the town the title of "Carrot Capital."

All these economic bases waxed and waned with the times. Grants's greatest boom occurred during the 1950s, when Paddy Martinez discovered uranium at Ambrosia Lake. Five mills were built, and Grants's population jumped from 2,200 in 1950 to 10,000 in 1960. New stores, banks, a hospital, library, and schools rode the construction wave, and a branch of New Mexico State University was awarded the town. However, prosperity was short-lived. By the 1980s the demand for uranium dried up, and the mines and mills closed, one by one.

Today Grants is still struggling, depending more and more on the development of its visitor services. Most motel chains have located off the interstate, and more players make their appearance every year. Among the many restaurants, three stand out: the Uranium Cafe across from the New Mexico Museum of Mining, El Cafecito on East Santa Fe Avenue, and La Ventana Steakhouse, hidden away on Geis Street a block off Santa Fe.

The Uranium Cafe serves breakfast and lunch with a funky 1950s flair. Owners Johnny and Kathy Calahan have used neon and old mining pictures to bring back Grants's glory days. Half a 1955 Chevy is the restaurant centerpiece. The menu sports a New Mexican flair, and daily blackboard specials are featured.

Angie and Larry Baca run the El Cafecito, where you'll find they live up to their motto of "authentic New Mexico cuisine." Whether it's a morning order of huevos rancheros, a lunch of a stuffed sopapilla with beans and meat, or a dinner combo plate of tacos, enchiladas, and chimichangas, the emphasis is on chile in its many and varied forms.

True carnivores will love La Ventana. This hideaway serves some of the best beef in the state. Partners Stephanie Matkovich and William Sorensen have been serving up charbroiled steaks, seafood, and an occasional New Mexican dish for 30 years. The restaurant is a trifle difficult to locate. It's directly in back of Republican Headquarters and next to Checker Auto Parts.

If you have time, stop in the New Mexico Museum of Mining. The first level traces the history of Grants from prehistoric times to the present, but it is the lower level that is special. It simulates an actual uranium mine. You are led to the "mine shaft" where you take a simulated ride in the "cage" 900 feet below the surface. Here you trek through dim caverns, visit the assignment station, and enter an open stope, an expanse stripped of ore. Kids, in particular, will enjoy this unusual museum.

Lastly, Grants provides access to 11,301-foot Mount Taylor, one of the four mountains sacred to the Navajos. Once an active volcano, Taylor now is popular for hikers, fishermen, campers, and photographers. Lobo Canyon and Coal Mine Canyon have campsites and picnic areas, and in winter cross-country ski trails lace the area. On cloudless days the scenic drive to the summit is well worth the effort.

For More Information

Socorro Chamber of Commerce, 103 Francisco de Avondo, P.O. Box 743, Socorro, NM 87801. Call 505-835-0424. Open Monday through Friday from 9:00 A.M. to 5:00 P.M., Saturday from 9:00 A.M. to 1:00 P.M. Website: www.socorro-nm.com.

Sundance Gallery, 115 North California Street, Socorro, NM 87801. Call 505-835-1781. Open Tuesday through Saturday from 9:30 A.M. to 5:30 P.M., Monday from 11:00 A.M. to 5:30 P.M.

Doug West Gallery, 102 Plaza, Socorro, NM 87801. Call 505-835-4445. Open Monday and Wednesday through Saturday from 10:30 A.M. to 5:30 P.M. Closed Sunday and Tuesday.

San Miguel Church, Otero Street, Socorro, NM 87801. Call 505-835-1620. Open Monday through Friday from 9:00 A.M. to noon and 1:00 to 4:30 P.M.

Hammel Brewery and Museum (on Sixth Street), Socorro Historic Society, P.O. Box 923, Socorro, NM 87801. Contact Ted Ellinger, call 505-835-5206. First Saturday of the month from 9:00 A.M. to 1:00 P.M. Website: www.nmt.edu/~nmtlib/LOCAL/hammel.html.

New Mexico Bureau of Mines and Mineral Resources Museum, Workman Addition, 801 Leroy Place, Socorro, NM 87801-4796. Call 505-835-5140. Open Monday through Friday from 8:00 A.M. to noon and 1:00 to 5:00 P.M., Saturday and Sunday from 10:00 A.M. to 3:00 P.M. Website: www.geoinfo.nmt.edu.

Martha's Black Dog Coffeehouse, 110 Manzanares, Socorro, NM 87801. Call 505-838-0311. Open daily from 7:30 A.M. to 9:00 or 9:30 P.M.

La Pasadita Cafe, 230 Garfield, Socorro, NM 87802. Call 505-835-3696. Open Monday through Friday from 8:00 A.M. to 8:00 P.M.

Val Verde Steak House, 203 Manzanares Avenue, Socorro, NM 87802. Call 505-835-3380. Open Monday through Friday from 11:00 A.M. to 2:00 P.M. and 5:00 to 9:30 P.M., Saturday 5:00 to 9:30 P.M., Sunday noon to 9:00 P.M. Lounge open daily noon to midnight.

Dana Book Store, 203 Manzanares, Socorro, NM 87802. Call 800-524-3434 (in New Mexico) or 505-835-3434. Open daily from 9:00 A.M. to 9:00 P.M.

Magdalena Chamber of Commerce, P.O. Box 145, Magdalena, NM 87825. Call 505-854-2261. Open Monday through Friday from 8:00 A.M. to 5:00 P.M.

Magdalena Cafe, P.O. Box 294, Magdalena, NM 87825. Call 505-854-2696. Open for breakfast and lunch Monday through Saturday from 6:00 A.M. to 1:00 P.M.; for dinner, Thursday from 5:00 P.M. to 7:00 P.M.; also open Sunday from 8:00 A.M. to 1:00 P.M.

Kelly Mine, Magdalena, NM 87825. Open May 15–October 15, Tuesday through Saturday from 9:00 A.M. to 4:00 P.M. Fee.

Very Large Array, National Radio Astronomy Observatory, Public Information Office, P.O. Box O, Socorro, NM 87801. Call 505-835-7000. Open daily from 8:30 A.M. to sunset. Website: www.nrao.edu/doc/tourist/visit.vla.html.

Los Olmos Guest Ranch, P.O. Box 127, Glenwood, NM 88039. Call 505-539-2311. Open for dinner Wednesday through Sunday by reservation for two or more only.

Blue Front Bar & Cafe, U.S. 180, P.O. Box 166, Glenwood, NM 88039. Call 505-539-2561. Open daily from 11:00 A.M. to 9:00 P.M.

The Catwalk National Recreation Trail, Glenwood Ranger District, U.S. Forest Service, Glenwood, NM 88039. Call 505-539-2481. Office open Monday through Saturday from 8:00 A.M. to 4:30 P.M. Trail always open except for flood damage. Website: www.fs.fed.us/r3/gila.

El Sarape Cafe, P.O. Box 132, Quemado, NM 87829. Call 505-773-4620. Open in summer, daily from 6:00 A.M. to 8:30 P.M.; in winter, from 7:00 A.M. to 7:00 P.M.

Pueblo of Zuni, P.O. Box 1029, Zuni, NM 87327. Call 505-782-5800.

A:shiwi A:wan Museum and Heritage Center, P.O. Box 1009, Zuni, NM 87327. Call 505-782-4403. Open in winter, Monday through Friday from 9:00 A.M. to 5:00 P.M.; in summer, daily from 8:30 A.M. to 6:00 P.M.

Pueblo of Zuni Arts and Crafts, P.O. Box 425, Zuni, NM 87327. Open in summer, Monday through Friday from 9:00 A.M. to 6:00 P.M., Saturday from 9:00 A.M. to 5:00 P.M.; in winter, Monday through Friday from 9:00 A.M. to 5:00 P.M.

Pueblo Trading Post, Highway 53, P.O. Box 1115, Zuni, NM 87327. Call 505-782-2296. Open in summer, Monday through Saturday from 9:00 A.M. to 6:00 P.M., Sunday from 9:00 A.M. to 5:00 P.M.; in winter, Monday through Saturday from 11:00 A.M. to 6:00 P.M., Sunday from 9:00 A.M. to 5:00 P.M.

Our Lady of Guadalupe, Old Zuni Mission, St. Anthony's Rectory, P.O. Box 486, Zuni, NM 87327. Call 505-782-2888. Open Monday through Friday from 8:00 A.M. to 4:30 P.M.

Ramah Navajo Weavers Association, P.O. Box 153, Pine Hill, NM 87357. Call 505-775-3253. Open by appointment.

El Morro National Monument, Highway 53, Route 2, Box 43, Ramah, NM 87321-9603. Call 505-783-4226. Open Memorial Day–Labor Day, visitors center daily from 9:00 A.M. to 7:00 P.M., trails daily from 9:00 A.M. to 6:00 P.M.; in winter, daily from 9:00 A.M. to 5:00 P.M. Upper trail may close in bad weather. Fee. Website: www.nps.gov/elmo.

Cimarron Rose Bed & Breakfast, 689 Oso Ridge Route, Grants, NM 87020. Call 505-783-4770.

El Morro RV Park, Cabins and Cafe, Highway 53, Route 2, Box 44, Ramah, NM 87321. Call 505-783-4612. Open daily from 7:00 A.M. to 8:00 P.M.

El Malpais National Monument, National Park Service, 11000 Ice Caves Road, Grants, NM 87020. Call 505-783-4774. Access NM 53 and 117. Website: www.nps.gov/elma.

Bandera Volcano and Ice Caves, 12000 Ice Caves Road, Grants, NM 87020. Call 888-423-2283. Open in summer, daily from 8:00 A.M. to 7:00 P.M.; in winter, daily from 10:00 A.M. to 4:00 P.M. Fee.

Grants/Cibola Chamber of Commerce, P.O. Box 297, Grants, NM 87020. Call 505-287-4802 or 800-748-2142. Open Memorial Day–September, Monday through Saturday from 9:00 A.M. to 6:00 P.M.; October–Memorial Day, Monday through Saturday from 9:00 A.M. to 4:00 P.M. Website: www.grants.org.

Uranium Cafe, 519 West Sante Fe Avenue, Grants, NM 87020. Call 505-287-7540. Open Tuesday through Friday from 7:00 A.M. to 2:00 P.M., Saturday and Sunday from 8:00 A.M. to 2:00 P.M.

El Cafecito, 820 East Santa Fe Avenue, Grants, NM 87020. Call 505-285-6229. Open Monday through Friday from 7:00 A.M. to 9:00 P.M., Saturday from 7:00 A.M. to 8:00 P.M.

La Ventana Steakhouse, 110 1/2 Geis Street, Grants, NM 87020. Call 505-287-9393. Open Monday through Saturday from 11:00 A.M. to 2:00 A.M.

New Mexico Museum of Mining, Business Loop 40, Grants, NM 87020. Call 505-287-4802 or 800-748-2142. Open May 1–September 30, daily from 9:00 A.M. to 6:00 P.M.; October 1–April 30, Monday through Saturday from 9:00 A.M. to 4:00 P.M. Website: www.grants.org.

9

The Silvered South

Getting there: From Albuquerque, take I-25 south to Truth or Consequences, exit 79. Take NM 187 south from Truth or Consequences 17 miles through the suburb of Williamsburg and along the western edge of Caballo Reservoir. Cross the interstate south of the town of Caballo, exit 63, and head west on NM 152, 51 miles through the towns of Hillsboro and Kingston, over Emory Pass to San Lorenzo. Here you can continue on NM 152 14 miles to its junction with U.S. 180, the direct road to Silver City.

Alternately, you can take NM 35 27 miles northwest to Lake Roberts, where you connect with NM 15 north, which winds 19 miles to Gila Hot Springs and dead-ends at Gila Cliff Dwellings National Monument. Returning south, you stay on NM 15 at Lake Roberts and traverse 18 miles of extremely narrow, winding roadway to Pinos Altos, eventually connecting with U.S. 180 outside of Silver City. Heading south from Silver City, take NM 90 44 miles southwest to Lordsburg, where you join I-10. Deming is 60 miles east on the interstate.

For the Columbus detour, you head south from Deming 32 miles on NM 11. Las Cruces is 59 miles east of Deming, and if you continue to Fort Selden, it's 19 miles north of Las Cruces, off I-25.

Highlights: A loop around southwestern New Mexico begins in Truth or Consequences, with its mineral hot springs and ends in Las Cruces, home of New Mexico State University and historic Old

Mesilla. The route winds through the Black Mountains; ranges into the Gila Wilderness, site of ancient cliff dwellings; and pauses in Silver City, once an old mining town and now a thriving retirement community.

This is your starting point for a foray into the southern plains and the communities of Lordsburg, with its ghost towns of Shakespeare and Steins, and Deming, with its exceptional community museum.

Detour south to Columbus, a Mexican border crossing and home to Pancho Villa State Park, commemorating the general's infamous 1916 raid into the United States. After a stint in Las Cruces and old Mesilla, hit the highway north to Fort Selden State Monument, where Douglas MacArthur spent his boyhood years.

Western towns have a look about them, a kinship with the lay of the land. The false-fronted stores define a strip called Main Street, or some variation, and development extends only a block or two in supplemental parallel roads. What defines the individual communities, makes the chambers of commerce sit up and point with pride, is not immediately obvious to the casual visitor. Truth or Consequences is a good example. Other than its unusual and puzzling name, there appears to be not much to intrigue the traveler. However, there's more than initially meets the eye in this town situated five miles from the recreational boating and fishing haven, Elephant Butte Lake.

T or C, as New Mexicans call it, was well known for its healing thermal waters long before Europeans settled the area. Native Americans frequently visited the site and bathed in its natural springs. It is said it was a place of peace where all tribes could gather without rancor.

The Spanish settlers called the place Alamocitos (Little Cottonwoods), and the spot was sparsely populated until the checking of the Rio Grande in 1912–1916 and the construction of Elephant Butte Dam. During this phase of its existence, the town was known as Hot Springs in honor of the mineral waters. Although the stream of visitors coming to the spas continued through the early decades of the 20th century, the stream gradually became a trickle by the 1950s.

In 1951 *Truth or Consequences*, hosted by Ralph Edwards, was one of television's most popular game shows. As a promotional tool, Edwards promised to broadcast his show from any town willing to change its name to that of the program. Hot Springs jumped at the chance. Not only would it give the town national prominence, it would eliminate the confusion with the many other U.S. towns called Hot Springs. In a special election, the conversion was approved 1,294 to 295. A protest was held, resulting in another election. This time the outcome was four to one in favor of the alteration. Through the years the town has polled its residents to determine if they wish to continue under their quirky name, and the response has always been a firm yes.

Edwards beamed his program from the small burg on the Rio Grande the first year, and he has continued his warm relationship with T or C since, returning with his Hollywood friends every year for its May fiesta. In honor of his unstinting support, the town named Ralph Edwards Park in his honor.

The first thing you notice as you turn off the interstate is the city's utilitarian water tower, a fixture in much of the Southwest. But here, the formerly unaesthetic structure is gloriously decorated by Las Cruces artist Tony Pennock in a rendition of Native Americans journeying to the sacred spring. Two other examples of Pennock's work may be viewed on the towers of his hometown.

Passing the tower, you discover your route branching, creating two main arteries. Main Street, which exits the interstate from the north, swings down the hill and becomes a one-way east-west thoroughfare near the fire station. Broadway meets Main west of town and travels east to its junction with Main. It's a bit confusing at first, but you get the lay of the land rather quickly.

As you descend the hill and before the roads diverge, you pass one of T or C's top restaurants, Los Arcos. Opened in 1969 and owned by Bob Middleton, proprietor of the popular Monte Vista Fire Station and Owl Restaurant in Albuquerque, Los Arcos is always busy. The manifold arches, crimson carpeting, and massive wood inlay tables and chairs might strike some as a bit labored, but there is no question about the artistry of the consistently good food. Basically a steakhouse with seafood and chicken alternatives, the restaurant prides itself on prime beef, cooked as ordered. The service is outstanding.

If you're searching for something more casual, stop in at Lewis Ludvigson's Bar-B-Que on Broadway. A great favorite with the locals, the café is jammed at lunchtime with folks seeking basic, tasty fare. The menu runs to a variety of barbecues, including sliced or chipped brisket, turkey, Polish sausage, and sliced pork, all served with mounds of skin-on fries. Additional items range from burgers and sandwiches to ribs and chicken-fried steak.

Fully fortified, you are ready to take in the sights. The Geronimo Springs Museum on Main Street traces the history of the area from frontier days to the present. Built beside the hot spring that gives the museum its name, the structure is laid out in multiple rooms devoted to varying aspects of town culture—ranching, farming, and the rise and fall of mining and cattle towns, and the construction of Elephant Butte Dam. The Ralph Edwards Wing relates the tradition of the annual fiesta, and the Heritage Wing displays artwork by local artist

Delmas Howe and Hivana Leyendecker, a Las Cruces sculptor and artist. The murals and bronze busts depict four historic figures important to area history: Juan de Oñate, Spanish explorer; Geronimo, Chiricahua Apache leader; Eugene Manlove Rhodes, cowboy author; and Pancho Villa, Mexican revolutionary.

Students and admirers of prehistoric Indian pottery should be sure to see the outstanding Fairs Watson Chestnut Indian Heritage Collection. The exhibit highlights artifacts from Casa Grande, El Paso, Tularosa, Mesa Verde, Hohokam, White Mountain, and Mimbres Mogollon cultures. A reconstructed settler's log cabin is bound to please the children, and there is a compact gift shop specializing in books on the Southwest.

T or C's wide choice of mineral baths offers travel-fatigued road warriors soothing respite. Most are registered and licensed by the state, and their temperatures range from about 98 to 115 degrees. There is no odor to the waters, and the pH is about seven, or neutral. An analysis by the Los Alamos National Laboratory revealed 38 different minerals.

Your selection of a spa should be determined by the proffered method of the soak. Some baths provide tubs and private or semiprivate rooms, while others offer natural flowing pools. All are enclosed against the weather, and most furnish massage or other therapies. If you like the experience of a natural pool, make a reservation at Marshall Miracle Hot Springs on Marr, Hay-Yo-Kay on Austin, or drop by Indian Springs Pools on Pershing. Other spas run the gamut from the popular Artesian Bath House, with five individual and three double-occupancy tubs, to funky Riverbend Hot Springs Hostel, whose pool is a converted minnow tank from the oldest live-bait store in New Mexico and whose deck overlooks the placidly flowing Rio Grande.

If you are searching for a place to stay combined with a full-facility spa, look no farther than the Charles Motel &

Bath House on Broadway. Built in the late 1930s, it has been nicely refurbished by Cathy Clark. There are 20 motel-style units, 18 with kitchens and two without, all individually and graciously decorated. The Charles's spa boasts the hottest water in town—110 to 112 degrees, and its immaculate facilities include nine individual tubs, sauna, and massage room.

If you are in T or C Wednesday or Thursday mornings, be sure to check out the small flea market across from the motel. You will find a good assortment of fruit trucked up from Mexico.

For those interested in shopping, there's Xochi's bookstore and gallery, chock-full of books, artifacts, art, coins, old furniture, and all sorts of merchandise not usually encountered in a book emporium. On Broadway, Second Hand Rose specializes in preworn boutique wear. If you love musty antique shops harboring dusty treasure lurking in the cobwebs, U-Name-It/Gift Shop on Main has 15,000 square feet of antiques, glass, jewelry, furniture, dolls, vintage kitchenware, and other collectibles.

While in the area, visit Chateau Sassenage winery in Engle, 26 miles west of town. A family business with its roots in the Burgundy region of France, the operation is the only local vineyard producing bottled wine. Its vintages include cabernet sauvignon, merlot, pinot noir, chardonnay, Riesling, and white zinfandel. Although tastings and tours are free, the proprietors request that you call ahead, because they are often out in the fields.

As you leave T or C and continue your journey south on Broadway, stop at Buffalo Bill's Cactus Ranch. Dave Lamb and Maryann "George" Lambert have assembled an astonishing variety of cactus and succulents for sale. In addition to the garden variety of prickly pear and hedgehog cactus, you'll find exotics such as wrinkled blue myrtle, elkhorn, and black rose tree. You might even be tempted to buy a rare golden saguaro, no small investment. A gift shop stocking pots and garden implements complements the greenhouse.

Broadway winds south and becomes NM 187 after passing the suburb of Williamsburg. You skirt the village of Las Palomas and flank Caballo Reservoir, another dammed waterway on the Rio Grande. In the town of Caballo you turn west, cross the interstate, and head toward the Black Mountains.

The first 10 miles or so are an arrow-straight two-lane road with roller-coaster dips, but shortly the complexion of both highway and terrain makes a drastic change. Approaching Hillsboro through the foothills of the Black Range, the route is tortuous.

In the 1800s Hillsboro was a gold- and silver-mining town and the seat of Sierra County (later moved to T or C). Today you'll discover a sleepy village that depends largely on tourists passing through en route to Silver City.

A popular stop, if you hit the hours right, is the Black Range Museum and Library, founded in 1961 by Eve Simmons as a volunteer service to the community. The first collection of relics was accommodated in the auditorium of the local elementary school. Moved to an adobe building when the school reclaimed its space, the museum quickly outgrew its quarters and was conveyed to a building that once housed a bordello and restaurant owned and operated by Miss Sadie Orchard. Sadie was the proverbial madam with a heart of gold. When Percha Creek flooded in 1914 and an influenza epidemic followed, she hiked up her skirts and went out to care for the sick and dying. History relates that she used her fine silk and velvet dresses to line children's coffins and her fancy buggy was pressed into service as a hearse to carry the deceased to burial in the cemetery above town.

The bordello cook, Tom Ying, assumed proprietorship of the restaurant when Miss Sadie retired, and his café was known as the Chinaman's Place. In addition to the usual flotsam and jetsam of a small town museum, you will encounter areas retained as Ying left them. The huge meat block and sharp knives wielded by the Chinese cook remain where he abandoned them, and his skullcap is exhibited in a showcase.

It's pleasant walking down the cottonwood-shaded main street lined with shops and cafés. Luanne Franklin, editor of the local *Percha Press*, presides over one of the best, Hidden Treasures, a multifaceted gift shop stocking everything from regional crafts to collectibles. Before you leave, walk up the hill to the site of the old courthouse and jail, a reminder of Hillsboro's more wild and woolly past.

Just west of Hillsboro, an affable gentleman identified only as J.R. operates Sweetwood Bar-B-Q and Hillsboro Orchard, the focal point of the annual Labor Day Apple Festival. Menu choices at the rustic stand run to applewood-smoked brisket or capon and homemade beans, soup, salads, and apple or pecan pies. Take a seat on a picnic bench in the orchard and watch the world go by while you satisfy your hunger pangs.

The road from Hillsboro to Kingston is another exercise in Grand Prix driving, and if you're not careful, you'll miss the side road that leads to the tiny community. There's not much left of the 1889 silver-mining town that had a population of 7,000 serviced by 22 saloons, three hotels, and three newspapers. A few historic buildings remain—the assay office, the Percha Bank (now a private museum), and The Black Range Lodge.

The Black Range Lodge is a rambling bed-and-breakfast built on the ruins of Pretty Sam's Casino and Monarch Saloon. While most of the construction was completed in 1940, the multilevel brick section dates back to the 1880s, when it housed miners and cavalry.

Catherine Wanek and Peter Fust operate the inn as a combination lodge and retreat center. Both Pete and Catherine are experts in natural building techniques such as strawbale construction, a discipline that engages many of their student groups. In addition to acting as lodge chatelaine, Catherine produces and directs feature films. *Paper Hearts*, which had its debut at the Sundance Film Festival, was shot in Kingston.

The lodge is a rustic, make-yourself-at-home sort of place where the resident cat is likely to join you for an afternoon nap, and breakfast is self-serve, featuring a plethora of wholegrain breads and fresh fruit. Evening activities may focus on tours of different natural building materials projects and systems or the occasional hike led by Pete to view the roosting of a large flock of turkey buzzards on the banks of Percha Creek.

From Kingston, you soldier on, climbing higher and higher until you crest Emory Pass, crossed in 1846 by the Army of the West, scouted by Lieutenant William H. Emory of the Topographical Engineers and guided by Kit Carson. Entering Grant County, you gradually descend the mountains toward San Lorenzo and enter the Mimbres valley.

If it is late afternoon, you should continue on NM 152 past Santa Rita and its huge open-pit copper mine. Turn onto U.S. 180/NM 90, and proceed through Arenas Valley to Silver City, a total of 24 miles. You need to be fresh for the trip to the Gila Cliff Dwellings, which is long and difficult due to the narrow, winding road offering the real possibility of an encounter with a highballing logging truck. The actual distance to the cliff dwellings does not accurately reflect on the time needed for the journey. Allow two hours to navigate NM 35 to the monument visitors center, at least two hours to hike to the ruins, and another two hours to drive NM 15 back to Silver City—more if you plan to stop at Pinos Altos. You do not want to drive this route after dark, if you can possibly avoid it.

If it's the shank of the day and you are still alert, head north on NM 35 out of San Lorenzo into the scenic Mimbres valley, named for the area's prehistoric inhabitants, a branch of the Mogollon people. As you leave the pastoral setting of the valley, you enter the juniper, piñon, and ponderosa pine country of the Gila National Forest. You pass Lake Roberts, a 72-acre man-made lake that offers fishing, boating, and camping. At Mile Marker 10.1, you may notice an abandoned Meerschaum mine, the only one in the United States. Meerschaum is a form of hydrous magnesium silicate, a fine, light, white, clayey mineral used in the crafting of fine smoking pipes.

Turn right where the highway reaches its junction with NM 15, and take the scenic mountain road toward the cliff dwellings, halting at Copperas Vista (Mile Marker 33.6) to view the headwaters of the three forks of the Gila River. You will pass the small community of Gila Hot Springs, where you can stop at Doc Campbell's Post for gas, a cold drink, or a taste of their special homemade ice cream.

Pass the road leading to the cliff dwellings and continue on a short distance to the visitors center, where you can watch a 15-minute film and check out the displays on Mogollon country and its people. When you've been well briefed, you can head for the monument. The trail to the cliff dwellings is about a mile in length and begins a short distance from the center. It climbs 175 feet above the canyon floor and is moderately steep as it ascends to the seven naturally formed caves, six of which contain prehistoric ruins. By all means, take the hike if you are able. Cliff Dweller Canyon is a beautiful place any time of the year, with its cloaking of Douglas firs standing tall against the warm dun walls of volcanic tuff.

Scientists believe that 40 to 50 people lived in the caves' 40 rooms from A.D. 1280 to 1300. They were dryland farmers, and their fields were along the valley of the West Fork and on the mesa across the canyon. They raised squash, corn, and beans, and they supplemented their harvest with wild foods they gathered and animals they hunted. They were weavers and skilled potters, producing brown bowls with black interiors and black-on-white vessels.

What made them leave such a snug harbor? Perhaps there was an extended drought, overuse of natural resources, a shortened growing season, a social schism, or a combination of factors. By the time the Mogollon left the area, their culture largely had been assimilated by other Southwestern groups. Their descendants can be found in today's Pueblo people.

After leaving the monument, you'll retrace your steps toward Gila Hot Springs and hook up with NM 15 south. The section between this junction and Pinos Altos makes your earlier route appear straight. It is a beautiful but serpentine drive, and you'll breathe a sigh of relief when you arrive in the old mining town, founded in 1860 by Thomas "Three-Fingered" Birch, a prospector who discovered gold in Bear Creek. Miners and settlers followed him, but Apache raids in 1861 and 1864 all but closed down the fledgling town. Today Pinos Altos is a pleasant, quiet village snuggled in the tall ponderosa pines. The liveliest spot in town is Karen Campbell's Buckhorn Saloon. Housed in an old adobe structure with 18-inch walls, the watering hole has two massive bars, both freighted in on wagons during some distant past. That special Buckhorn ambiance is assured by the establishment's resident characters, Indian Joe and Debbie DeCamp. Debbie, perched on the balcony overlooking the entrance, gives handsome gents the eye. Dressed in a bar girl's net stockings and low-cut gown, the soft-sculpture mannequin commemorates the original Debbie, who is said to have died in a public brawl. Members of her sisterhood penned a rhyme for her:

> Shed a tear for Debbie DeCamp,
> Born a virgin, and died a tramp.
> For 17 years she retained her virginity,
> A real good record for this vicinity.

Poor old Indian Joe, another full-size sculpture, warms the end barstool, reportedly waiting day upon day, month upon month, for someone to buy him a drink. His sad visage, beat-up felt fedora, and hand-me-down clothes reflect his dejection and despair. Myopic or inebriated customers have been known to offer him a beer, but the offer is never acknowledged.

With all its high jinks, the Buckhorn is a good-time bar, and the dining room, decorated with gaslights and scenes of early days, is held in high repute. Offering a basic menu of steaks, seafood, baby back ribs, and homemade desserts, the restaurant draws customers from distant points. On most Friday and Saturday nights, the Pinos Altos Melodrama Theatre performs in the restored opera house.

Other town attractions are the Fort Cobre Trading Post, selling a variety of Native American crafts, and the adjoining Fort Santa Rita del Cobre, a re-creation of the fort built by the Spanish to protect their copper interests against the Apaches. In addition to the fort itself, you'll visit a homestead compound with all the signatures of life on the frontier—stables and corrals, a blacksmith shop, a windmill, and chicken coop with active inhabitants. Another section depicts the region's early mining past.

The Pinos Altos Museum and adjoining Log Cabin Curio Shop are a stop for hardcore small-town museum buffs. Housed in the old schoolhouse, the museum has room after room of household items, arrowheads, pottery shards, an old switchboard, a mineral collection, row upon row of old photographs, and a cider press. You get the idea. The curio shop, which was originally the George Schafer store, carries a selection of souvenirs, T-shirts, books, jewelry, Navajo kachinas, and Casas Grandes pottery.

Leaving Pinos Altos, you have a less arduous route to Silver City. With its spring and marsh, the site was a popular Apache camping site, and when the Spanish miners discovered copper in the region, they called it San Vincente Cienega and judiciously left the valley to the Indians.

When in 1869 the English-speaking settlers unearthed the area's silver deposits just above the marsh, they were not so wise and incurred the predictable hostile repercussions from the Apache. In spite of this, the municipality, renamed Silver City, grew from one cabin to a boomtown of more than 80 buildings. Prosperity lasted until 1893, when silver prices crashed. Instead of dying a quick death, Silver City survived, first as an industrial center and later at the turn of the century as a haven for invalids and tubercular patients.

With new mineral discoveries, growth stabilized, and Silver City was named the seat of Grant County. Today the town is a trade center and is becoming an increasingly popular travel destination and retirement haven. Blessed with a beneficent climate and a 6,000-foot elevation, the city is home to an active arts community and Western New Mexico University, in addition to serving as gateway to the spectacular Gila Wilderness.

Upon arriving, your first stop should be the Murray Ryan Visitor's Center on Hudson Street, where you'll find a plethora of information, including material detailing four historic and scenic tours. Loop tour one is an excellent guide to the city's attractions, including several sites reminiscent of Billy the Kid's youth. His mother, Catherine McCarthy Antrim, is buried in a town cemetery. Another stop on the tour is Big Ditch Park, where from 1895–1906 floodwaters destroyed buildings and dropped the level of Main Street 55 feet. In 1980 the city turned the eyesore into what is now a graceful, shaded park.

Don't miss the Silver City Museum, housed in the H. B. Ailman House. Located on West Broadway in a handsome mansard/Italianate brick Victorian mansion, the building was constructed in 1881 as home to the owner of one of the richest silver mines in the area.

Through the years it morphed into a boarding house, city hall, and the town fire department. In 1967 it had its final evolution into the Silver City Museum.

The first-floor galleries include a period parlor with a Jewett grand piano, velvet double-camelback sofa, and marble-top table. Additional rooms display local architectural styles and the history of Silver City from the time of the Apache to the present. A new wing, the Cleveland E. Dodge Memorial Gallery, depicts regional involvement in the Mexican War and the Civil War in the West. A well-stocked gift shop carries a bonanza of Mexican Casas Grandes pots, books, Mimbres reproductions, T-shirts, and children's toys.

The second floor houses a room of mining memorabilia, another area devoted to local commerce, and a re-creation of a working mine office complete with an old Underwood Standard typewriter, Addressograph, two oak desks with matching filing cabinets, and a wide-eyed stuffed bobcat. The third-floor cupola features a vista of the historic area of the city.

Broadway's lures do not end with the museum. Galleries line the sidewalks up and down the street. Silver City Trading Company functions as a 29-dealer mall specializing in antiques and collectibles. Fire Cloud Traders sells handcrafts by local artists.

On nearby North Bullard, Yankie Creek Gallery is a cooperative of 20 Grant County artists working in diverse media, and on Arizona, What's A Pot Shop is the studio and home of Harry Benjamin, an artist working his eccentric designs in clay and oils. No shrinking violet, Harry is as much fun as his idiosyncratic constructions.

O'Keefe's Bookshop on Broadway is bound to attract the inveterate reader with its shelves brimming over with used and rare books, tomes of local and Southwestern lore, and photographic prints and cards by owner Dennis O'Keefe.

If all this shopping leaves you hungry, hop over to the Adobe Springs Cafe at the I-80/90 split. The restaurant is located in what was the office and owner's quarters of Clark Court, a motel built in 1937. Named for the natural spring still active beneath the building, the café is a favorite for the local business crowd—and justly so—for its good food, lovingly prepared. Try their special green-chile-chicken chowder. Served with a fresh muffin or roll, it's guaranteed to fill that hollow spot.

After lunch, be sure to visit the Western New Mexico University Museum in Fleming Hall. Anyone fascinated with the Southwest's prehistoric Indian heritage will be well rewarded by the collection of artifacts relating to the Mimbres Mogollon and Casas Grandes cultures. What draws so many visitors to this small college museum is the largest exhibit of Mimbres painted pottery on permanent display in the world. Extracted mainly from the collection of Richard Eisele, these pots are stylized renditions of men and animals in a great variety of whimsical displays. The museum gift shop plays on this theme, with Mimbres pottery replicas, jewelry, books, T-shirts, and cards.

For a place to lay your weary head, consider The Cottages, at the edge of town. The complex of a great house and cottages was built in the 1930s and was the parental home of Harrison "Jack" Schmitt, the United States' first astrogeologist and one of the last men to walk on the moon. The French country brick construction has undergone a complete renovation, and the 80 gated acres provide the traveler with a private and pristine preserve.

The master suite in the main house is elegant and spacious, with private entrance, fireplace, decorator fabrics and bed linens, and hardwood floors accented by braided rugs. A touch of '30s detailing is the dressing room with lady's mirrored table and appointed closets. The three individually decorated cottages are self-catering, with well-stocked refrigerators and pantries.

Bear Mountain Guest Ranch is an alternate possibility. Innkeeper Myra McCormick maintains the 1928 Spanish Territorial on 160 acres, and the ranch has great appeal to visitors interested in the area's natural attractions, especially its abundant bird life. A living guidebook of the area, Myra can tell you where to find a canyon with prehistoric petroglyphs or a hiking trail tailored to your interests. The atmosphere is congenial, with guests sharing talk about their occupations and hometowns around the breakfast table. The accommodations are comfy if not luxurious.

When you leave Silver City, you pass Tyrone, with its strip mines, and head south through the Burro Mountains. Descending through Thompson's Canyon, you pass the place where Apaches ambushed and killed Judge H. C. McComas and his wife and kidnapped their young son, Charlie. The abduction touched off one of the West's widest searches, but the child was never found.

En route you also pass the remains of Gold Hill, a silver-mining town spared by Geronimo and his band of 90 Apaches in 1885. By pure luck the citizens had erected two American flags for Independence Day, and when spotted from afar, Geronimo assumed cavalry troopers were there, and he withdrew without attack.

Traversing a section of Gila National Forest and crossing the Continental Divide, you pass into New Mexico's Bootheel, with its seemingly endless creosote flats and small volcanic mountain ranges shimmering like mirages in the desert heat.

Lordsburg is an old Southern Pacific town, the kind where every head of household worked for the railroad and people set their watches by the daily comings and goings of the freights. As the fortunes of the railroad diminished, so waned the town. Evidence of the depressed economy stares out of empty store windows up and down the old business district. You can still find a little action at El Charro Cafe across the tracks, where 70-year-old twins Inez and Irene Hood feed the dwindling populace as they have for the past 50 years. Most folks become acquainted with Lordsburg as a stop along I-10, which runs from Arizona to the Texas border, or as a jumping-off point for visiting the ghost towns of Steins and Shakespeare.

Shakespeare, a National Historic Site, is the remains of a small settlement on the stage and emigrant trail to California. When silver was discovered in 1870 and news of a diamond mine circulated, Ralston City—or Burro Mines, as it was then called—prospered until the counterfeit source of the diamond story was determined. For a while only a few die-hard miners remained, but during the silver-mining boom of 1879–1893 and the copper boom of 1908–1932, the city was again fully occupied with an assortment of wild and lawless characters.

Owned since 1935 by the Hill family, Shakespeare is blissfully noncommercial. Tours guided by family member Manny Hough run about two hours. Except for months where a holiday intervenes, they are given the second Saturday and preceding Sunday of the month at 10:00 A.M. and 2:00 P.M. The town is open to the public only at those times or by special appointment.

Manny takes you back in time, reciting colorful anecdotes from Shakespeare's history as you stroll along the old main street. You'll visit Grant House, the back portion once the old Butterfield Stage station and the front rooms doubling as a restaurant and hanging parlor. You'll examine the Stratford Hotel (where Billy the Kid is said to have washed dishes), the powder magazine, mail station, saloon, gun museum, blacksmith shop, and assay office. Special reenactments from town history are staged four times yearly.

Steins is west of Lordsburg, just off I-10. Like Lordsburg, it was a railroad town. Named for Enoch Steins, a captain of the U.S. Dragoons, who camped there in 1856, Steins was a stop on the Butterfield Stage line. After the Southern Pacific pushed track through Steins Pass and established a work station, the tiny community grew. When the railroad switched from steam to diesel after World War II, the work station was closed, and the town began its slow death.

Currently owned by Larry and Linda Link, Steins still sits by the track, looking like some forlorn, jilted Casanova. Crumbling stagecoach station walls, a section house (rumored to be haunted), and 10 buildings filled with artifacts and furniture await the visitor, who can take one of Larry's guided tours or wander at will.

If ghost towns are not on your list of must-sees, you could bypass Lordsburg by driving east and south from Silver City on U.S. 180 to Deming. This route takes you through the towns of Central, Bayard, and Hurley. If you leave U.S. 180 south of Hurley and take NM 61 four miles northeast, you'll arrive at City of Rocks State Park. These wild, eroded formations of Kneeling Nun rhyolite tuff were created 35 million years ago from an ash flow originating in a large volcanic caldera in the Black Range. With a desert garden and picnic and camping areas scattered in the shade of the boulders, the park is a superb place for a bag lunch or an overnight stay.

Returning to U.S. 180, you pass Faywood Hot Springs on your left, just 1.5 miles from the park. The planned construction of a multipurpose building eventually will house a visitors center, museum, gift shop, and restaurant. The springs historically are a popular spot for "taking the waters," and facilities include massage and both public and private flow-through soaking pools and hot tubs, some of which are "clothing optional."

Although hardly a "country road," I-10 provides the only reasonable route between Lordsburg and Deming, approximately an hour's drive at interstate speeds. Your first stop in town should be the old railroad depot, now the Deming visitors center, where you'll find a collection of information on Deming and nearby Columbus.

Deming is best known in the wide world for its Great American Duck Races, held the fourth weekend of August. The brainchild of local businessmen who decided to enliven life in a small town, the speedster fowls have been racing since 1980 to continued coverage by national and international media such as *Sports Illustrated* and commentator Paul Harvey. Over the years, the festival has grown to include a balloon rally, parade, Main Street outhouse race, chile cook-off, classic car show, tortilla toss, and other special events.

Whether you arrive for the festival or another time of year, you need to reserve a couple hours to visit the Deming Luna Mimbres Museum, one of the finest small-town museums in the West. There is a great deal to see, and most people regret not giving more time to their visit. Originally the National Guard Armory, the museum is a community project operating with all volunteer personnel and public contributions. The 25,000 square feet of exhibit space houses an art gallery; the Gilmore Quilt Room, with textiles dating back to 1847; the Southerland Doll room, with specimens ranging from china-headed dolls of the late 1800s to today's Barbies; an extensive geode and thunder egg array; and the Indian Gallery, with its collection of crafts from the Mimbres, Pueblo, and Alaskan peoples. A new wing is devoted to a transportation exhibit hall.

Across the street from the museum, the restored Historic Custom House was the port of entry from Old Mexico from 1848 to 1900. The all-adobe building is furnished and decorated with period pieces. The main room is especially charming, with its marble-topped tables and Victorian chairs, carved oak server, and display of fine china and glass.

St. Clair Vineyards is a short distance east of town on NM 549. Master winemaker Florent Lescombes, a seventh-generation vintner, blends a wide selection of wines from grapes grown in nearby fields. The creation of personalized wine bottles is a distinctive service of the winery. Their resident artist paints a bottle with one-of-a-kind designs for birthdays, anniversaries, or other special occasions. The tasting room is open daily, and visitors may sample a selection of still and sparkling wines.

Deming is a mineralogist's heaven, with its multiple rock shops featuring agate, chert, dipside, garnet, and jasper garnered from nearby sites. If you're a rock hound, you'll want to visit Rock Hound State Park in the nearby Florida Mountains. The park encourages visitors to take home the agate, jasper, and opal they find.

To fuel all these forays around town, stop at Si Señor Restaurant on East Pine. Raul and Margarita Granillo run a justly popular local spot where you'll find excellent New Mexican food and fast service in pleasant surroundings. Their carne adovada is especially recommended.

While in the Deming area, devote a halfday to an excursion south to Columbus, a small town on the Mexican border noted primarily as the site of Pancho Villa's raid of March 9, 1916. Villa attacked both Columbus and the nearby 13th Cavalry at Camp Furlong in an attempt to embarrass President Wilson for having given recognition to Venustiano Carranza as president of the Republic of Mexico instead of Victoriano Huerta, backed by Villa. Although the town and its population suffered considerable damage, Villa lost many men to cavalry fire, and the day following the attack, Wilson ordered a punitive expedition commanded by General John J. "Black Jack" Pershing to capture the outlaw. After many skirmishes, Villa's forces were decimated, but he was not apprehended. Pershing returned to Columbus with his troops on February 5, 1917.

The military post at Camp Furlong was closed in 1926 and the extensive cactus gardens of Pancho Villa State Park now cover the site. The old customs house, built in 1902, is the park visitors center, and its exhibits describe the histories of Villa, the raid, and the Pershing expedition.

In addition to the park, Columbus's Historical Museum is worth a stop. Housed in the restored Southern Pacific Railroad Depot, the museum's rooms contain Indian artifacts, military and town memorabilia, and Villa mementoes, including his death mask. A collection highlight is the telephone switchboard of Susan Parks Kendrick, the town operator who, even though injured, stayed at her post during the raid and summoned help from Fort Bliss and El Paso.

The border crossing between Columbus and Palomas, Chihuahua, Mexico, is New Mexico's only international port of entry open 24 hours a day. You can park your car in the United States and walk across into Palomas, a hardscrabble border town. Other than the novelty of strolling into a foreign country, there's little compelling reason for visiting Palomas. However, if you do go, a respectable place for lunch is The Pink Store, also known as Casa de Pancho Villa Restaurant and Bar. The restaurant is to the rear of the shop, which sells a variety of Mexican arts and crafts. The dining room is attractive, and the menu predictable. For gringos cautious about Mexican food, they advertise, "we disinfect our vegetables and utensils with NOE-BAC. We use distilled ice and water. Our beef is USDA choice from Luna County Meat Company."

Las Cruces is your last stop on this tour. With a population of 67,000 and the campus of New Mexico State University, Las Cruces is a bustling town. Situated in the Mesilla Valley with the rugged Organ Mountains to the east, the city's long history begins with Paleo-Indian habitation circa 200 B.C., extends through the rise and fall of Puebloan people around A.D. 300, and includes the Spanish Entrada by Alvar

Nunez Cabeza de Vaca in 1535 as he made his way from a shipwreck in the Gulf of Mexico. Five years later Coronado captained the first organized expedition through the Mesilla Valley, and in 1598 Don Juan de Oñate led colonists along El Camino Real, which passed through Las Cruces and Mesilla.

With the ratification of the Gadsden Purchase in 1854, Las Cruces became a major supply center for Organ Mountain miners and soldiers stationed at Fort Selden. Nearby Mesilla was a major stopover on the Butterfield Overland Stage route.

Today Las Cruces is both a cultural and agricultural center. Fields of cotton, groves of pecans, and acres of vineyards dot the outskirts. One of the largest single growers of pecans, with several million pounds harvested annually, Stahmann Farms groves are positioned on the site of an ancient lake bed south of the city. Their company store is a good place to buy pecans and pecan candy, and a drive through their groves is a cool treat on a sunny day.

Local products are featured every Wednesday and Saturday morning, when over 200 local growers sell fruit, vegetables, herbs, honey, and baked goods at the Farmer's & Crafts Market at the open-air market on the Downtown Mall. Artists and craftspeople add their wares to the mélange.

At the north end of the mall, the Bicentennial Log Cabin, originally located in the Black Range, houses authentic furnishings and artifacts. Open only the first and third Saturday of the month, special tours may be arranged by contacting the Branigan Cultural Center.

Among the city's galleries and museums, the New Mexico State University Museum in Kent Hall stands out. Fronted by a beautifully landscaped courtyard, the museum's eclectic collection includes pottery by San Ildefonso's famous Blue Corn; a Zuni woman's manta (or shawl); the leather helmet, football, and shoes belonging to Homer Powers, class of 1916, who captained the Aggies to the Southwest championship; and a lariat said to have belonged to Pancho Villa. A whole gallery and the front room are reserved for changing exhibits, and every object is well displayed and labeled. An excellent gift shop stocks Southwestern jewelry, tin and clay work from Mexico, and other crafts.

Anyone visiting Las Cruces should take time to drive out Dripping Springs Road (the western extension of University Avenue) to visit New Mexico's newest state museum. Located on 47 acres at the base of the Organ Mountains, the New Mexico Farm and Ranch Heritage Museum chronicles the 3,000-year history of New Mexico's agricultural and rural life. Children in particular will enjoy visiting the corrals populated by longhorn cattle, dairy cows, churro sheep, Jerusalem donkeys, and all their furry progeny. In the dairy barn twice daily milking demonstrations are conducted, with the resulting milk bottle-fed to the baby calves.

The museum building itself is a commodious structure of 25,000 square feet with space for permanent and changing exhibits, a state-of-the-art theater, a kitchen, and classrooms. The expansive lobby, with a clerestory and a truss-and-beam pitched roof, is designed to resemble a hacienda or ranch house. The massive stone floor-to-ceiling fireplace wall is reminiscent of early buildings at Chaco Canyon, while the polished concrete floor is reflective of the hardened-blood floors found in early Spanish colonial structures. Adjacent to the lobby, the Museum Mercantile gift shop imitates an old-time general store with its tin ceiling. It offers books, gardening supplies, New Mexican food products, jewelry, cowboy gear, and more.

Wings stretch out to right and left. The main gallery in the north wing features a diverse range of artifacts focusing on key aspects of agriculture and rural life. Set against giant suspended backdrops illustrating turn-of-the-century photographs, the exhibit explores a variety of themes: hand tools, horse-drawn implements, harness and tack, making hay, windmills and water, "making do," mercantiles, and mail order. Each area includes a segment entitled "Voices of New Mexico," a first-hand account of people whose lives were spent in the fields and ranch lands of the state. In addition, the north wing houses a smaller gallery for changing exhibits.

The south wing contains the theater and a full-service restaurant, the Purple Sage, specializing in New Mexican cuisine such as grilled chicken with chile-cream sauce or lighter fare such as black bean nachos or fajita salad. The porches, or *portillos*, stretch the width of the building, and during the summer, a farmers market with native produce is held beneath their sheltering frame. There's an outdoor amphitheater for special events, and special living history demonstrations are conducted throughout the year.

After catching glimpses of the nearby Organ Mountains from almost every vantage point of the museum, you may be inclined to inspect them up close and personal. Continue east on Dripping Springs Road, up beyond the pavement's ending to the A. B. Cox visitors center of Dripping Springs Natural Area. From this location, you may access the popular La Cueva and Dripping Springs Trails.

La Cueva leads to a rock shelter, an archaeological site associated with the Jornada branch of the prehistoric Mogollon culture. In the late 1860s the cave was home to Giovanni Maria Agostini, an Italian nobleman, faith healer, and bona fide hermit who was murdered in the spring of 1869. His assailant was never found.

Dripping Springs Trail leads from the visitors center to the site of a resort complex built by Colonel Eugene Van Patten in the 1870s. Hikers pass the ruins of the sanatorium, the resort, and the old coach stop. The rocky but beautiful 1.5-mile trail climbs 560 vertical feet and dead-ends above the spring. Be sure to take water and wear sturdy walking shoes.

Las Cruces is blessed with a variety of accommodations, none more appealing than the Inn of the Arts in the historic district across from the First National Towers Building. A combined gallery and bed-and-breakfast, the inn is owned by Linda and Gerald Lundeen, who restored two homes constructed by William Henry Harrison Llewellyn, a member of the New Mexico House of Representatives. Gerald, a noted architect whose passion is the preservation of old structures, designed the addition that joined the two buildings and provided room for both his office and an art gallery for Linda.

All 20 guest rooms are named for well-known Southwestern artists and are furnished with original art and antiques. The common area, the Merienda Room, soars two stories with massive arched French doors leading to two of many patios and outdoor seating areas. Guests gather here for the ample breakfast or to gossip about the day's adventures. The inn is popular with visitors in the arts community, and frequently hosts special Elderhostel programs.

Searching the nearby streets for signs of a pleasant dining experience, you may recoil from the proliferation of same old, same old, chains. If you're a devotee of Asian cooking, Tatsu on nearby El Paseo, with its Japanese and fusion cuisine, is a more satisfying choice. You can sit at the sushi bar and order any number of nigiri, maki te-maki, or sashimi preparations or choose to dine at a banquette framed by cormandel screens and hangings of silk kimonos. The adventurous might try the "Taste of Japan" special, with miso soup, salad, yakitori (grilled chicken on skewers with teriyaki sauce), negi maki (spring onions wrapped in sliced beef), harumaki (spring roll), gyoza (dumplings), sushi (California maki), and shrimp and vegetable tempura. Ordered for two or more, the meal is a sensate experience.

Most visitors to the area spend a day in neighboring Mesilla, a historic village dating to the 1500s. The Gadsden

Purchase was signed on the plaza in 1854, annexing Mesilla to the United States and fixing the international boundaries of New Mexico and Arizona. In 1861 the village was the western headquarters of the Confederacy. The shady plaza is highlighted by San Albino Church, one of the oldest in the valley, and ringed by upscale shops selling everything from fancy Southwestern duds to fine art. The Galeria on the Plaza specializes in folk art; Del Sol stocks Navajo and Zuni jewelry, imported cottons, South American and Mexican handicrafts, Zapotec rugs and souvenirs. Sister store, La Zia features Indian jewelry, pottery, storytellers, fetishes, sand paintings, and Navajo rugs. You can buy an ice-cream cone or a pound of homemade fudge at J. Eric Chocolatier, browse tomes on the Southwest and Americana at the Mesilla Book Center, or taste vintages at the Blue Teal Winery.

Hungry or thirsty? Sip a latte at the Kokopelli Cafe, treat yourself to lunch or dinner in elegant surroundings at the Double Eagle, specializing in American and Continental cuisine, or visit El Patio Restaurante, founded by Arthur and Celia Fountain in 1934 and currently run by Barbara Fountain-Johnson.

Perhaps the plaza's most popular restaurant is La Posta. Earliest records indicate the building was constructed in the 1840s and in the 1850s served as a freight and passenger stop for service to Pinos Altos. After the Civil War, it became a stage station on the Butterfield Overland Mail Route, and during the 1870s and 1880s the Corn Exchange Hotel operated from the structure.

In 1939 Katy Camuñez Meeks originated the Posta de Mesilla restaurant in the northwest corner of the old adobe, and she operated it, expanded it, and left her indelible imprint upon it until her death, when the property was acquired by her great-niece Jerean Camuñez Hutchinson and Hutchinson's husband, Hutch. The list of habitues runs the gamut from famous to infamous: Billy the Kid, Kit Carson, Pancho Villa, and General Douglas MacArthur.

La Posta's unassuming exterior belies a surprisingly exotic interior. You enter through what once was a *zaguan*, a wide sheltered entry, and pass several small shops—a jeweler, a clothing boutique, and a store selling New Mexico products. Entering the enclosed patio, with its tangle of plants and commodious aviary, you're greeted by the squawks and whistles of parrots, cockatiels, a cockatoo, and Simon, an ancient African gray. Red piranha swim lazily in their tanks.

The dining room fronting Calle de Guadalupe was the original eating house, but as the years passed, additional structures were added and parts of the building devoted to other uses were converted to dining. The Lava Room is their most requested seating, with its wall covered with basalt boulders, its abundance of plants, and its romantic atmosphere. Food is traditional New Mexican, and steaks are an additional specialty.

Military history buffs should make the short journey north to Radium Springs, where Fort Selden State Monument is located. This post, built in 1865, quartered the famous Buffalo Soldiers, the unit of black cavalry charged with protecting valley settlers from Apache raids. In later years Fort Selden was the boyhood home of General Douglas MacArthur, whose father was post commander. The visitors center has a 10-minute video on the fort's history and exhibits on day-to-day military life.

Fort Selden's adobe walls are now ruins gradually melting back into the earth, but walking the sunlit path among sheltering cottonwoods you can almost hear the echoes of bugle calls and the commands of the calvary officers mustering their troops.

For More Information

Truth or Consequences/Sierra County Chamber of Commerce, 201 South Foch, P.O. Box 31, Truth or Consequences, NM 87901. Call 505-894-3536.

Los Arcos, 1400 North Date, Truth or Consequences, NM 87901. Call 505-894-6200. Open in summer, Friday and Saturday from 5:00 to 11:30 P.M., Sunday through Thursday from 5:00 to 10:30 P.M.; in winter, Monday through Friday from 5:00 to 9:30 P.M., Saturday and Sunday from 5:00 to 10:30 P.M.

Bar-B-Que on Broadway, 308 Broadway, Truth or Consequences, NM 87901. Call 505-894-7047. Open daily from 6:00 A.M. to 4:00 P.M.

Geronimo Springs Museum, 211 Main, Truth or Consequences, NM 87901. Call 505-894-6600. Open Monday through Saturday from 9:00 A.M. to 5:00 P.M. Fee.

Marshall Miracle Hot Springs, 311 Marr, Truth or Consequences, NM 87901. Call 505-894-9286. Open daily from 8:00 A.M. to 8:00 P.M.

Hay-Yo-Kay Hot Springs, 300 Austin, Truth or Consequences, NM 87901. Call 505-894-2228 for hours. Closed Wednesday.

Indian Springs Pools, 200 Pershing, Truth or Consequences, NM 87901. Call 505-894-3823. Fee.

Artesian Bath House, 312 Marr, Truth or Consequences, NM 87901. Call 505-894-2684. Open Friday and Saturday from 8:00 A.M. to 7:00 P.M., Sunday, Tuesday, and Thursday from 8:00 A.M. to 6:00 P.M. Closed Wednesday. Fee.

Riverbend Hot Springs Hostel, 100 Austin, Truth or Consequences, NM 87901. Call 505-894-6183. Open daily from 10:00 A.M. to 9:00 P.M.

The Silvered South 197

Charles Motel & Bath House, 601 Broadway, Truth or Consequences, NM 87901. Call 505-894-7154. Fee.

Xochi's, 430 Broadway, Truth or Consequences, NM 87901. Call 505-894-7685. Open Tuesday through Saturday from 9:00 A.M. to 5:00 P.M.

Second Hand Rose, 311 Broadway, Truth or Consequences, NM 87901.

U-Name-It/Gift Shop, 108 Main, Truth or Consequences, NM 87901. Open in summer, daily 9:00 A.M. to 6:00 P.M.; in winter, 9:00 A.M. to 5:00 P.M.

Chateau Sassenage, P.O. Box 1606, Truth or Consequences (Engle), NM 87901. Call 505-894-7244. Call for appointment.

Buffalo Bill's Cactus Ranch & Succulent Farm, 1600 South Broadway, Truth or Consequences, NM 87901. Call 505-894-0790. Open Monday and Wednesday through Sunday from 9:00 A.M. to 6:00 P.M. Closed Tuesday.

Black Range Museum and Library, Main Street, P.O. Box 454, Hillsboro, NM 88042. Call 505-895-5233. Open March 1–December 31, Tuesday through Saturday from 11:00 A.M. to 4:00 P.M. Call to confirm hours.

Hidden Treasures Gift Shop, 101 Main Street, Hillsboro, NM 88042. Call 505-895-5631. Open Monday through Saturday from 10:00 A.M. to 5:00 P.M.

Sweetwood Bar-B-Q & Hillsboro Orchard, NM 152 (one mile west of town), Hillsboro, NM 88042. Call 505-895-5642/3317. Open in summer, daily from 11:00 A.M. to 7:00 P.M.; in winter, Thursday through Sunday from 11:00 A.M. to 7:00 P.M.

Black Range Business Association , P.O. Box 152, Hillsboro, NM 88042.

The Black Range Lodge, Star Route 2, Box 119, Kingston, NM 88042. Call 505-895-5652. Website: www.vianet.com \blackrange.

Doc Campbell's Post, NM 15, Gila Hot Springs. Mail: HC 68, Box 80, Silver City, NM 88061. Call 505-536-9551. Open in summer, daily from 8:00 A.M. to 6:00 P.M.; in winter, daily from 9:00 A.M. to 4:30 P.M.

Gila Cliff Dwellings National Monument, NM 15, Gila Hot Springs. Mail: HC 68, Box 100, Silver City, NM 88061. Call 505-536-9461. Visitors center open in summer, daily from 8:00 A.M. to 5:00 P.M.; in winter, daily from 8:00 A.M. to 4:30 P.M. Fee. Website: www.nps.gov/gicl.

Buckhorn Saloon and Opera House, Main Street, Pinos Altos, NM 88053. Call 505-538-9911. Dinner served Monday through Saturday from 6:00 to 10:00 P.M. Saloon open Monday through Saturday 3:00 to 11:00 P.M. Reservations requested.

Fort Cobre Trading Post and Fort Santa Rita del Cobre, 25 Main Street, Pinos Altos, NM. Mail: 22112 Pinon Street, Silver City, NM 88061. Call 505-388-2211. Open in summer only, Tuesday through Saturday from 10:00 A.M. to 5:00 P.M.

Pinos Altos Museum and Log Cabin Curio Shop, 33 Main Street, Pinos Altos, NM. Mail: P.O. Box 53083, Pinos Altos, NM 88053. Call 505-388-1882. Open in summer, Monday through Saturday from 9:00 A.M. to 6:00 P.M., Sunday from 9:00 A.M. to 5:00 P.M.; in winter, daily from 9:00 A.M. to 5:00 P.M.

Silver City/Grant County Chamber of Commerce, 201 North Hudson (corner of Hudson and Broadway), Silver City, NM 88061. Call 505-538-3785. Open Monday through Saturday from 9:00 A.M. to 5:00 P.M.

Silver City Museum & Museum Store, 312 West Broadway, Silver City, NM 88061. Call 505-538-5921. Open Tuesday through Friday from 9:00 A.M. to 4:30 P.M., Saturday and Sunday from 10:00 A.M. to 4:00 P.M. Closed Monday.

Silver City Trading Company Antique Mall, 205 West Broadway, Silver City, NM 88062. Call 505-388-8989. Open Monday through Saturday from 10:00 A.M. to 6:00 P.M., Sunday from noon to 4:00 P.M.

Fire Cloud Traders, 209 West Broadway, Silver City, NM 88061. Call 505-538-5376. Open Monday through Saturday from 10:00 A.M. to 5:30 P.M.

Yankie Creek Gallery, 217 North Bullard Street, Silver City, NM 88061. Call 505-538-5232. Open daily from 10:00 A.M. to 5:00 P.M.

What's a Pot Shop, 300 North Arizona, Silver City, NM 88061. Call 505-388-2007. Open Monday through Saturday from 9:00 A.M. to 5:00 P.M.

O'Keefe's Book Shop, 102 West Broadway, Silver City, NM 88061. Call 505-388-3313. Open in summer, Monday through Saturday from 10:00 A.M. to 5:00 P.M.; in winter, Tuesday through Saturday from 10:00 A.M. to 5:30 P.M.

Adobe Springs Cafe, Pinon Plaza, 1617 Silver Heights Boulevard (corner Silver and Bullard), Silver City, NM 88061. Call 505-538-3665. Open Monday through Saturday from 11:30 A.M. to 8:00 P.M., Sunday from 8:00 A.M. to 3:00 P.M.

Western New Mexico University Museum, Fleming Hall, 10th Street, Silver City, NM 88061. Call 505-538-6386. Open Monday through Friday from 9:00 A.M. to 4:30 P.M., Saturday and Sunday from 10:00 A.M. to 4:00 P.M.

The Cottages at Pinon Canyon Hideaway, 2037 Cottage San
Road, P.O. Box 2562, Silver City, NM 88062. Call 505-388-
3000 or 800-938-3001.

Bear Mountain Guest Ranch, 2251 Bear Mountain Road, P.O. Box
1163 CC, Silver City, NM 88062. Call 505-538-2538 or 800-
880-2538. Website: www.BearMtGuestRanch.com.

El Charro Cafe, 209 Southern Pacific Boulevard, P.O. Box 428,
Lordsburg, NM 88045. Call 505-542-9121. Open daily 24
hours.

Lordsburg/Hidalgo County Chamber of Commerce, 208 Motel
Drive, Lordsburg, NM 88045. Call 505-542-9864. Website:
www.gila.net.com/lordsburgcoc.

Lordsburg Visitor Information Center, I-10, exit 20. Call 505-542-
8149. Open daily from 8:00 A.M. to 5:00 P.M.

Shakespeare Ghost Town (2½ miles south of Lordsburg),
P.O. Box 253, Lordsburg, NM 88045. Call 505-542-9034.
Tours at 10:00 A.M. and 2:00 P.M. on the second Sunday
and preceding Saturday of the month. Other times by
appointment only. Fee.

Steins, exit 3, I-10. Mail: P.O. Box 2185, Roadforks, NM 88045.
Call 505-542-9791. Open daily from 9:00 A.M. to dark. Fee.

City of Rocks State Park (28 miles northeast of Deming via U.S.
180 and NM 61), P.O. Box 54, Faywood, NM 88034. Call 505-
536-2800. Gates open daily at 7:00 A.M., close at 9:00 P.M.
Fee.

Faywood Hot Springs (NM 61) HC 71, Box 1240, Faywood, NM
88034. Call 505-536-9663. RV park, tepee, and travel trailer
lodging. Fee. Website: www.faywood.com.

Deming-Luna County Chamber of Commerce and Visitors Center, Deming Depot, 800 East Pine, Deming. Mail: P.O. Box 8, Deming, NM 88030. Call 505-546-8757 or 800-848-4955.

Deming Luna Mimbres Museum, 301 South Silver, Deming, NM 88030. Call 505-546-2382. Open Monday through Saturday from 9:00 A.M. to 4:00 P.M., Sunday from 1:30 to 4:00 P.M.

Historic Custom House, 304 South Silver, Deming, NM 88030. Call 505-546-2382. Open Monday through Saturday from 12:30 to 4:00 P.M., Sunday from 1:30 to 4:00 P.M.

St. Clair Vineyards, NM 549, three miles from exit 85, I-10. Mail: P.O. Box 11880, Deming, NM 88031. Call 505-546-9324. Open Monday through Saturday from 10:00 A.M. to 6:00 P.M., Sunday from noon to 5:00 P.M. Tours on Saturdays.

Rockhound State Park, 14 miles southeast of Deming via NM 11 and Road 141. Mail: P.O. Box 1064, Deming, NM 88031. Call 505-546-6182. Open daily from 7:00 A.M. to sundown.

Si Señor Restaurant, 200 East Pine, Deming, NM 88030. Call 505-546-3938. Open daily from 9:30 A.M. to 8:30 P.M.

Pancho Villa State Park, P.O. Box 450, Columbus, NM 88029. Call 505-531-2711. Visitors center open daily from 8:00 A.M. to 5:00 P.M.

Columbus Historical Society Museum, P.O. Box 562, Columbus, NM 88029. Call 505-531-2620. Open daily from 10:00 A.M. to 4:00 P.M.

The Pink Store (Casa de Pancho Villa Restaurant and Bar), Puerto Palomas, Chihuahua, Mexico. Phone: 01152-166-60106.

Stahman's Store, P.O. Box 130, San Miguel, NM 88058-0130 (NM 28, seven miles south of Las Cruces). Call 505-526-8974 or 800-654-6887. Open Monday through Friday from 9:00 A.M. to 5:30 P.M., Saturday and Sunday from 10:00 A.M. to 5:00 P.M.

Las Cruces Farmers & Crafts Market, Downtown Mall, Las Cruces, NM. Open Wednesday and Saturday mornings.

Bicentennial Log Cabin, north end of Downtown Mall, Las Cruces, NM. Call 505-541-2155. Open first and third Saturday of the month.

Las Cruces Convention & Visitors Bureau, 311 North Downtown Mall, Las Cruces, NM 88001. Call 505-524-8521 or 800-343-7827. Open daily from 8:00 A.M. to 5:00 P.M.

New Mexico State University Museum, Kent Hall, University Avenue at Solano, Silver City, NM 88061. Call 505-646-3739. Open Tuesday through Saturday from noon to 4:00 P.M. Closed Sunday, Monday, and university holidays.

New Mexico Farm and Ranch Heritage Museum, 4100 Dripping Springs Road, P.O. Drawer 1898, Las Cruces, NM 88004. Call 505-522-4100. Open Wednesday through Saturday from 9:00 A.M. to 5:00 P.M., Sunday from noon to 5:00 P.M. Milking demonstrations Wednesday through Sunday at 11:00 A.M. and 3:00 P.M. Will be open six days a week starting in late 1999, so call for hours. Fee.

Dripping Springs Natural Area and La Cueva, A. B. Cox Visitors Center, 15000 Dripping Springs Road, Las Cruces, NM 88001. Call 505-522-1219. Open year-round, daily from 8:00 A.M. to sunset. Dripping Springs Trail closes at 3:00 P.M. in winter. Fee.

Inn of the Arts, 618 South Alameda, Las Cruces, NM 88005. Call 505-526-3327 or 3326.

Tatsu, 930 El Paseo, Las Cruces, NM 88001. Call 505-526-7144. Open Monday through Saturday from 11:00 A.M. to 2:30 P.M., Sunday through Thursday from 5:00 to 9:00 P.M., and Friday and Saturday from 5:00 to 10:00 P.M.

San Albino Catholic Church, 2280 Calle Principal, Old Mesilla Plaza, Mesilla. Mail: P.O. Box 26, Mesilla, NM 88046. Call 505-526-9349. Visiting hours daily except Monday from 1:00 to 3:00 P.M. Call to confirm.

Galleria on the Plaza, 2310 Calle Principal, Old Mesilla Plaza, Mesilla. Mail: P.O. Box 1017, Mesilla, NM 88046. Call 505-526-9771. Open Monday through Saturday from 10:00 A.M. to 5:00 P.M., Sunday from noon to 5:00 P.M.

Del Sol, 2322 Calle Principal, Mesilla Plaza, P.O. Box 1098, Mesilla, NM 88046. Call 505-524-1418. Open daily from 10:00 A.M. to 6:00 P.M.

La Zia, 2340 Calle Principal, Old Mesilla Plaza, P.O. Box 1098, Mesilla, NM 88046. Call 505-523-2213. Open daily from 10:00 A.M. to 6:00 P.M.

J. Eric Chocolatier, 2379 Calle de Guadalupe, Old Mesilla Plaza, Mesilla. Mail: P.O. Box 1073, Mesilla, NM 88046. Call 505-526-2744. Open Tuesday through Saturday from 10:30 A.M. to 6:00 P.M., Sunday and Monday noon to 5:00 P.M.

Mesilla Book Center, 2360 Calle Principal, Old Mesilla Plaza, Mesilla. Mail: P.O. Box 96, Mesilla, NM 88046. Call 505-526-6220. Open Tuesday through Saturday from 11:00 A.M. to 5:30 P.M., Sunday from 1:00 to 5:00 P.M. Closed Monday.

Blue Teal Vineyards Wine Tasting Room, 2461 Calle de Guadalupe (next to Old Fountain Theater), Old Mesilla, NM 88046. Call 505-524-0390. Open Thursday through Saturday from 10:00 A.M. to 5:00 P.M., Sunday through Wednesday from 1:00 to 5:00 P.M.

Kokopelli Cafe, 2210 Calle de Parian, Old Mesilla Plaza, Mesilla, NM 88046. Call 505-524-1929. Open Monday through Saturday from 11:00 A.M. to 5:00 P.M., Sunday from noon to 5:00 P.M.

Double Eagle de la Mesilla, 3255 Calle de Guadalupe, Old Mesilla Plaza, Mesilla. Mail: P.O. Drawer 905, Las Cruces, NM 88004. Call 505-523-6700. Open Monday through Saturday from 11:00 A.M. to 10:00 P.M., Sunday till 9:00 P.M.

El Patio Restaurante, 2171 Calle de Parian, Old Mesilla Plaza, Mesilla. Mail: P.O. Box 1202, Las Cruces, NM 88001. Call 505-524-0982. Open Monday through Thursday from 11:00 A.M. to 2:00 P.M. and 5:00 to 9:00 P.M., Friday and Saturday from 5:00 to 9:30 P.M.

La Posta de Mesilla, 2410 Calle de San Albino, Old Mesilla Plaza, P.O. Box 116, Mesilla, NM 88046. Call 505-524-3524. Open Sunday through Thursday from 11:00 A.M. to 9:00 P.M., Friday and Saturday from 11:00 A.M. to 9:30 P.M. Closed Monday.

Fort Selden State Monument, P.O. Box 58, Radium Springs, NM 88054. Call 505-526-8911. Open daily from 8:30 A.M. to 5:00 P.M. Fee.

Other Sources of Information

Albuquerque Bed & Breakfast Association, 414 C de Baca Lane NW, Albuquerque, NM 87114. 505-897-0431.

Albuquerque Visitors Guide, Albuquerque Convention & Visitors Bureau, 20 First Plaza, Suite 601, P.O. Box 26866, Albuquerque, NM 87125. 800-284-2282 or 505-842-9918. Website: www/abqcvb/org.

Bureau of Land Management (1474 Rodeo Road), P.O. Box 27115, Santa Fe, NM 87505. 505-438-7400. Website: www.publiclandsinfo.org.

Highway hotline, call 800-432-4269. Website: www.nmshtd.state.nm.us.

Indian Pueblo Cultural Center, 2401 12th Street NW, Albuquerque, NM 87102. 800-766-4405 outside New Mexico; in state, 505-843-7270.

Jicarilla Apache, Jicarilla Game and Fish, P.O. Box 507, Dulce, NM 87528. 505-759-3242.

Mescalero Apache, P.O. Box 176, Mescalero, NM 88340. 505-671-4495.

National Forest Service, Southwest Regional Office, 517 Gold Avenue SW, Albuquerque, NM 87102. 505-842-3898. Website: www.recreation.gov or www.fs.fed.us/r3.

National Park Service, Southwest Regional Office, 1100 Old Santa Fe Trail, Santa Fe, NM 87501. 505-988-6100. Website: www.nps.gov.

Navajoland Tourism Department, Window Rock, AZ. 520-871-6436 or 505-871-7371.

New Mexico Bed & Breakfast Association, P.O. Box 2925, Santa Fe, NM 87504-2925. 800-661-6649 or 505-766-5380. Website: www.nmbba.org.

New Mexico Department of Fish and Game, P.O. Box 25112, Santa Fe, NM 87504. 800-862-9310. Website: www.gmfsh.state.nm.us.

New Mexico Office of Cultural Affairs, 228 East Palace Avenue, Santa Fe, NM 87503. 505-827-6364. Website: www.nmmnh-abq.mus.nm.us/oca/oca.html.

New Mexico Park and Recreation Division (408 Galisteo Street), P.O. Box 1147, Santa Fe, NM 87504-1147. 888-NM-PARKS or 505-827-7473. Website: www.emnrd.state.nm.us.

Public Lands Information Center. Santa Fe Office, 1474 Rodeo Road, Santa Fe, NM 87505. 505-438-PLIC. Roswell Office, 2909 West Second Street, Roswell, NM 88201. 505-627-0210.

New Mexico Road & Recreation Atlas, Benchmark Maps, 25 East Mason Street, Santa Barbara, CA 94707. 800-898-NMEX or 805-965-4402.

New Mexico Vacation Guide and/or Outdoor and Recreation Guide, Department of Tourism, 491 Old Santa Fe Trail, Santa Fe, NM 87501-2753. 800-545-2040, ext. 751. Website: www.newmexico.org.

Online New Mexico information: www.NMSource.com.

Pueblos:

Acoma, P.O. Box 309, Acoma, NM 87034. 800-747-0181 or 505-252-1139.

Cochití, P.O. Box 70, Cochití, NM 87072. 505-465-2244.

Isleta, Box 317, Isleta, NM 87022. 505-869-3111.

Jemez, P.O. Box 100, Jemez, NM 87024. 505-834-7235.

Laguna, P.O. Box 194, Laguna, NM 87026. 505-552-6654 or 505-243-7616.

Nambe, Route 1, Box 117BB, Santa Fe, NM 87501. 505-455-2036 or 800-94NAMBE.

Picuris, P.O. Box 127, Penasco, NM 87553. 505-587-2957.

Pojoaque, Route 11, Box 127, Santa Fe, NM 87501. 505-455-2278.

San Filipe, P.O. Box 4339, San Felipe Pueblo, NM 87001. 505-867-3381.

San Ildefonso, Route 5, Box 315A, Santa Fe, NM 87501. 505-455-2273.

San Juan, P.O. Box 1099, San Juan, NM 87566. 505-852-4400.

Sandia, P.O. Box 6008, Bernalillo, NM 87004. 505-867-3317.

Santa Ana, 2 Dove Road, Santa Ana, NM 87004. 505-867-3301.

Santa Clara, P.O. Box 580, Española, NM 87532. 505-753-7326.

Santo Domingo, P.O. Box 99, Santo Domingo, NM 87052. 505-465-2214.

Taos, P.O. Box 1846, Taos, NM 87571. 505-758-1028.

Tesuque, Route 5, Box 360T, Santa Fe, NM 87501. 505-983-2667.

Zia, 135 Capital Square, Zia Pueblo, NM 87053. 505-867-3304.

Zuni, P.O. Box 339, Zuni, NM 87327. 505-782-4481.

Santa Fe Visitors Guide, City of Santa Fe Convention & Visitors Bureau, 201 West Marcy Street, Santa Fe. Mail: P.O. Box 909, Santa Fe, NM 87504-0909. Call 800-777-2489. Website: www.santafe.org.

Ski New Mexico, P.O. Box 1104, Santa Fe, NM 87504. 800-755-7669. Website: www.skinewmexico.com.

Taos Bed & Breakfast Association, P.O. Box 2772, Taos, NM 87571. 800-876-7857 or 505-758-4747. Website: www.taoswebb.com/BedandBreakfast.

Taos Visitors Guide and Visitor Center, Taos County Chamber of Commerce, 1139 Paseo del Pueblo Sur, P.O. Drawer I, Taos, NM 87571. 800-732-8267 or 505-758-3873. Website: www.taoswebb.com/TAOS.

U.S. Army Corps of Engineers, Albuquerque District, 4101 Jefferson Plaza NE, Albuquerque, NM 87109. Website: www.usace.army.mil.

Welcome Centers:

Anthony Welcome Center, P.O. Box 1270, Interstate 10, Anthony, NM 88021. 505-882-2419.

Chama Welcome Center, P.O. Box 697, U.S. 64/84, Chama, NM 87520. 505-756-2235.

Gallup Welcome Center, 701-A East Montoya Boulevard, Gallup, NM 87301. 505-863-4909.

Glenrio Welcome Center, 37315 C I-40, exit 373, Glenrio, NM 88434. 505-576-2424.

La Bajada Welcome Center, 17 miles south of Santa Fe on I-25. 505-424-0823.

Lordsburg Welcome Center, P.O. Box 132, I-10 rest area, exit 20, Lordsburg, NM 88045. 505-542 8149.

New Mexico/Santa Fe Welcome Center, 491 Old Santa Fe Trail, The Lamy Building, Santa Fe, NM 87503. 505-827-7336.

Raton Welcome Center, 100 Clayton Road, Raton, NM 87740. 505-445-2716.

Texico Welcome Center, No. 336 U.S. Highway 60-70-84, Texico, NM 88135. 505-482-3321.

Index

Abiquiu, New Mexico, 24, 28–33
Abiquiu Inn, 31, 43
Acoma, New Mexico, 207
Adams, Ansel, 28
Adobe Spring Cafe, 182, 199
Aguilar, Irene, 4
Alamogordo, New Mexico, 136–37
Alamogordo Chamber of
    Commerce, 143
Albuquerque Bed and Breakfast
    Association, 205
Albuquerque Visitors Guide, 205
Allison, Clay, 80
Alvarado, Hernando de, 107
American Museum of Natural
    History, 55
Anasazi people, viii, x, 112
Anderson, Robert, 132
Anderson-Freeman Museum, 131
Angel Fire, New Mexico, 78,
    86, 87
Angel Fire Resort Chamber of
    Commerce, 87
Angel Fire Ski Area, 78, 86
Anthony Welcome Center, 209
Antique Accents, 76, 86
Antiques, 73, 76, 85, 86
Antonio, Johnson, 60
Antonio, Sheila, 60
Antrim, Catherine McCarthy, 181
Apaches, x, 180, 184
    living conditions, xi–xii
Aragon, Kelly, 51
Archaic period, viii
Arcos, Los, 172, 196
Armstrong, Neil, 137
Art Space, 98, 103
Artesian Bath House, 173, 196

A:shiwi A:wan Museum and
    Heritage Center, 157, 166
Atchison, Topeka & Santa Fe
    Railroad, 71, 97, 123, 147
Atencio, Larry, 26
Atencio, Pete, 26
Attic, The, 60, 67
Aztec, New Mexico, x, 54–55
Aztec Chamber of Commerce, 66
Aztec Mill, 81, 87
Aztec Museum, 56, 66
Aztec Ruins National Monument,
    55, 66

Babbitt's Cottonwood Trading Post,
    17, 22
Baca, Adolfo, 123
Baca, Angie, 163
Baca, Della, 147
Baca, Donald, 147
Baca, Larry, 163
Baca, Richard, 2
Baca, Rowena, 123
Badelier, Adolph Francis, 10
Baker's Hearth Restaurant, 64, 68
Balagna, John, 12
Balagna Winery, 12, 20
Ball, Marion, 5
Bandelier, New Mexico, x
Bandelier National Monument, 10,
    11, 20
Bandelier volcanic tuff, 6
Bandera Volcano and Ice Caves, 162,
    167
Bar-B-Que on Broadway, 172, 196
Barns, Charliene, 61
Batchelor, Carol, 54
Batchelor, Don, 54

Batchelor, Harry, 54
Battleship Rock hot springs, 8
Beadwork, 157
Bear Mountain Guest Ranch, 183, 200
Beasley, Jack, 59–60
Beasley Folk Art, 59, 67
Bed and breakfasts
   Albuquerque Bed and Breakfast Association, 205
   Black Range Lodge, The, 176, 198
   Carriage House Bed and Breakfast, 74–75
   Casa Blanca Bed and Breakfast, 58–59, 66
   Cimarron Rose Bed & Breakfast, 161, 167
   Elaine's: A Bed and Breakfast, 90
   Hacienda Grande, La, 3, 19
   Inn of the Arts, 193, 202
   New Mexico Bed & Breakfast Association, 206
   Renata's Orange Street Bed & Breakfast, 17, 22
Bedre, Linda, 9
Belen, New Mexico, 110
   Greater Belen Chamber of Commerce, 118
Benally family, 60
Bernalillo, New Mexico, 2–4
Best Kept Secrets Emporium, 2, 19
Bicentennial Log Cabin, 191, 202
Big Ditch Park, 181
Big Rock Shopping Center, 25
Billing, Gustav, 151
Billy the Kid, 130–31, 181
Billy the Kid Casino, 133, 142
Birch, Thomas, 179
Bird, Doren, 96
Black Jack's Restaurant, 75
Black Mesa, 107
Black Mountains, 175

Black Range Business Association, 197
Black Range Lodge, The, 176, 198
Black Range Museum and Library, 175, 197
Blanco Trading Post, 54, 66
Blea, Jesus, 162
Blue Front Bar & Cafe, 153, 166
Blue Teal Vineyards Wine Tasting Room, 194, 203
Blue Window bistro, 16, 22
Bluewater Dam, 162
Bode's General Merchandise, 32, 43
Bonney, William, 130–31
Bootheel, 184
Borrego Pass Trading Post, 61, 68
Bosque del Apache National Wildlife Refuge, 124, 139
Box Car Museum, 151
Bradbury, Norris, 15
Bradbury Science Museum, 15–16, 21
Bradford, Anne, 74
Bradford, John, 74
Brady, William, 131
Branigan Cultural Center, 190
Brett, Dorothy, 32
Brewer, Linda, 93
Brook, Harold H., 13
Brown, C. T., 149
Brown, Patricia, 98
Brown, Todd, 98
Bruno's Resterante y Cantina, El, 49, 65
Buck, Delbert, 60
Buckhorn Saloon and Opera House, 179–80, 198
Buffalo Bill's Cactus Ranch & Succulent Farm, 174, 197
Buffalo Soldiers, 195
Buffalo Tours, 22
Bultos, 100

Index 213

Bureau of Land Management, 127, 205
Burnside, Bob, 56
Burnside, Faith, 56
Byron T's Saloon, 72

Cabezon Peak, 49
Cafe Rio, 134, 142
Cafecito, El, 163, 167
Cambio, 96, 102
Camino Real, El, 2, 99, 111, 147
Campbell, Barbara, 37, 44
Campbell, Karen, 179
Candelaria, Felix, 108
Capitan, New Mexico, 128–29
Capitan Chamber of Commerce, 141
Capitol Saloon, 148
Carine's Jewelry, 97–98, 103
Carne Seca de Santa Fe, 109
Carr, William H., 34
Carriage House Bed and Breakfast, 74–75, 85
Carrizozo, New Mexico, 127
Carrizozo Chamber of Commerce, 140
Carson, Kit, 131
Casa Blanca Bed and Breakfast, 58–59, 66
Casa de Patrón, 130, 141
Casa Grande Trading Post, 98, 103
Cash, Maria Romera, 35
Casita gift shop, La, 94, 101
Catwalk National Recreation Trail, The, 153–54, 168
Cedar Crest, 90
Cerrillos, New Mexico, 97–98
Cerrillos petting zoo, 98
Cerrillos Turquoise Mining Museum, 98
Cerro de Tome, El, 109–10
Chaco, New Mexico, x, 52–54
Chaco Culture National Historical Park, 48, 65

Chaffin, Shane, 54
Chaffin, Tiffany, 54
Chama River, 24
Chama River Canyon Wilderness Area, 35
Chama Welcome Center, 209
Chamizal, New Mexico, 123
Charles Motel & Bath House, 173–74, 197
Charro Cafe, El, 184, 200
Chateau Sassenage winery, 174, 197
Chatters Restaurant and Lounge, Ramada Inn, 59, 67
Chavez, Manuela, 110
Chavez, Pablo, 110
Chihuahuan desert, 138
Children's Field, The, 116–17
Chilili, New Mexico, 116
Chimayo Trading Post / The Marco Polo Shop, 27, 42
Chinaman's Place, 175
Chisum, John, 130
Chitenden, Stanley, 58
Christ of the Desert Monastery, 34, 43
Cibola National Forest, 93
Cicuye, New Mexico, 71
Cienega, La, 99
Cimarron, New Mexico, 79
Cimarron Chamber of Commerce, 87
Cimarron River, 79
Cimarron Rose Bed & Breakfast, 161, 167
City of Las Vegas Museum and Rough Riders Collection, 72, 84
City of Rocks State Park, 186, 200
Clark, Cathy, 174
Cloudcroft, New Mexico, 135
Cloudcroft Chamber of Commerce, 143
Coal Mine Canyon, 164
Coal mining, 94, 97, 151

Cochití, New Mexico, 207
Colalillo, Nancy, 73
Colin Neblett Wildlife Area, 79
Columbine Pottery, 5, 19
Columbus, New Mexico, 188
Columbus Historical Society Museum, 189, 201
Company Stores Building, 96
Connell, A. J., 15
Conner, Wayne, 62
Copperas Vista, 178
Cordova, Jose, 111
Cordova, Kathy, 111
Coronado, Francisco Vásques de, ix, 4, 156
Coronado State Monument, 4, 19
Cottages at Piñón Canyon Hideaway, The, 183, 200
Cottonwood Picnic Area, 12
Counselor, Ann, 51
Counselor, Jim, 51
Counselor, New Mexico, 50
Counselor Trading Post, 50–51, 65
Coyote Creek State Park, 77
Crafts, xi, 3, 17–18, 24, 49, 50, 51, 60, 61, 94, 123. See also specific shops
Crest Trail, 93
Cristo Rey church, 74
Crownpoint, New Mexico, 62–63
Crownpoint Rug Auction, 62, 68
Cuba, New Mexico, 49
Cuba's visitors center, 50, 65
Cueva, La, 192, 202
Cuisine, xii
   Adobe Spring Cafe, 182, 199
   Arcos, Los, 172, 196
   Baker's Hearth Restaurant, 64, 68
   Bar-B-Que on Broadway, 172, 196
   Black Jack's Restaurant, 75, 86
   Blue Front Bar & Cafe, 153, 166
   Blue Window bistro, 16, 22
   Bruno's Resterante y Cantina, El, 49, 65
   Byron T's Saloon, 72
   Cafecito, El, 163, 167
   Carriage House Bed and Breakfast, 75, 85
   Casa Blanca Bed and Breakfast, 58–59, 66
   Charro Cafe, El, 184, 200
   Chatters at Ramada, 59, 67
   Deb's Deli and Mercantile, 8, 20
   Dick's Deli, 76, 86
   Farolito Restaurant, El, 32, 43
   Heck's Hungry Traveler restaurant, 79, 87
   Hill Diner, 15, 21
   Hotel Chango Restaurant and Art Gallery, 129, 140
   Java Junction, 96
   Kokopelli Cafe, 194, 204
   La Lorraine, 135, 143
   Landmark Grill, 72
   Luna Mansion, 108–9
   Matilda's Restaurant, 26, 42
   Meadows Bar and Grill, 75, 86
   Michelenas Italian Restaurant, 135, 143
   Olmos Guest Ranch, Los, 153, 165
   Outpost, The, 127–28, 140
   Paragua, El, 26, 42
   Parasol, El, 26, 42
   Pasadita Cafe, La, 150, 165
   Patio Restaurante, El, 194, 204
   Pete's Cafe, 110, 118
   Poppy's Cafe, 38, 44
   Range Cafe, 2–3
   Rialto's, El, 73, 85
   Saint James Hotel, 81
   San Marcos Cafe, 98–99, 103
   Santa Clara Cafe, 83, 88
   Señor Peppers, 59, 67
   Serape Cafe, El, 155, 166

Shaffer Hotel and Dining Room, 115, 119
Si Señor Restaurant, 188, 201
Silver Bar and Cafe, 49
Silver Dollar Saloon and Restaurant, 131–32, 141
Sweetwood Bar-B-Q & Hillsboro Orchard, 176, 197
Teofilo's, 109, 118
Uranium Cafe, 163, 167
Val Verde Steak House, 150, 165
Curtin, Leonora, 99

Dana, Gladys, 150
Dana Book Store, 150, 165
Dar al Islam Foundation, 36, 43
David Westphall Veterans Foundation, 78
de Baca, Luis Maria C., 71
Dear, David, 24–25, 41
Deb's Deli and Mercantile, 8, 20
Del Sol, 194, 203
Deming, New Mexico, 186–87
Deming-Luna County Chamber of Commerce, 201
Deming Luna Mimbres Museum, 187, 201
Deschillie, Mamie, 60
Dice apartments, 73
Dick's Deli, 76
DiGregory, Matt, 2
Dimit, Paula Saville (studio), 2, 19
Dinosaurs, 4–5
Dinsmore, Dave, 64
Doc Campbell's Post, 178, 198
Dolan, James, 130
Dominguez (Father), 55
Double Eagle de la Mesilla, 194, 204
Doug West Gallery, 148, 164
Dragon River Herbals, 39, 45
Dripping Springs Natural Area, 192, 202

Duke Antiques, 76, 86
Dunnill, Linda, 96
Dwyre, Gay, 123

Eagle Nest, New Mexico, 78–79
Eagle Nest Chamber of Commerce, 87
Eagle Nest Lake, 78
Eames, Charles, 30
"East Mountain," 90
Edwards, Ralph, 171
Eiffel, Alexandre-Gustave, 151
El Rito, New Mexico, 37
El Turquillo, New Mexico, 77
Elaine's: A Bed and Breakfast, 90, 101
Elephant Butte Lake, 170, 172
Engine House Theatre & Mine Shaft Tavern, 95
Entrada, the, ix, 112
Escabosa, New Mexico, 116
Escalante (Father), 55
Española, New Mexico, 24–25
Española Chamber of Commerce, 24–25
Estancia Basin, 112
Excavation of Mound Seven, The, 115

Fabian, Jim, 58
Fabian, Mary, 58
Farmington, New Mexico, 58–61
Farmington Convention & Visitors Bureau, 68
Farolito Restaurant, El, 32, 43
Fathy, Hassam, 36
Faywood Hot Springs, 186, 200
Fenton, Tom, 2
Fenton Lake State Park, 9
Festival of the Cranes, 124, 139
Fire Cloud Traders, 182, 199
Fishing, 78–79
Fitch, Jack, 76

Florence Hawley Ellis Museum of
 Anthropology, 33, 43
Fogelson, E. E. "Buddy," 71
Folk Art Environmentalist, 115
Forked Lightening Ranch, 71
Fort Cobre Trading Post, 180, 198
Fort Meigs, 132
Fort Santa Rita del Cobre, 180, 198
Fort Selden State Monument, 195,
 204
Fort Union National Monument,
 83–84, 88
Fort Worth Spudder Drilling rig, 56
Foutz Indian Room, 60, 67
Franklin, Luanne, 176
Fred Harvey Tours, 27
Free Spirits at Noisy Water, 133, 134
Frijoles Canyon, 10
Fuente, Peter de la, 132
Fuller Lodge, 15, 21
Fust, Peter, 176

Gadsden Purchase, 190, 193–94
Galaviz, Beatriz, 94
Galleria on the Plaza, 194, 203
Galleria West, 134, 142
Gallery of the Sandias, 93, 101
Gallina, New Mexico, 50
Gallup Welcome Center, 209
Garrett, Pat, 131
Garson, Greer, 71
Gateway to Past Heritage Center, 34
Georgia O'Keeffe Foundation,
 29–30, 42
Georgia O'Keeffe Museum, 41, 45
Germain, Mary Jo, 134
Germain, Neil, 134
Geronimo, 173, 184
Geronimo Springs, 172, 196
Geronimo Springs Museum, 172, 196
Ghost Ranch, 24, 29, 32–34
Ghost Ranch Conference Center, 43
Ghost Ranch Living Museum, 34, 43

Ghost towns, 128, 151, 152
Gifted Hand, The, 96, 102
Gila Cliff Dwellings National
 Monument, 178, 198
Gila Hot Springs, 179
Gila National Forest, 154
Glenrio Welcome Center, 209
Gluckman, Richard, 41
Gold Hill, New Mexico, 184
Golden, 93–94
Good Friday pilgrimage, 110
Graham, John T., 153
Granillo, Margarita, 188
Granillo, Raul, 188
Grants, New Mexico, 162
Grants/Cibola Chamber of
 Commerce, 167
Great American Duck Races, 187
Griffo, Joseph, 17
Gross, Billie, 161
Gross, Lou, 161
Groves, Leslie, 13
Gruber, Bernardo, 125
Guadalupita Canyon, 77
Guillen, Matilda, 26
Guillen, Phillip, 26
Guisewa, New Mexico, 8
Guitierrez, Mary, 5
Gutierez de la Chica, Juan, 115–16

Hacienda Grande, La, 3, 19
Hamilton, Greg, 59
Hammel Brewery and Museum, 149,
 164
Hammer, Armand, 73
Harnack, Barbara, 98
Harris, Wayne, 63
Hartman, Lynda, 17
Hartman, Mark, 17
Harvey, Fred, 110
Harvey Girls, 110
Harvey House Museum, 110, 118
Hathale brothers, 60

Háwikuh, New Mexico, viii
Hay-Yo-Kay Hot Springs, 173, 196
Hayes, Alden, 115
Hayes, David, 63
Hayes, Helen, 132, 133
Heath, David, 40
Heck's Hungry Traveler restaurant, 79, 87
Heritage Park, 57
Hermanos de Nuestro Padre Jesus Nazareno, Los (Penitentes), 29, 99
Hernandez, New Mexico, 28
Herrera, Bruno, 49
Herrera, Hazel, 49
Herrera, Nick, 37, 44
Hidden Treasures Gift Shop, 176, 197
High Finance Restaurant and Tavern, 93, 101
Highway hotline, 205
Hiking, 53–54, 93, 127, 153, 154, 161, 177, 178, 192
Hill Diner, 15, 21
Hillsboro, New Mexico, 176
Hilton, Conrad, 123
Hilton Drugstore, 148
Historic Custom House, 187, 201
Hollander, Seri, 96
Home at the Range gift shop, 2, 3, 18
Hondo valley, 132
Hood, Inez, 184
Hood, Irene, 184
Horgan, Paul, 132
Horlick, Iris, 93
Hot springs, 74, 170
   Artesian Bath House, 173, 196
   Battleship Rock hot springs, 8
   Charles Motel & Bath House, 173–74, 197
   Faywood Hot Springs, 186, 200
   Geronimo Springs, 172, 196
   Gila Hot Springs, 179
   Hay-Yo-Kay Hot Springs, 173, 196
   Indian Springs Pools, 173, 196
   Jemez Springs, 7, 20
   Marshall Miracle Hot Springs, 173, 196
   Ojo Caliente hot springs, 37–38
   Riverbend Hot Springs Hostel, 173, 196
   Spense hot springs, 8–9
Hotel Chango Restaurant and Art Gallery, 129, 140
Howe, Delmas, 173
Hubbard Foundation, 131
Hubbard Museum of the American West, 133, 142
Hurd, Michael, 132
Hurd, Peter, 132
Hurd Ranch Guest Homes, 132–33, 141
Hurd Rogers, Carol, 132
Hurd-Wyeth family, 132
Hurd-Wyeth La Rinconada Gallery, 132, 141
Hutchinson, Daniel, 93
Hutchinson, Hutch, 195
Hutchinson, Jerean Camuñez, 194

Indian Arts and Crafts Gallery, 24
Indian Pueblo Cultural Center, 205
Indian Springs Pools, 173, 196
Inn at Ojo, 39, 44
Inn of the Arts, 193, 202
Inn of the Mountain Gods, 135, 143
Isaacson, Jody, 3
Isleta, New Mexico, 107–8, 117, 207
Isleta Reservation, 107–8

J. Eric Chocolatier, 194, 203
Jackalope, 4, 19
Jacquez, Lawrence, 54
James, Jefferson, 94
James, Will, 81

Jaramillo, Irene, 155
Jaramillo, Jim, 155
Jarimillo, Renee, 49
Java Junction, 96, 102
Jemez, New Mexico, 207
Jemez Falls, 9
Jemez Mountains, 2
Jemez Pueblo, New Mexico, 5
Jemez Springs, 6, 7, 20
Jemez State Monument, 8, 20
Jewel Box Pawn Shop, 60, 67
Jewelry, 25, 60, 67, 96, 97, 98, 147, 156, 194. *See also* Crafts
Jicarilla Apache Indian Reservation, 205
Jicarillo Apache Indian Reservation, 50
Jo Ann's Ranch O Casados, 25, 42
Johnson, Arlene, 51
Johnson, Eleanor, 51
Johnson, Howard, 60
Johnson, John H., III, 40
Johnson, Louise, 51
Jordan, Charlie, 39
Jordan, Cleis, 130
Jordan, Jerry, 130
Jornada del Muerto, 125
Junction Cave Trail, 161

Kachinas, 159, 180
Kayser, Axel, 115
Kearny, Stephen, ix, 73
Kelly, New Mexico, 151
Kelly Mine, 151, 165
Kendrick, Susan Park, 189
Kenyon Thomas Gallery, 134, 142
Kimbrel, Ken, 75
Kin Kletso ruin, 52
Kingston, New Mexico, 176
Kit Carson Museum, 83, 88
Kittrel, L. W., 148
Kittrel Park, 148
Kiva murals, 4

Kiva Trading Post, 56, 66
Kivas, 55–56, 71, 117
Klinglesmith, James, 148
Kluck, Michael, 96
Kokopelli Cafe, 194, 204
Kostka, Shirley, 134
Kuaua (Tiwi pueblo), 4

La Bajada Welcome Center, 209
La Castaneda Hotel, 75
La Cueva, New Mexico, 76–77
La Lorraine, 135, 143
Labor Day Apple Festival, 176
Labor Day New Mexico Wine Festival, 2
Laguna, New Mexico, 207
Lake Roberts, 178
Lamb, Dave, 174
Lambert, Henri, 80
Lambert, Mary, 80
Lambert, Maryann "George," 174
Lancaster, N J, 98
Land of Enchantment (Sloan), xiii
Landmark Grill, 72
LaPointe, Carine, 97–98
Largo, Robert, 94
Las Cruces, New Mexico, 189–90
Las Cruces Convention & Visitors Bureau, 202
Las Cruces Farmers & Crafts Market, 190, 202
Las Nutrias, New Mexico, 111
Las Vegas—San Miguel Chamber of Commerce, 84
Las Vegas, New Mexico, 70, 71–76
Las Vegas Citizen's Committee for Historic Preservation, 72
Lawrence, D. H., vii
Lemitar, New Mexico, 123
León y Contreras, Diego de Vargas Zapata Lujan Ponce de, ix
Leonov, Alexei, 137

Index 219

Lescombes, Florence, 187
Letrado (Father), 114
Leyendecker, Hivana, 173
"Lily of the Mohawks," 108
Lincoln, New Mexico, 130–32
Lincoln Historic District, 130–31, 141
Lincoln National Forest, 128
Lincoln State Monument, 131, 141
Link, Larry, 186
Link, Linda, 186
Little Black Peak, 127
Llano de Albuquerque, 106
Llano Mercantile, El, 37
Llewellyn, William Henry Harrison, 193
Lobo Canyon, 164
Locke, Linsay, 9
Lodge, The, 135, 143
Log Cabin Curio Shop, 180, 198
Lordsburg, New Mexico, 184
Lordsburg Visitor Information Center, 200
Lordsburg Welcome Center, 209
Los Alamos, New Mexico, 12–17
Los Alamos Historical Museum, 14, 21
Los Alamos National Laboratory, 14
Los Alamos Ranch School, 13, 14
Los Alamos Visitors Centers, 21
Los Lunas, New Mexico, 108
Los Lunas Chamber of Commerce, 117
Low riders, 25
Ludvigson, Lewis, 172
Ludwig, Dave, 73
Luga, Fray Alonso de, 8
Luhan, Mabel Dodge, 33
Luna, Antonio José, 108
Luna Mansion, 108–9, 117
Lundeen, Gerald, 193
Lundeen, Linda, 193

MacArthur, Douglas, 195
MacDonell, Susan, 98–99
MacDonell, Tom, 98–99
Madrid, New Mexico, 94–96
Magdalena, New Mexico, 150–52
Magdalena Cafe, 151, 165
Magdalena Chamber of Commerce, 165
Malpais National Monument, El, 161, 167
Manderfield Otero, Josefita, 108
Manhattan Project, The, 13
Manzano, New Mexico, 116
Marion, Ann, 41
Marion, John, 41
Marshall Miracle Hot Springs, 173, 196
Martha's Black Dog Coffeehouse, 149, 165
Martin, Joe, 128
Martinez, Julian, 18
Martinez, Maria, 2, 18
Martinez, Paddy, 162
Martin's General Store, 37, 44
Matilda's Restaurant, 26, 42
Matkovich, Stephanie, 163
Mauro, Gary, 38
Maxwell, Lucien, 79
Maxwell Grant, 79
May Fiesta, 171
Maya Jones Imports, 96, 102
McCormick, Myra, 183
McDonald, Harold, 51
McDonald, Jane "Turk," 51
McDonald Ranch, 126
McGary, Dave, 133, 134
McGary Studios: Expressions in Bronze, 134, 142
McKuen, Jim, 54
McSween, Alexander, 130
McWethy, Sheri, 161
Meadowland Antiques & Spice Company, 73, 85

Meadows Bar and Grill, 75, 86
Meeks, Katy Camuñez, 195
Meem, John Gaw, 15
Meerschaum mine, 178
Meigs, John, 132
Mendoza, Antonio de, 155
Mercantile at Ojo. *See* Shops at the Mercantile
Mercantile Building, 77
Mescalero Apache Indian Reservation, 135, 205
Mesilla, New Mexico, 193–94
Mesilla Book Center, 194, 203
Mexican War, ix
Michelenas Italian Restaurant, 135, 143
Middleton, Bob, 172
Miera y Pacheco, Bernardo, 55
Miller, Harry, 80
Mitchell, E. J., 97
Moen, Andrée, 7
Moen, Rodney, 7
Mogollon, New Mexico, 152
Mogollon people, viii, 112, 138, 178
Mohr, Judy, 96
Monastery of Christ in the Desert. *See* Christ of the Desert Monastery
Montezuma, New Mexico, 73
Montezuma Castle, 73
Moore, Merle, 61
Moore, Rosilla, 61
Mora, New Mexico, 77
Morris, Earl H., 55
Morro National Monument, El, 160, 167
Morro rv Park, El, 161, 167
Mount Taylor, 163–64
Mountainair, New Mexico, 114–15
Mountainair Chamber of Commerce, 119
Movie making, 97, 177

Murphy, L. G., 130
Murray Ryan Visitor's Center, 181

Nageezi Trading Post, 54, 65
Nairn, Jack, 81
Nakashima, George, 35
Nambe, New Mexico, 207
National Forest Service, 205
National Park Service, 206
Navajoland Tourism Department, 206
Navajos, x
 crafts, xi, 3, 17–18, 49, 50, 51, 60, 61, 94, 180
 living conditions, xi
 nation, 61
 trading posts, 61
Naylor, Patricia, 96
New Mexico. *See also* specific towns
 climate, viii, xii–xiii
 cuisine. *See* Cuisine
 cultural diversity, ix–x
 history of, viii–x, 189–90
 Indian population, x
 land, viii
New Mexico Bed & Breakfast Association, 206
New Mexico Boys Ranch, 111
New Mexico Bureau of Mines and Mineral Resources Museum, 149, 164
New Mexico Department of Fish and Game, 206
New Mexico Farm and Ranch Heritage Museum, 191–92, 202
New Mexico Highlands University, 75
New Mexico Institute of Mining and Technology, 147
New Mexico Museum of Mining, 163, 168
New Mexico Museum of Natural History, 4

New Mexico Office of Cultural Affairs, 206
New Mexico Park and Recreation Division, 206
New Mexico Road & Recreation Atlas, xiii, 206
New Mexico/Santa Fe Welcome Center, 209
New Mexico State University Museum, 190, 202
New Mexico Vacation Guide, 206
Newberry, John S., 55
Niza, Marcos de, viii, 155

O'Hagan, Duane, 40
Oil Field Exhibit, 56
Ojo Caliente, New Mexico, 38–39
Ojo Caliente hot springs, 37–38, 44
O'Keefe, Dennis, 182
O'Keeffe, Georgia, 24
  house, 29–31
O'Keefe's Book Shop, 182, 199
Old Coal Mine Museum, 95, 102
Old Wagon Boutique, The, 7
Ollinger, Robert, 131
Olmos Guest Ranch, Los, 153, 165
Oñate, Juan de, ix, 146, 160, 173, 190
O'Neil, Elaine, 90
Online New Mexico information, 206
Oppenheimer, J. Robert, 13
Orchard, Sadie, 175
Otowi Station Science Museum Shop & Bookstore, 16, 21
Our Lady of Guadalupe church, 157–58, 166
Outpost, The, 127–28, 140
Owl Bar and Cafe, 123, 139

P & M Farm Museum, 110, 118
Pack, Arthur (Mr. and Mrs.), 32, 34

Pajarito Plateau, 9
Paloheimo, Y. A., 99
Palomas, Mexico, 189
Pancho Villa State Park, 188–89, 201
Paragua Restaurant, El, 26, 42
Parasol, El, 26, 42
Pasadita Cafe, La, 150, 165
Patio Restaurante, El, 194, 204
Patterson, Marilyn, 134
Pecos National Historical Park, 70, 84
Pecos River, 13
Pedernal, 24
Pennock, Tony, 171
Peralta, Pedro de, ix
Percha Bank, 176
Percha Press, 176
Pershing, Black Jack, 131
Pete's Cafe, 110, 118
Petroglyphs. *See* Rock art
Petrogylph National Monument, 93
Phillips, Waite, 81–82
Philmont Scout Ranch, 79, 81, 88
Philmont Museum, 82, 88
Picuris, New Mexico, 207
Pilabo, New Mexico, 146
Pink Store, The, 189, 201
Pinos Altos, New Mexico, 179
Pinos Altos Museum, 180, 198
Pinto, Eugene, 60
"Pinto Bean Capital of the World," 115
Pioneer Village, 56, 66
Piro people, 146
Plaza Antiques, 76, 86
Plaza Hotel, 72, 85
Pojoaque, New Mexico, 207
Pojoaque Pueblo's Poeh Center, 24, 41
Polo-Trujillo, Leo, 27
Polvadera, New Mexico, 123
Pond, Ashley, 13

Ponderosa Valley Vineyards &
    Winery, 6, 20
Popé, ix
Poppy's Cafe, 38, 44
Posta de Mesilla, La, 194, 204
Pottery, 3, 5, 7, 17–18, 37, 96, 98,
    123, 173, 190
  Art Space, 98
  Columbine Pottery, 5
  Indian Arts and Crafts Gallery, 24
  San Ildefonso Pueblo, 18, 22
  Sun and Fire Pottery House, 6
  White Mountain Pottery, 134, 142
Powell, Debbie, 5
Powell, Kellie, 5
Powell, Shirley, 5
Predock, Antoine, 134
Primitiva, 96, 102
Prisby, (Grandma), 91–92
Public Lands Information Center,
    206
Pueblo de las Humanas, 114
Pueblo of Zuni Arts and Crafts, 157,
    166
Pueblo Revolt (1680), 107, 114, 148,
    156
Pueblo Trading Post, 157, 166
Pueblos, x, 71, 146, 155, 179
  languages of, x
  visiting rules, x–xi
Purísima Concepción de Cuarac,
    115

Quarari, New Mexico, 115
Quebradas Scenic Byway, 123
Quemado, New Mexico, 155

Ra Paulette, 40
Radium Springs, New Mexico, 195
Rainbow Trading Company, 63, 68
Rajkovic, Rosa, 150
Ralph Edwards Park, 171
Ramah, New Mexico, 159

Ramah Navajo Weavers Association,
    159–60, 166
Ramona Hotel, 27
Rancho Bonito, 115
Rancho de las Golondrinas, El,
    99–100, 103
Rancho de los Burros, 33
Rancho de San Juan, 39, 45
Range Cafe, 2–3, 18
Rankins, Linda, 83
Raton Welcome Center, 209
Rayado, New Mexico, 81
Rayado Rancho, 83
Redbird, Robert, 49
Renata's Orange Street Bed &
    Breakfast, 17, 22
Restaurants. See Cuisine
Retablos, 100
Rhodes, Eugene Manlove, 173
Rialto's, El, 73, 85
Richards, 50, 68
Rimmel, Martha, 149
Rio Abajo, viii
Rio Arriba, viii
Rio Bonito, 132
Rio Grande, viii, 106, 107
Rio Grande River, 12
Rito de los Frijoles, El, 10
Riverbend Hot Springs Hostel, 173,
    196
Riverdancer Inn, 9, 20
Roberts, Penne, 5
Rock art, 53, 144, 160
Rock collecting, 149
Rock House at Vista Point, 93
Rockhound State Park, 188, 201
Romero, Ronald, 75
Romero, Vincente, 77
Romero's Fruit Stand, 28, 42
Roperito, El, 49
Rose Festival, 138
Rose's Pottery House and Art
    Gallery, 2, 18

Index 223

Rough Rider Trading Company, 73, 85
Roybal, Max, 33
Rugs, 51, 60, 62, 159–60
Ruidoso Downs, New Mexico, 133
Ruidoso Downs Race Track, 133, 142
Ruidoso Valley Chamber of Commerce, 141
Ruth Hall Museum of Paleontology, 33, 34, 43

Saarinen, Eero, 30
Sacramento Mountains Historical Museum, 135, 143
Sager, Salem, 132
Saint Augustine mission church, 107
Saint Clair Vineyards, 187, 201
Saint Francis de Paula Fiesta, 138
Saint James Hotel, 79–81, 87
Saint John Baptist Church, 151
Salinas Pueblo Missions National Monument, 113–14, 114, 118
Salman, William, 76
Salmon, George, 57
Salmon Raspberry Ranch, 77, 86
Salmon Ruins, 57, 66
Salt Missions Trail, 105–19
San Acacia, New Mexico, 122–23
San Acacia Gallery, 123, 139
San Albino Catholic Church, 194, 203
San Antonio, New Mexico, 123, 125
San Antonito, New Mexico, 90
San Buenaventura, 114
San Clemente Grant, 108
San Filipe, New Mexico, 207
San Gregorio de Abó, 114
San Ildefonso, New Mexico, 207
San Ildefonso Pueblo, 18, 22
San Isidro Chapel, 114
San José de los Jémez, 8
San Juan, New Mexico, 207

San Juan County Archaeological Research Center and Library, 57
San Marcos, New Mexico, 98–99
San Marcos Cafe, 98–99, 103
San Miguel Historic Area, 148
San Miguel mission, 147, 149, 164
San Patricio, New Mexico, 132
San Rafael Mission Church, 77
Sanchez, Carmen, 116
Sanchez, Val, 116
Sandia, New Mexico, 207
Sandia Cave, viii
Sandia Crest House, 93
Sandia Crest Scenic Byway, 90
Sandia Mountains, 90, 106
Sandia Peak Aerial Tramway, 93, 101
Sandia Peak Ski Area, 92, 101
Sandia Ranger Station, 117
Sandoval, Sammy, 50
"Sandstone Shrine, Windows in the Earth," 39
Sangre de Cristo Mountains, 12
Santa Ana, New Mexico, 4, 207
Santa Clara, New Mexico, 207
Santa Clara Cafe, 83, 88
Santa Fe, New Mexico, ix, 41
Santa Fe Railroad, 108, 110, 115
Santa Fe Trail, 71
Santa Fe Visitors Guide, 207
Santeros, 33–34, 37
Santo Domingo, New Mexico, 207
Santos, 122
Sapello, New Mexico, 76
Schafer, George, 180
Schindler, Rudolf, 30
Schmidt, Franz, 126
Schmitt, Harrison "Jack," 183
Second Hand Rose, 174, 197
Señor Peppers, 59, 67
Seowtewa, Alex, 158, 159
Sera (Father), 80
Serape Cafe, El, 155, 166

Seton, Ernest Thompson, 82
Seton Memorial Library, 82, 88
Seven Springs Fish Hatchery, 9
Shaffer, Clem "Pop," 115
Shaffer Hotel and Dining Room, 115, 119
Shakespeare, New Mexico, 185
Shakespeare Ghost Town, 185, 200
Shangri-La West Gallery and Trading Post, 7, 20
Shops at the Mercantile, 39, 44
Si Señor Restaurant, 188, 201
Sierra Blanca Regional Airport, 134
Sierra Farms, 116, 119
Sikh Dharma Community, 26
Silva, Rose, 2
Silver Bar and Cafe, 49
Silver City, New Mexico, 180–81
Silver City/Grant County Chamber of Commerce, 198
Silver City Museum & Museum Store, 181, 199
Silver City Trading Company Antique Mall, 182, 199
Silver Dollar Saloon and Restaurant, 131–32, 141
Simmons, Eve, 175
Sitzberger, Ed, 80
Ski Apache, 135
Ski Cloudcroft, 135
Skiing, 78, 86, 92, 135, 207
Sloan, Marion, xiii
Smokey Bear Historical Park, 128, 140
Smokey Bear Museum, 129, 140
Smouse, Don, 61
Smouse, Vern, 61
Socorro, New Mexico, 124–25, 147–50
Socorro Chamber of Commerce, 139, 164
Soda Dam, 8

Something Special Bakery and Tea Room, 61, 67
Sorenson, William, 163
Space Center, The, 137–38, 144
Spencer, A. N., 134
Spencer, Jackie, 134
Spencer Theater for the Performing Arts, 134, 142
Spense hot springs, 8–9
Springer, Frank, 74, 81
Staehle, Albert, 128
Stagner, Paul, 73
Stahmann's Store, 190, 202
Stalgren, Pat, 5
Stauder, Roberta, 63
Stauder, Sherwood, 63
Stauder's Navajo Lodge, 63, 68
Steins, 185, 200
Steins, Enoch, 185
Steuart, Beryl D., 27
Stevens, Jaqui, 96
Storrie Lake State Park, 76
Stradling, Anne C., 133
Street, Henry, 6
Street, Mary, 6
Strickfaden, Georgia, 16
Sun and Fire Pottery House, 6, 19
Sundance Gallery, 147, 164
Sunset Foods, 109, 118
Sweetwood Bar-B-Q & Hillsboro Orchard, 176, 197

Taft, Leonard, 51
Taft, William Howard, ix
Tajique, New Mexico, 116
Talamantes, Cindy, 37
Taos, New Mexico, 207
Taos Bed and Breakfast Association, 207
Taos Visitors Guide, 208
Tarango, Ricardo, 96
Tatsu, 193, 203
Taylor, Antonio J., 15

Taylor, Merrill, 58
Taylor, Miriam, 58
Tekakwitha, Kateri, 108
Teofilo's, 109, 118
Tesuque, New Mexico, 207
Texico Welcome Center, 209
Three Rivers Petroglyph National
    Recreation Site, 138, 144
Tijeras, New Mexico, 117
Tijeras Canyon, 90
Tijeras Pueblo Archaeological Site,
    117, 119
Tinkertown Museum, 91–92, 101
Tinnie, New Mexico, 131–32
Tito's Gallery, 73, 85
Tome, New Mexico, 109–10
Tome on the Range, 73, 85
Torreon, New Mexico, 116
Torres, Eligia, 109, 110
Torres, Pete T., 109
Torres, Tenci, 109
Tovar Hotel, El, 73
Towayálane, 159
Trading posts, 61
    Babbitt's Cottonwood Trading
        Post, 17, 22
    Blanco Trading Post, 54, 66
    Borrego Pass Trading Post, 61, 68
    Casa Grande Trading Post, 98, 103
    Chimayo Trading Post/The Marco
        Polo Shop, 27, 42
    Counselor Trading Post, 50–51, 65
    Fire Cloud Traders, 182, 199
    Fort Cobre Trading Post, 180, 198
    Kiva Trading Post, 56, 66
    Nageezi Trading Post, 54, 65
    Pueblo Trading Post, 157, 166
    Rainbow Trading Company,
        63, 68
    Rough Rider Trading Company,
        73, 85
    Shangri-La West Gallery and
        Trading Post, 7, 20
    Silver City Trading Company
        Antique Mall, 182, 199
    Turquoise Trail Trading Post, 96,
        102
    Zuni Mountain Trading Company,
        63, 68
Traveling precautions, xii–xiii
Traylor Shaft, 151
Treaty of Córdova, ix
Treaty of Guadalupe Hidalgo, ix
Trinity Site, 126, 140
Trujillo, Carmen, 32
Trujillo, Dennis, 32
Trujillo, E. D., 27
Truth or Consequences, New
    Mexico, 170–71
Truth or Consequences/Sierra
    County Chamber of Commerce,
    196
Tsosie, Edie, 50
Tsugwevaga, New Mexico, 107
Tularosa, New Mexico, 138
Tularosa Chamber of Commerce,
    144
Tunstall, John, 130
Turquoise Trail, 1, 89–103
Turquoise Trail Association, 101
Turquoise Trail Trading Post, 96,
    102
Twentieth Century Store, 75, 86
Twitchell, Burton, 81
Tyree, Eileen, 5

U-Name-It/Gift Shop, 174, 197
United World College of the
    American West, 73, 85
Upshaw, Dwayne, 94
Upshaw, Ron, 94
Uranium Cafe, 163, 167
Uranium mining, 162–63
U.S. Army Corps of Engineers, 208
U.S. Fish and Wildlife Service, 124
Ute Park, 79

Vaca, Alvar Nunez Cabeza de, 190
Val Verde Steak House, 150, 165
Valencia County Historical Society Museum, 110
Valencia Flour Mill, 111, 118
Valle Grande, 9–10
Valley of Fires, 127, 140
Van Winkle, Alanna, 151
Vanderbrook, Kathleen, 37
Vanderbrook, Terry, 37
Vanderbrook Studios, 37, 44
Vargas, Don Diego de, 80
Vega y Coca, Miguel, 99
Veguita, New Mexico, 111
Ventana Steakhouse, La, 163, 168
Verlarde, Cleo, 50
Verlarde, Richard, 50
Very Large Array, 147, 152, 165
Victorio (Chief), 131
Vidal, Gore, 15
Vietnam Veterans National Memorial, 78, 87
Vigil, Paul, 50
Villa, Pancho, 173, 188
Villa Philmonte, 82, 88
Voepel, Karlene, 147
Volcanos, 6, 93, 106, 109–10, 127, 161, 184

Wagon Mound, New Mexico, 83
Walatowa Visitors Center, 5, 19
Wall, Aelred, 35
Wallace, Lew, 131
Wanek, Catherine, 176
Ward, Ross, 91–92
Warren, Jack, 98
Wax Poetic Workshop, 2, 3, 19
Welcome centers, 209
West, Bob, 60
West, Carol, 60

West, Doug, 123
Western New Mexico University Museum, 183, 199
Westphall, Victor, 78
What Not Shop, 97, 102
What's a Pot Shop, 182, 199
White Dove, 134, 142
White Mountain Pottery, 134, 142
White Oaks, 128, 140
White Rock Canyon, 12
White Sands Missile Range, 137, 147
White Sands National Monument, 136–37, 143
Whitewater Canyon, 153
Whittemore, Earl, 108
Willetos family, 60
Wimmett family, 39
Woods House, 131
Wright, T. J., 80
Wyeth, Jamie, 132
Wyeth, N. C., 132
Wyeth-Hurd, Henriette, 132

Xochi's bookstore and gallery, 174, 197

Yankie Creek Gallery, 182, 199
Ying, Tom, 175

Zeniceros, Tate, 96
Zia, La, 194, 203
Zia, New Mexico, 207
Zimmer, Barbara, 73
Zimmer, Ray, 73
Zimmerman, Shoshana, 3
Zuni, New Mexico, 155, 166, 207
Zuni-Acoma Trail, 161
Zuni Mountain Trading Company, 63, 68